May Made Me

May Made Me

An Oral History of the 1968 Uprising in France

Mitchell Abidor

This edition © 2018 AK Press (Chico, Oakland, Edinburgh, Baltimore)

ISBN: 978-1-84935-310-6
E-ISBN: 978-1-84935-299-4
Library of Congress Control Number: 2017947342

AK Press
370 Ryan Ave. #100
Chico, CA 95973
USA
www.akpress.org
www.akuk.com
akpress@akpress.org

The above addresses would be delighted to provide you with the latest
AK Press distribution catalog, which features books, pamphlets, zines,
and stylish apparel published and/or distributed by AK Press. Alternatively,
visit our websites for the complete catalog, latest news, and secure ordering.

People say about me: You're someone who made May, and I answer that it's May made me.

—Thierry Porré

Ce qu'il avait vu, était-ce une bataille? Et en second lieu, cette bataille, était-ce Waterloo?

—Stendhal, *La Chartreuse de Parme*

Contents

Acknowledgements

I would like to thank all those who participated in this project, as well as those who made it possible. Jean-Pierre Duteuil (who I never had the opportunity to meet), Helen Arnold, Sebastian Budgen, Yves Coleman, Lou Marin, Marie-Pierre Fournier, Philippe Dubacq, and Christophe "Patsy" Patillon all assisted me in locating participants willing to be interviewed. Marie-Pierre is owed extra thanks for having located most of the participants in Saint-Nazaire and Nantes, as well as for having hosted me during my stay in the region and providing a home for the interviews.

Space constraints forced me to omit several interviews, and I apologize to those involved. Every person I interviewed brought something new and interesting, and performing this triage was a difficult task. I apologize to Frank Cassenti, Yves Coleman, Helen Arnold, Daniel Blanchard, Eric Hazan, Catherine Lévy, Colette Danappe, Rémi Drouet, Scylla, and Joël Quélard. Transcripts of their interviews can be found at the Marxists Internet Archive— www.marxists.org—in the May '68 archive of the French history section.

I can't speak highly enough of the people I interviewed, of their warmth and generosity; people were generous not only with their time, but with the books and newspapers they'd saved since May '68, feeling these would be more beneficial for this book and its readers than for them.

I would like to thank Jim Brook, for his invaluable editorial assistance. And finally, I thank my wife, Joan Levinson, for her patience during the time spent on this voyage through space and time.

* * *

Note on the interviews: All of the interviews that follow, except that with Jean-Jacques Lebel, were conducted in French. I wanted all of the interviewees to be able to express themselves fully and freely, so even those who speak English told me of their experiences in French. Jean-Jacques, having spent much time in the US, preferred to carry out the interview in English, which he speaks as well as he does French.

—Mitchell Abidor

Abbreviations

CA	Comités d'Action
CAL	Comité d'Action Lycéen
CARL	Comité d'Action Révolutionnaire Lycéen
CFDT	Confédération Française Démocratique du Travail
CGT	Confédération Générale du Travail
CNT	Confédération Nationale du Travail
CRS	Compagnies Républicaines de la Sécurité
ENS	Ecole Normale Supérieure
FLN	Front de Libération Nationale (Algeria)
ICO	Informations et Correspondances Ouvrières
JC	Jeunesse Communiste
JCR	Jeunesse Communiste Révolutionnaire
LCR	Ligue Communiste Révolutionnaire
LO	Lutte Ouvrière
OCI	Organisation Communiste Internationaliste
ORTF	Office de Radiodiffusion Télévision Française
PCF	Parti Communiste Français
PSU	Parti Socialiste Unifié
SNESUP	Syndicat National de l'Enseignement Supérieur
SouB	Socialisme ou Barbarie
SRF	Société des Réalisateurs de Films
UEC	Union des Etudiants Communistes
UJCML	Union de la Jeunesse Communiste Marxiste-Léniniste
UNEF	Union Nationale des Etudiants de France
VO	Voix Ouvrière

Timeline of Events in 1968

January 8	Protest against François Misouffe, Minister of Sports and Youth, at the inauguration of a pool at Nanterre.
February	Demonstrations in support of Henri Langlois, director of the Cinématheque Française, who was fired by Minister of Culture André Malraux.
March 20	Offices of American Express near the Opéra attacked by anti-Vietnam War demonstrators.
March 22	Occupation of the administration tower at Nanterre.
April 30	Nanterre campus closed.
May 3	Closing of the Sorbonne, occupied by the police prior to the disciplinary hearings for the students arrested at the American Express demonstration.
May 6	Violent incidents in the Latin Quarter. Strike begins at the university in Lyon.
May 7	Mass demonstration in Paris.
May 8	Day of regional action in the region of Nantes and Saint-Nazaire, attracting 10,000 demonstrators in Nantes.
May 10–11	Night of the Barricades.
May 13	Worker-student demonstrations throughout France.
May 14	Occupation of Sud-Aviation Bouguenais, first factory occupied.
May 15	Occupation of the Odéon. Strike at Cléon.
May 20	Between 6,000,000 and 10,000,000 on strike across the country.
May 22	Daniel Cohn-Bendit expelled from France.
May 24	In Paris, attack on the Stock Exchange, which is set aflame. In Lyon, a violent demonstration results in the death of a police officer. In Nantes, huge peasant demonstration.

May 27	Grenelle Accords. Meeting at Charléty.
May 29	Disappearance of de Gaulle.
May 30	National Assembly dissolved. Massive pro-de Gaulle demonstration in Paris on the Champs-Elysées.
June 1	Gaullist demonstration in Nantes.
June 6–10	Incidents at Flins. Death of Gilles Tautin.
June 11	Demonstration at the Gare de l'Est.
June 12	Dissolution of the left-wing groups.
June 16	Sorbonne evacuated.
July 10	Alain Krivine arrested.

CHAPTER ONE

Introduction: May '68 Revisited

On March 15, 1968, the journalist Pierre Viansson-Ponté published an article in *Le Monde*. Echoing the words of the nineteenth-century liberal Alphonse Lamartine, his article was headlined "Quand la France s'ennuie" (When France is bored). He entered into the heart of the matter immediately, saying that "what currently characterizes our public life is boredom." The French "don't participate in any way in the great convulsions shaking the world." The Vietnam War "moves them, but doesn't really touch them."

In a world of guerilla warfare in Latin America, mass murder in Indonesia, war and starvation in Biafra, the French view all this "as their business, not ours." Viansson-Ponté mocks French students who, while their fellows around the world demonstrate and fight, "are concerned with knowing if the girls of [the universities] in Nanterre and Antony can freely access boys' rooms." Young workers, for their part, "look for work and don't find it." Caring nothing for politicians, "television is there to divert their attention towards the real problems: [skier Jean-Claude] Killy's bank account, traffic jams, and horse race results."

Boredom is everywhere: even General de Gaulle is bored. Viansson-Ponté's final words were a warning: "A country can also perish from boredom."

Five days later, on March 20, an anti-Vietnam War demonstration turned violent at American Express near the Opéra and several students from Nanterre were arrested. On March 22, exactly a week after Viansson-Ponté's article, 142 students at Nanterre occupied the administrative tower in support of the arrested students. The March 22 Movement, its most famous face that of the German

Jew Daniel Cohn-Bendit, is born. Everything was now in place for the explosion that would occur on May 3 at the Sorbonne, setting off the May–June events. Two months, almost to the day, from the article's publication, France experienced its first general strike since the Popular Front of 1936, and the most massive popular movement in Western Europe in the twentieth century.

In retrospect, Viansson-Ponté's article seems foolish. But was it?

France was, indeed, in a state of political quiet. Still in the middle of the post-war *trente glorieuses*, the thirty glorious years of economic expansion, France was modernizing at a furious pace under the un-modern figure of de Gaulle. Though there had been strikes of varying degrees of importance in the previous couple of years, there was no sign of the kind of worker discontent that would lead anyone to predict what would occur in May and June. No one would have thought that student protests about dorm visitation rights would lead to an upsetting of French society. But it would be the students Viansson-Ponté mocked who would set it all off.

After the occupation of the recently opened University of Nanterre by the students who would become the first members of the March 22 Movement and the temporary closing down of classes there, on May 3 a gathering took place in the courtyard of the Sorbonne in support of the seven students who had been called before the disciplinary committee for their actions on March 20. The police were on the scene, and inexplicably, spontaneously, confrontations between students and police broke out. The May events had begun.

The authorities closed the Sorbonne after the police-student battles, and the following Monday, when the disciplinary hearings were scheduled to occur, demonstrations criss-crossed Paris. Word of the May 3 events had spread across France, and students all around the country began to follow Paris's example; demonstrations occurred daily. Early on, the leading voices of the Parisian students were Daniel Cohn-Bendit for the March 22 Movement, Alain Geismar for the Syndicat National de l'Enseignement Supérieur (SNESUP, the union of professors), and Jacques Sauvageot of the student union, the Union Nationale d'Etudiants de France (UNEF). If the Trotskyists of the Jeunesse Communiste Révolutionnaire (JCR) supported the movement from the start, indeed participated in Nanterre in the March 22 Movement, the Maoists of the Union de la Jeunesse Communiste Marxiste-Léniniste (UJCML), based at the elite Ecole Normale Supérieure, stood aloof.

The working-class was beginning to join the fight, though on its own terms for the most part, firmly controlled by (and supporting the line of) the French Communist Party (PCF) and its union, the Confédération Générale du Travail (CGT), both deeply suspicious of the students. If the students' demands were in a sense more poetic, for "all power to the imagination," for a change of the university, for a more open educational system, one that refused to serve capitalism and those in power, the workers more prosaically demanded a raise in wages, but also a less inhumane workplace. On May 10 a huge march in Paris ended in the Latin Quarter, and rather than disperse, barricades went up and street fights with the police and the Compagnies Républicaines de la Sécurité (CRS) occurred on what came to be known as the Night of the Barricades.

Over the intervening weekend all the major trade union federations called for a general strike beginning May 13, and huge demonstrations occurred on that date, while the following day workers began to occupy factories, the first occupation taking place at Sud-Aviation, outside Nantes.

As the strikes and occupations spread, so did the student-originated movement, as the Odéon theater was occupied. General Assemblies occurred in universities and high schools everywhere, and the Cannes film festival was shut down. Dany Cohn-Bendit, who was not a French citizen, was expelled from France for saying that "the tricolor flag is made to be ripped and turned into a red flag," though he famously was able to sneak back into the country, his red hair dyed black.

On May 24 the CGT called for demonstrations throughout France, and the date would also be perhaps the most violent one of the events, as the Stock Exchange in Paris was set on fire (though the participant accounts below vary as to the gravity of the event), while in Lyon a policeman died during the demonstration that night (see the account of Jacques Wajnsztejn, leader of the March 22 Movement in Lyon for a full account of those events).

This would perhaps be the high-water mark of the events, though it didn't seem so at the time. The following day, negotiations between the workers and the bosses and government began that would result in the Grenelle Accords of May 27, after which the workers returned to work within the following two weeks. The accords, which granted wage increases, union recognition, and a rise in the minimum wage, would be rejected in some larger enterprises. Communist functionaries like CGT head Georges Séguy were booed over them, but the accords were finally accepted and the return to work would begin on a large scale on June 5.

Until then, though, the demonstrations and occupations continued, and the first signs of a political recuperation by the left-wing parties also appeared, with a major rally at Charléty Stadium, called by, among others, the independent left-Socialists of the Parti Socialiste Unifié (PSU) and former Prime Minister Pierre Mendès-France. At the same time, the pro-government forces, which had been silenced for the first few weeks, also shook themselves from their torpor, and on May 30 in Paris and May 31 in the provinces, massive pro-de Gaulle demonstrations occurred and de Gaulle dissolved the National Assembly.

This, as most of those interviewed below admit, signaled the beginning of the end. Strikes continued, as well as violent confrontations, as students went to factories still occupied to give their support, leading on June 10 to the death of the student Gilles Tautin outside the Renault factory in Flins.

The demonstrations petered out, and after all the workers had returned to their factories, legislative elections were held on June 30, with the right tightening its grip on power, obtaining over 43 percent of the vote. Revolution in the streets had failed to overturn bourgeois power (but was it a revolution?). The electoral road, as most of the far left had predicted, had solidified the right's position.

It was time for the left to reflect on what had occurred, to define the possibilities for the future, to continue to organize and act. One of the great slogans chanted everywhere had been "*Ce n'est qu'un début, continuons le combat*" (It's only a beginning, continue the fight)! In order to continue the fight, the lessons from May had to be drawn.

Five decades later, we continue to question May, to try to learn from it.

* * *

In May 2018 we will be fifty years from the events of May '68 in France, as far from May as May was from the trenches of World War I. May '68 seemed to portend the beginning of a revolutionary period in Europe, but it didn't. Even so, in France and in so much of the world, it remains a marker, a moment when it was forbidden to forbid, when it seemed the imagination was about to seize power.

Even as a 16-year-old living in the deepest depths of Brooklyn, I was one of those profoundly influenced by the events in Paris. The images on TV of the results of the Night of the Barricades, May 10, 1968, were, along with the war in Vietnam, a catalyst for a life of political activism.

Reading the interviews that follow, the accounts by Isabelle Saint-Saëns and Prisca Bachelet of the occupation of Nanterre on March 22, 1968, which set off all that was to follow, of peoples' activities throughout the period, the excitement and hopes of those weeks in May and June fifty years ago are still fresh. Life was different during the events, and not just because of barricades and battles with the police. The barriers between people fell. As Alain Krivine, the leader of the Trotskyist JCR told me: "I saw people talking to each other on the street, people you would pass every day and never say hello and then everyone was talking to everyone. On the metro too everyone talked. It was fantastic. You never drove alone, you picked people up and took them, it was absurd to be alone. People became unrecognizable. I never saw it before and never saw it again."

Suzanne Borde, who would live on a commune and eventually become a nuclear physicist, told me of how she was a girl in pleated skirts before the events, but as soon as the events kicked off she went home and made herself a miniskirt, around the hem of which she wrote in magic maker: "The problem is not with the length of my skirt, but with your gaze." People discovered the thrill of speaking in public and inspiring others to action, of sharing ideas on the streets with total strangers.

It seemed that life would never be the same, and for the people I interviewed it never was. People literally discovered their voices. Myriam Chédotal, a high school student in Saint-Nazaire at the time, told me of how she went around to the classes in her high school as events began to encourage the students to go out on strike. And as she did so, "My life shifted. I realized I had a gift for speaking, for finding the right words. It was that day I gained confidence in myself. It was brilliant."

Social movements grew out of May: feminism, prisoners' rights, gay rights ... Everyone I interviewed admitted they might have come about anyway; all insisted that given the sclerotic nature of French society it would have taken much longer to happen without May.

May as it was lived, May '68 during May '68, the "great lyrical community," as Jean-Michel Rabaté describes it below, was an irreplaceable, extraordinary event, one we are unlikely to see again in the West. But beyond that there is another side to any recounting of May that must be confronted, and that is its failure to overturn the state and establish a new and different order. To make a revolution. To change class relations. This is far less cheery a subject, and yet it became clear from my conversations that it, too, has haunted the minds of those who took part. Almost all found positive results flowing from the events, in their bringing about greater openness, greater individual freedom, in their smashing of the Gaullist myth and the complacency of the *trente glorieuses*, the three decades of prosperity that followed World War II.

6

The first question May raises, indeed the central one, is whether revolution in the West is possible. But even before addressing that larger question, there is the question of how to name the period. Was May '68 a revolution? If we were to say that a revolution is an uprising that results in the overturning of the power structure and a change in the ownership of the means of production, then May obviously wasn't one, not only because it failed to accomplish either of these things, but because there is no indication that the seizure of power was ever even seriously considered. In fact, it was in many ways scrupulously avoided. And further, when the period drew to a close the Gaullist state was more firmly entrenched than it was at the beginning, sweeping the elections in late June with a greater majority than it had held before. And as for a change in ownership of the means of production, those who could have posed that question—the workers—never considered asking it. Quantitative demands were the order of the day for the workers, while the students wanted to completely change society.

Also standing in the way of calling it a revolution is the lack of intentionality: when the events began it was a call for the liberation of students arrested for their involvement in an anti-Vietnam War demonstration at an American Express office on March 20, 1968. On May 3, 1968, when students gathered at the Sorbonne to support those students who would pass before the disciplinary council the following Monday, they spontaneously exploded against the police. It grew and grew from that, but though many I spoke to admitted that they thought revolution would be the end result at some point during those six weeks, it was not a stated goal.

But if the fact that it didn't succeed in changing power disqualifies May from being defined as a revolution, then no mass activity that fails to change society to its foundations can be called one.

What then is the proper word for an event which sees virtually every factory in France on strike and occupied; schools shut down and occupied and end-of-year exams cancelled; daily demonstrations all over the country; barricades set up in the hearts of cities; the police and the forces of order confronted violently; unions taking over the distribution of food and gas; people organizing in their neighborhoods and schools; and strangers engaging each other in conversation, breaking the barriers that had formerly stood between them, all while the authorities are helpless to put a stop to it? "Events," which is the word most often used, seems to be a pale reflection of what was occurring.

Is avoiding the word "revolution," which is what the veterans of the event do today, simply another way of conjuring away the fact that it ended so poorly? Was May a revolution that failed, or was it really something else entirely, something sui generis?

Several people I interviewed described May as their 1905, the preparation for 1917 (a 1917, it must be pointed out, that never occurred). Indeed, Henri Weber and Daniel Bensaïd, then leaders of the JCR, wrote a book titled *Mai 68: Une Répétiton générale* (A Dress Rehearsal) positing precisely the notion that May was the precursor of the *grand soir*: the violent, rapid, and total overturning of the old order. This was the opinion as well of several of the people I interviewed:[1] they were active in May as a way of pushing things as far as the circumstances allowed, and—in the case of the most Bolshevik among them—in the hope that a united revolutionary working-class party taking in all tendencies would be a result.

Viewing May as 1905 has a serious flaw. In 1905 the Russians thought they were living 1917, i.e., they were engaged in a fight that was not the preparation for something greater that would occur later: they intended to seize power in that moment. In fact, the Soviets, the organs of dual power, date from that revolution (and it is worthy of note that despite its failure the events are called precisely that: The Revolution of 1905). The hope of the revolutionaries of the day was that this would be the end of Tsarism, and Trotsky wrote unambiguously at the time, "The Revolution has come."[2] In the heat of the struggle they had no thought of laying

---

1   See interviews with Prisca Bachelet and José and Hélène Chatorussat below.
2   Leon Trotsky, "The Events in Petersburg." www.marxists.org/archive/trotsky/1918/ourrevo/cho3.htm.

the groundwork for a second attempt. They intended to win in 1905. That there were second and third chapters was the result of the revolutionaries' defeat in 1905 and later of an event no one would base their strategy on: a world war.

And if many of my interviewees said they didn't think this was the *grand soir*, many admitted that *at the time* they did, so the notion of a dress rehearsal has no validity: no one takes to the streets and confronts the CRS having in mind a hypothetical victory in some indefinite future.

But that leads to a further question, one that is essential: if you have a situation such as that in France in May–June '68 and power is not taken, and it is denied the name "revolution," what would or could a revolutionary situation look like? An entire country on strike, normal life brought to a halt, hundreds of thousands of people marching daily throughout the Hexagon ... It was a situation totally unlike that of the Paris Commune (in *many* ways), where it was Paris against the rest of France, for in May all of France was a field of struggle. If power was not shaken and taken, what possibility is there for this to ever occur? No Western country has had a situation remotely like May, except perhaps Portugal in 1974, though that was significantly different due to the involvement of the armed forces in overthrowing the government and advancing working-class power (and even so the revolution failed to overthrow capitalism). There could be no more propitious circumstances for the overthrow of capital, yet it didn't occur. That being the case, can it ever occur? Is the revolutionary project dead?

Many of my interviewees spoke of the lack of interest in attacking the seats of power as if it was an irrelevancy. Alain Krivine, his role already established, spoke to me of how there were only three guards in front of the parliament building, yet it never occurred to anyone to steer the march into it and seize it, even for symbolic reasons. As I was told by one of its organizers, Jean-Jacques Lebel, the Stock Exchange, as the obvious stand-in for capitalism, was attacked and set on fire on May 24 as a symbolic gesture. Prefectures were attacked in a couple of cities, yet the main seat of power never was.

Some of the explanation for this can be marked down to the spirit of the March 22 Movement, founded at the University of Nanterre and led by the anarchists Daniel Cohn-Bendit and Jean-Pierre Duteuil.[3] All of their actions during the six weeks of struggle would be aimed at disorganizing centralized power and relocating it to the base. "Self-organization" was their goal, as I was told, with committees in universities, in high schools, in neighborhoods; committees uniting workers and students, intellectuals and workers: their new society would be from the bottom up, so a seizing of power as represented by its buildings with the new authority emanating from a single locus would have been anathema to them. Cohn-Bendit wrote that had Paris awakened on May 25, the day after the attack on the Stock Exchange, "with several ministries occupied, Gaullism would have immediately collapsed." But he was clear that the seizing of buildings would not have aimed at occupying them as the holders of power, but rather it would have "provoke[d] the awareness in the entire population of the fact that the state apparatus was no longer anything, that it had no power, and that henceforth everything was to be reconstructed on new bases."[4] This explains the anarchists' inaction in this regard, but what of the rest of the left?

The role of the PCF in the failure to pose the question of power is key. The PCF looked askance at the movement from the start, and if the strikes that started about a week into the events were inspired in part by the students (one interviewee told me that for the workers the thought was "if the students can do it, why can't we?"), the fact remains that the PCF and its allied union, the CGT, did all they could to put a brake on the movement, to ensure that the utopian demands of the students didn't penetrate to the working-class.

3 Jean-Pierre Duteuil (1944–) was an anarchist student in sociology at Nanterre and, along with Cohn-Bendit, participated in the founding of the March 22 Movement.
4 Daniel and Gabriel Cohn-Bendit, *Le Gauchisme, remède à la maladie sénile du communisme.* Seuil, Paris, 1968, p. 75.

Some of those who were students in '68, like Eliane Paul-Di Vicenzo of Nantes, spoke of warm receptions from workers when they went to the factories to meet with them, to distribute flyers. But far more spoke of being ignored by the workers, some placing the blame on the CGT, others on the simple observation that the workers were just not interested.

The workers I interviewed, in Paris and the provinces, presented a uniform picture, and it was of a working-class that was anything but militant. All of them said that their first act upon declaring a strike was to sweep the floors and clean their machines and tools, so they wouldn't be looked on as destructive, so they'd be seen as "responsible," as "serious." This attitude set the tone for the rest of the strike.

For the workers, it was not the qualitative demands of the students that mattered, but their own quantitative, bread-and-butter issues. I spoke to workers from factories in several cities, all of whom occupied their workplaces, none of whom said they had any interest in the students. In fact, Guy Texier, a CGT leader at the naval shipyards in Saint-Nazaire, a hotbed of working-class activity, spoke with pride of kicking in the ass those students who came to speak to the workers. They did so, he said to me, "On principle, and also because the work of union militants is complicated, it's not something where you come and everything is immediately decided. There are discussions … We built and then the others came and instead of attacking the bosses they attacked the union."

The *ouvriérisme*—the workerism—so strong on the French left led the students to think the workers were the motor of any revolution, which left the vehicle immobile because the engine was dead. (An alternative way of looking at things is that the students, whose demands and actions were infinitely more radical than anything the workers did—who aspired at the very least to fundamentally changing their corner of the world, i.e., the high schools and universities of France—were Marxist in words, Marcusean in deeds. They spoke and wrote ad nauseam of the need for worker-student unity, for the workers to lead the way to a new France, yet they had no hesitation about throwing paving stones, building barricades, placing society in question without the assistance of the workers. Despite their outdated rhetoric, they acted as if *they* were the revolutionary class. And if they weren't a revolutionary class, they were unquestionably revolutionary actors. In fact, "actors" is what the Communists accused them of being, playing at revolution. And what some of the then-young admitted to.)

The image we on the left have carried in our heads for decades has been that of workers and students standing united, but it was Alain Krivine who perhaps put it best when he explained that the JCR had about twenty workers who they trotted out whenever they could, but in reality they had no real base in the working-class. (This syndrome could also be found in the late, lamented Socialisme ou Barbarie (SouB), whose token worker, D. Mothé, served as proof of their working-class attachments. Mothé, though a worker, was not a simple factory hand who saw the light when he read Cornelius Castoriadis. He had been a Trotskyist militant prior to SouB, so his consciousness had already been raised.) But even more significantly, Krivine explained to me that at the monster worker-student demonstration of May 13, the beginning of the general strike, the workers and the students occupied nothing more than the same physical space: mentally and politically they remained miles apart. When I interviewed Krivine, he said, "[T]here was a gap between the workers and the students; there was never a junction." The correctness of this analysis was borne out by events.

The harmful influence for decades of the PCF cannot be underestimated here, but the Communists' profound reformism should not be seen as the sole cause of the working-class not being as revolutionary as the students hoped and as the Marxist vulgate demands. France was not the USSR: There were few social benefits accruing to membership in the Communist Party; some within the party and in its bastions; none in greater French society. No one forced a worker to join the PCF or back its line: they did so in full awareness of what they were doing, and viewed the PCF as their true voice; there is no reason to believe that workers to any large extent disagreed with them. When workers attended student General Assemblies it was always specified to me that they were "young workers" who were not representative of the class as a whole. Cornelius Castoriadis wrote of how "In France in May '68 the industrial proletariat was not the revolutionary vanguard of society, but rather its ponderous rear guard. If the student movement attacked the heavens, what stuck society to earth … was the attitude of the proletariat, its passivity in regard to its leadership and the regime, its inertia, its indifference to everything that was not an economic demand."[5]

So when Communists explained to me that they knew the working-class and that the working-class was not ready for more than bread-and-butter demands, the fault was partly theirs for failing in their role as a Communist Party in encouraging revolutionary ideas. But whatever the cause, the workers were, indeed, not ready or interested in the overthrow of capitalism. There is no surprise then that when the Grenelle Accords were signed, the workers voted to return to work almost everywhere.

There were of course instances of the workers refusing to accept the bosses' offer, of their rejecting the Grenelle Accords that were aimed at ending the strikes, and these are now held up as examples of what could have been had the Communists not acted as a brake. And though it's true that the workers at factories like Flins (where the Maoist student Gilles Tautin drowned fleeing the police on June 10, 1968) and Renault at Billancourt (where the Maoist Pierre Overney would be murdered in 1972) booed and drove out CGT secretary Séguy and refused the contract three times, that doesn't necessarily mean the workers' opposition to what they considered a poor settlement meant they wanted to take the strike to the next level and use the general strike as a means of bringing down capitalism. In fact, perhaps the most militant worker in all of France was the young woman captured in the classic documentary

5   Cornelius Castoriadis, *La Société française*. Union Générale d'Editions, Paris, 1979, p. 193.

La Reprise du travail aux usines Wonder. This anonymous woman (later attempts to locate her were futile), captured on film entirely by chance, refuses under any circumstances to return to the vile job she had and is outraged that everyone else is ready to do so. *This* is working-class rage in its most primal form. It is not, however, a desire to establish socialism immediately.

Self-management, an important intellectual current in France for decades, would not make an appearance in France in practice until the occupation of the Lip factory in Besançon in 1972, though the subject was broached by the Confédération Française Démocratique du Travail (CFDT) in May '68. However, forms of auto-distribution were developed, particularly in Nantes and Saint-Nazaire, where food, vegetables, and milk passed directly from farmers to striking workers, bypassing the normal distribution networks. Here we truly had the hammer and sickle joined, on however small a scale.

Nothing better testifies to the worker indifference to their student supporters than the fact that when Gilles Tautin, a Maoist high school student, drowned when fleeing the police at Flins, the workers did not go on strike. And among the most optimistic of my interviewees May continued until 1972, and ended when the member of the Mao-spontex Gauche Prolétarienne Pierre Overney was shot at point-blank range by a Renault security guard and again the workers didn't move.

So in May we see clearly limned the historical dilemma: students, certain from their reading and from the strong French *ouvriériste* tradition that it is the working-class that must guide the revolution, seek an alliance with the workers, recognizing that on their own they could not bring down capitalism and its state. But for all the student advocacy and boasting of a worker-student alliance, in the first instance it was more apparent than real, and in the second instance, the revolutionary class was not revolutionary, not viewing either itself as such or the situation as being one propitious for revolution. The *trente glorieuses* had been very good to them, and they weren't going to risk losing all their material gains.

The anarchist Wally Rosell told me that May's most positive lasting effect on France was the beginning of the end of the PCF. And in the long run that might indeed be true, though it was only one factor. Oddly, several people I met with told me that though they hated the role of the PCF in May, they joined the party afterwards because, after the failure of the utopian dreams of May, they felt a need to do something concrete, and concrete in France in the '60s and '70s meant the PCF. The filmmaker Pascal Aubier told me of attending a meeting of Pouvoir Ouvrier, a successor group to Socialisme ou Barbarie: "There were about 30 people there. And there was one worker. That struck me. I said to myself we can't do without the working-class in making the revolution. So as simplistic as it might sound, the PCF represents the working-class, and so I joined it."

However despicable the PCF might have been, however restricting a role it played in the events of May (and in 1936 and in 1944 and in 1947 and during the war in Algeria ...), the death of the PCF, which the far left is fond of painting positively, was, ironically, a disaster for the left.

The death of the PCF would have been a fine thing if there had been something to take its place as the representative of the working-class, but there was nothing to assume this role. The working-class lost its home, and discontent lost a place where it could be expressed. Yes, for us on the left, the PCF was exemplary of all that was wrong with the Communist movement. But you can know a party by its enemies, and no party was as hated by the French right, by the bourgeoisie, as the PCF. And it is difficult to maintain that the most radical sections of the working-class thought any other party represented its interests. But more importantly, however attenuated a voice of discontent it was, it was nevertheless a voice. Its diminishment leaves the field free to the bourgeoisie. As Alain Badiou wrote: "What we suffer from on a world-wide scale is a politics disjoined from any interiority to capitalism ... Our affliction comes from the historic failure of communism."[6]

---

6   Alain Badiou, *Notre mal vient de loin*. Fayard, Paris, 2016, pp. 60–1.

Violence is part of the image of the revolutionary process, and there was no shortage of that: buildings set aflame in Paris and Lyon, barricades in too many cities to count (those in Nantes denigrated by the Communist Guy Texier as being "constructed of vegetable crates"), paving stones thrown, cars overturned and set on fire, tear gas launched at the demonstrators ... And yet, many of those I interviewed spoke of how relatively relaxed their experiences were with the police when they were arrested, and despite millions of people taking to the streets, the number of deaths was amazingly small. Gilles Tautin drowned, and one policeman in Lyon died, as well as two workers at Sochaux and one right-wing student in Paris. But these numbers are debated. I was told by Jacques Wajnsztejn, one of the leaders of the March 22 Movement in Lyon, that the two workers killed at Sochaux were bystanders, not strikers, and the cop in Lyon died of a heart attack, not as was thought at the time when hit by a truck driven by a demonstrator. To put this in perspective, on May 4 and May 14, 1970, more students were killed at Kent State University and Jackson State College than in France in the six weeks that the events lasted. And of course in the same year, 1968, student demonstrators—from the dozens to the hundreds—were killed in Mexico City. What explains the relative moderation of the violence in France?

Not that there weren't those who felt violence on the part of the students wouldn't be salutary. Pierre Goldman, veteran of the student left, son of Jewish Communist Resistance fighters, and a man who spent his life trying to act like the members of the Communist Resistance during World War II, had nothing but scorn for the students, describing their actions as "joyful and masturbatory"; "collective onanism." He had other ideas than mass demonstrations "spreading on the streets and in the Sorbonne the unhealthy tide of a hysterical symptom." He went to see a leader of March 22 "and proposed an armed action to him. I told him that the peace in which the situation was frozen had to be blown up. It sufficed to resort to serious, real violence, to open fire on the forces of order ... The government would oppose a military response to this surprising violence and the situation would be beneficially worsened and radicalized. In this way the possibility of communication with the workers would be created … The people had to be given a guarantee in blood."[7] And in fact Michel Andrieu, a filmmaker who knew Goldman, told me that one day, as he was at a demonstration, a man flashed a gun, a man he recognized as Goldman. But the fact remains that with the exception of the night of May 24, when the Stock Exchange was ignited, and when in Lyon, during fights with the police, a policeman died, violence on the part of the students was spontaneous and restricted to stone throwing and barricade building. Alain Krivine told me with a certain pride that he was thanked by the prefect of police for his role in ensuring that violence was no worse than it was, and Krivine doesn't deny that he and the other leaders did not push for attacks.

Needless to say, the state had all the means of repression at hand, yet they never fired into the crowds, limiting themselves to arrests, tear gas, and truncheons. Perhaps Goldman is right and a few dead students would have set off a wave of revolutionary violence, outside student ranks and outside Paris. It's far more likely that such a suicidal tactic would have led to a quick end to the events as well. I was frequently told that police prefect Grimaud handled the affairs with great deftness, allowing the demonstrators a certain leeway in their violence without a murderous riposte, which certainly would have reflected poorly on him. But as Jean-Michel Rabaté, who experienced May in Bordeaux, explained to me, "The French cops had orders not to kill, so this wasn't Tiananmen. Why? Because they knew the people who'd be killed were children of ministers and judges." In a sense those on the streets, despite their rebellion against their parents' world, were still protected by their families. Goldman diagnosed the situation perfectly: "The regime's art was that of maintaining the confrontation within peaceful limits, from which the use of arms was banned, while the rebels imagined themselves in the midst of an insurrection and in this way fictionally fulfilled their dreams of revolution."[8]

7   Pierre Goldman, *Souvenirs obscurs d'un juif polonais né en France*. Seuil, Paris, 1975. Editions Points, pp. 70–1.
8   Ibid., p. 70.

Several of my interviewees spoke of the fear that the army—whose support de Gaulle had ensured during a visit to General Massu in Baden-Baden—was preparing to repeat the feats of the army in 1871 in crushing the Paris Commune. And there is some basis to this belief. However—and we see here again the ambiguity of the PCF's position in France at the time and how little convinced the bourgeoisie was that it was the reformist party it was in reality—it was only preparing to move when the workers went out on strike, convinced that the PCF was preparing to seize power![9]

Everyone who took part in the events in May and June speaks of how speech was freed, how it was democracy in action. But was it? Certainly people spoke out in ways and in forums never before available. But there can be no question that the movement had leaders: Jacques Sauvageot, Alain Geismar, Daniel Cohn-Bendit, and to a lesser extent men like Alain Krivine, Jean-Pierre Duteuil, and Jean-Jacques Lebel. Who appointed them? The answer, of course, is no one; they simply rose to the top almost immediately. Cohn-Bendit in particular became a symbol of the period thanks to his gift for provocation and his willingness to confront anyone of any title at any time and any place. No one voted him the head of the March 22 Movement, and yet he played a vital role in animating the events (an early book about May, published a month after it ended, was a collection of interviews called *Les Animateurs parlent*, The Leaders Speak). They were not interested in exercising any kind of control over the movement or the events, but there is equally no question that they led and gave the movement a face and a voice and direction. How? Again, though our image of May is the General Assemblies at the Sorbonne and the Odéon, in fact there was a smaller group that met every evening to review the day's events and prepare the next day's.

In today's frenzy for horizontality, where the notions of majority rule and representation are anathema, a situation like that in May

---

9 Jean-Pierre le Goff, *Mai 68. L'héritage impossible*. La Découverte, Paris, 1998, p. 118.

would be considered reactionary. And yet, it was thanks to the strong presence and voices of the leaders that May was able to leave the Sorbonne, the Latin Quarter, and Nanterre and insert itself into every sector of French life. Action Committees in the neighborhoods and workplaces and high schools were formed, enabling activity in every corner of France. These committees were in many ways the outgrowth of previously existing committees dedicated to opposing the Vietnam War, but there is no reason to believe that the creation of these committees grew out of discussions: a leaflet went out calling for their creation and the call was taken up.

As for the General Assemblies, far from being action groups or deliberative bodies, they were rather a forum for the tearing apart and remaking of the world.

Finally, when asked what May brought that was lasting, the answer was always the same: it freed up French life, removed sexual and social constraints, opened the door to feminism and gay rights. The question I had to ask was, since all of these appeared in the US without a May (though certainly in the wake of the Civil Rights and anti-war movements), might this not have reached France a little later anyway, as part of the normal modernization of capitalism?

Though many I spoke with agreed this was a possibility, for Jean-Jacques Lebel, a cultural as well as political revolutionary, this was not necessarily the case: France and Europe are far more hierarchically structured than the US, so an explosion like May was needed to clear the way. As he put it, "Yes. We really needed it. You can't compare the US and old Europe. The cultures and societies were different. Capitalism doesn't function on Wall Street as it does here, in London, or Milan. It's not because we're all capitalist societies that they all work the same way. It doesn't work that way."

But though May opened the road to these movements, and led to a loosening of society's constraints, to changes in the educational system, to greater union rights, in the end it paradoxically served to strengthen capitalism.

May serves to prove the flexibility of capital, its ability to absorb shocks, to adapt itself to new situations, and then move on. Greater rights for women? Fine. A less mandarin-ruled education? Fine as well. Even a certain change in relations at the workplace was perfectly acceptable. As long as the fundamental matter isn't touched: the ownership of the means of production.

May '68 was another step in the modernization of French capitalism. It goes without saying that this is not what the people on the streets wanted. But it was perhaps Prisca Bachelet, a veteran of the fight against the war in Algeria, who joined the student struggle from the beginning, on March 22, who expressed it best, describing the years after May: "Many of us worked at our workplaces at transforming things; we acted as if we'd seized power and were post-revolution. But while we were doing this, while we assumed intellectual hegemony, we didn't notice that the bosses were reorganizing ... We missed the central axes."

But capital didn't.

CHAPTER TWO

Veterans in the Struggle

So if we're all crazy nobody's crazy.
—Jean-Jacques Lebel

JEAN-JACQUES LEBEL

Jean-Jacques Lebel was born in 1932 and so was older than the students by some ten years, but he "was never a student... Never went to university." He began his political life "on the left of the left" during the war in Algeria, protesting the war and doing support work for the FLN (National Liberation Front). But along with politics, Lebel, son of the important gallerist Robert Lebel, "was completely engaged as a so-called experimental artist ... I thought art was a good way of expressing the non-belonging to the capitalist system and to try to invent and imagine alternatives not only to the dominant culture, but the dominant way of life." He organized Happenings throughout Europe, befriended and translated the Beats ...

Close to the Situationists, to Socialisme ou Barbarie, to the Surrealists (from which he was expelled: "They just sent me a letter and telling me they didn't like what I was doing and that I should fuck off"), Lebel was constantly on the move in the '60s between Europe and the US, introducing Happenings to Europe, one of which, in 1967 in Nanterre, was interrupted when "some guys got up and started throwing tomatoes and bullshitting, and it was Daniel Cohn-Bendit and Jean-Pierre Duteuil." Underlying all of his activities in the years before 1968 (and after) "was my idea to blend the subversion of art and poetry and philosophy into the mass movement in the social field." Resolutely opposed to strict organizational structures, he likens his political ideas to that of the drip paintings of Jackson Pollock: "It's always the drippings in a situation that are more important than what you had planned to paint."

Absent from Paris and Nanterre when the events began, he soon returned.

Was there any connection between your work with the Beats and the May events?

In '65 I published an anthology of Beat Generation poetry. It was the first anthology, with Allen Ginsberg and Gregory Corso when they lived in Paris, and so I gathered this anthology of poems, which I chose with them. I translated them and published them with a wonderful publisher named Maurice Nadeau, who was an old Trotskyite, a very important publisher, and this anthology was a tremendous success. Which I didn't expect, of course. People liked the book and it was very influential. And in May '68, by the way, anonymous individuals tagged quotations from my translations in French on the walls, which was an extraordinarily wonderful experience. "At last it was happening," I said.

So things started; the police had surrounded the Sorbonne, and there was a lot of street fighting in which I was extremely active.

Had Daniel Cohn-Bendit been in touch with you between March 22 and May?

Yes, yes, we became good friends, and Jean-Pierre Duteuil especially. I lived right near the Sorbonne; it just so happens I had a studio at Maubert, a stone's throw from the Sorbonne, so I was right in the middle of everything, with the police everywhere. Then I went to Nanterre to be in the General Assembly (GA) and the idea was we had to find a way to get the police away from the Sorbonne and have the phenomenon spread. Stop being a fucking students' thing and become a social thing which involved all the classes of society, all the institutions, all the walks of life, and to get out of that ridiculous student business, which was boring. It was not a thing between the students and the rector, it was a thing between the young people and the entire society.

There was one-on-one repression/provocation bullshit between the students, who had no experience and no in-depth consciousness of what they were doing with the police, of the need to get out of that trap and to, of course, involve people who were not students; people of other age groups and especially other social groups. And spontaneously I thought of the Odéon, because if this turned into a real social upheaval, which we wanted it to, there would be a lot of blood. The police might become really serious and might shoot. So we needed to prepare for that, we needed to see ahead, to find a place on the middle of the Latin Quarter, in the middle of Paris, where the people who worked in hospitals could bring plasma, could bring medicine, could bring things to fix broken arms and legs: we were thinking positively. There were a lot of doctors around who in their profession were in the same position of revolt as we were. So that was very positive. We needed a place, but we couldn't do it in the Sorbonne, since the police were around, and I thought let's do it at the Odéon, which is just around the corner. They said, "Brilliant, do it!" so I proposed it at the GA in Nanterre—we couldn't get into the Sorbonne, the police were surrounding it—where everything was happening then, and I argued the case and it was voted on, getting an overwhelming "yes." Of course there were some plainclothes policemen in the Assembly, but they understood fuck all, and we decided the very next day to occupy the Odéon.

And so I set a time to meet at place de l'Odéon, where the metro is, and thousands of people showed up. Thousands. And the police didn't understand that it was open. We'd said what we were going to do, but they didn't comprehend. So we walked up the street, a whole bunch of demonstrators, into the Odéon and there was a performance going on: it was Alvin Ailey—a conventional dance company, a modern one but not all that modern—and we stormed the stage and said it was over. Then Jean-Louis Barrault[1] came and we had these public arguments, which was something that happened all over the world in the '60s, in the US, Japan, Germany, everywhere there were arguments like this. So that's how the Odéon was taken over and as soon as that was done, people said, "You took over the Odéon," and I'd answer "Wait a minute, I only suggested it. First of all, everybody took it, and second of all the next day I'd gone somewhere else, I didn't stay there, I didn't conquer an institution to take the place of Jean-Louis Barrault for crying out loud. I just took it over to give it to everybody."

So who was it that came up with the list of demands?

I did.

---

1 Jean-Louis Barrault (1910–1994), one of the great French actors and at the time director of the Théâtre de France.

There's a video of them being read to the press. Was that you?

I read them to everybody from the stage. There were thousands of people there by then. What was extraordinary for me was not what we did, because actually it was extremely easy. What was really wonderful—and that's why it was a question of learning what we were doing while we were doing it—was that people, middle-aged guys with beer bellies, came up crying on stage—we'd opened the stage to everybody—y'know: "I'm from the CGT, I've been in the Communist Party since I'm 18 and I realized it was bullshit and I didn't know what to do, and all of a sudden I realized there is an alternative and you're showing us there is an alternative; here's my party card," and he tore it up.

Guys were crying and I realized we were onto something really important, because they were transforming their very lives. People had been railroaded into being slaves, either of the boss in the factory or of the union or of the party, they were always subdued into obeying orders by the bureaucrats or the bosses. And all of a sudden they realized they could be freer if they joined forces with other human beings who wanted the same things. And we saw this in front of our own eyes. And we saw a social movement growing, thanks to this small little thing that we had done. We saw people coming from all walks of life, there was a general strike, and people hitchhiked from Marseilles, from all over France, and even from other countries to say, "We're with you." People who were the age of our grandparents. And then we realized we were onto something really fundamental. I saw this happening right before my eyes, and I want to tell you that to this day it's the most important and radical thing I'd ever dreamt I could live in my whole life.

And for me it's the high point of my entire existence.

What types of people were at the Odéon compared to the Sorbonne?

Well, the Sorbonne was mainly university people, because it was the Sorbonne. But in fact, it was more or less the same kind of people, though the Sorbonne already had politicized people, you know, the Trotskyites, the Maoists, the anarchists ... The people who already belonged to some kind of -ism. In the Odéon it was more like everybody, because it was a theater; it had no connotation as a place of learning. It was just a theater.

When people spoke, did they come up on stage or did they speak from the audience?

They came up on stage and the mics were all over the place, and the stage was full of people. There was no stage anymore; the whole thing was a stage. And people were talking, they were in dialogue; they never stopped. They didn't stop at midnight; they went on and on and on. People were sleeping there. And we'd secretly organized on the top floor medicines and things like that, and we had a lot of mattresses we'd stolen. That May was a warm and beautiful month, and the whole roof was covered with mattresses. Of course with these kids, what did they do? Everybody was fucking all over the place. It was like Woodstock: everybody was fucking everybody in the dark. It was paradise, it was like Hieronymus Bosch, *The Garden of Earthly Delights*. And it wasn't meant to be that way; it just happened. Nobody said we're going to do *The Garden of Earthly Delights* by Hieronymus Bosch but it just occurred that way because people were too tired to go home, and besides, the metro was on strike, everything was on strike. So what are you gonna do? You sleep where you are. And that's how it started.

When people spoke, did they, like the guy you mentioned, talk about their personal lives?

People talked about their own lives, how they felt. There was one guy I remember because I befriended him afterwards, he worked for Hachette, a distribution company, and he said something extremely interesting. He created the Comité d'Action Hachette, he was an employee, he wasn't a student, he was a worker. And he took the mic and he said something really extraordinary. "All my life I thought I was crazy because I couldn't obey. I fought everything the bosses or the union leaders wanted, I was against everything, but I was alone and felt in total revolt, and I don't know why, but I just knew it was wrong and I thought I'd internalized the fact that I was crazy. Then one day in May '68 we were at a demo and I looked behind and there were people with their flags and banners, and I saw three quarters of a million to a million people there and I said, "We're all crazy." So if we're all crazy nobody's crazy.

"All of a sudden I realized I wasn't crazy and that everybody was and we were right to be crazy. To be against the rules of capitalism."

You were at the heart of all this, so at this point did you think something was going to be forever changed?

Yes. That was the problem. We did have some notions of history; we knew what had happened at the Commune, that there was the Bloody Week[2] and on the anniversary of the Commune we took the Stock Exchange, though at first we were going to go to the Hôtel de Ville, since it was the anniversary of the Paris Commune, but somebody in the police told us not to do it, that they had machine guns there. Too important, too monstrously out of hand. So the police set up machine guns in the courtyard of the Hôtel de Ville, and if they break down the doors, you shoot. In other words, a bloodbath. A fucking bloodbath. There would have been hundreds of dead. So we heard this and I think it was some of the Freemasons who were in the police who came up and said they're waiting for you, it's a trap. So we had a secret meeting of about twenty of us, and said we have to find an alternative and we have to celebrate the anniversary of the Commune, but we can't go to the Hôtel de Ville, so I said we'll pretend we're going there, with a mass demonstration of 1,000,000 people, but just when we get to the right place on the Grands Boulevards we turn and head to the Stock Exchange instead. We don't tell anybody that, but at the last minute, when we pass near it, we say "This way" and we take over the Stock Exchange. It was as simple as that. There was nobody in the building, it was easy to break down the doors, and somebody

---

2 The final week of the Commune, from May 21–28, 1871, when the Communards were massacred by government forces.

took some gasoline and set it on fire. And the next day the stocks dropped 30 percent. We were right in the heart of capitalism, and it was a game, but it was also a serious game.[3]

We didn't burn the building down, we burned a bunch of papers, but the impact, the symbolic impact of that was tremendous; it rippled all around the world. Then we realized it wasn't a student thing anymore, because first of all there was a general strike, and then the Stock Exchange ... everybody knows what that is, it was like Occupy Wall Street, but it lasted longer and was more coherent, though it was the same type of thing. That's why I thought it was so wonderful when they did that thing in New York, because we're going straight to the heart of the beast, you see. And it was like we were living a dream, but we were realizing it as we were living it.

You were only three weeks into it at this point, and you're still optimistic that this is going to lead to something.

I was always optimistic. Even when things started getting bad. When I realized things were trapped into old models is when a bunch of Trotskyites formed a chain to try to stop the demonstrations. These young Trots were controlling and authoritarian in '68, just like the 1917 Bolchos were: it was a repetitive pattern. Mechanical historical reruns, going nowhere fast. How to break that archaic mold and invent viable alternatives. You must have read Trotsky's *History of the Russian Revolution*. In it there's one point where Trotsky is really sincere, where he says that we were always running after the movement, because the movement was far ahead of the party. That's exactly what was going on ... It was Rosa Luxemburg's theory of the spontaneity of the masses. That the masses have an intelligence of their own based on intuition, class-consciousness, and creativity, and that what bureaucrats do is try to stop that dynamic and fix it so that they have power over the movement. That's the history of Bolshevism. Having read and studied all that I realized that the mechanism was repeating itself.

---

3   See interviews with Henri Simon and Wally Rosell for alternative accounts.

You're talking about spontaneity. But I've spoken to a whole bunch of workers in the suburbs and the provinces, and all of them say that all they wanted were higher wages, a raise in the minimum wage, and that they weren't interested in politics.

Yeah, Mitch. You know what a human being is ... Freud was right: there's three levels of consciousness, there's no doubt about that. Some things you know but you don't know that you know them. And when you're talking about more wages, in fact you're up against the whole structure in which not only the owners of the factories, but also the unions are against the workers ... You know that this thing that happened at Renault, when the GA of several thousand workers said "Fuck you" to the Communist Party, so in fact, on the conscious level it's true what they told you, and on the other hand it's not true, because of their desire to take control over their own existence and to transform their relationship to their own work ... So at one point of course they'd say all we want is more money and want to be respected more as human beings, but read between the lines ... There's a censorship within each one of us, there is an id, a superego that says don't say those things they'll get you in trouble, so they refuse to admit to themselves that what they really want is fucking freedom. It's not a question of getting $100 a month more; it's a question of not having to punch the clock like a robot, to do what the guys on the assembly line force you to do. It's much more than just the money. If you look at it with a magnifying glass into all those peoples' discourse ... Although maybe after more than forty years they don't want to hear about their adolescent yearnings for another life, but the ones that came to the Odéon, the ones we met at Renault and everywhere else we went to, they couldn't say it in the same way that you and I would say it; of course not. But they would say it in their words, like the guy from Hachette, that he realized he wasn't crazy after all. To dream, to desire more.

With all the speaking going on in the Odéon, all the liberated speech, how were you organizing within the theater so that things got done?

They did it themselves. As I told you, I didn't spend more than twenty-four hours there, I was part of a group, these things organized themselves.

So no one saw to it that bathrooms were cleaned ...

They were doing that spontaneously; they were self-organizing; it's called self-management. Of course they were. People who had medical knowledge would come together and create a committee for this or that, and you had to go out and get food, so they went out and asked restaurants for food, and when the restaurants gave them food someone had to pick it up and distribute it. It was self-organizing and I saw it happening before my eyes. That was also an extraordinary event. But not only at the Odéon, everywhere.

It sounds like this was the culmination of everything you'd been trying to do ...

Of everything that I dreamt was possible but didn't know was possible. We just did it. We gave ourselves permission to act upon our instincts. Our good instincts to transform not only the social and economic structures, but the mental and libidinal structure. All these things being linked, of course, as Wilhelm Reich brilliantly explained.

So everything's going great, and there are things happening all over France ...

It was going on all over. There was New York, with Columbia, there was Berlin ... It was enormous.

So it would have been perfectly normal to think this is it.

Something's happening that is of a different quality. It's not revolution in the sense of armed revolution, because we know that leads to a bloodbath. We're not cowboys, we're not playing cowboys and Indians with the police, because we know we'd be annihilated, since they have machine guns and tanks; it's ridiculous. What we have to do is invent a way for these situations of personal, intimate subversion of peoples' lives without the military impact. In other words, we have to integrate the paranoia of the adversary into the game. And that was very difficult. And then we started realizing that the PCF was in fact the main enemy of this movement.

Even more than the crowds at the pro-de Gaulle demo on May 30?

But before that the Communists were saying you have no right to destroy the unions, the party. In fact, the reality of this was that the CP was crumbling from within for many years, since '56, since the workers' uprising in Budapest, which was an extremely important date for Europe, when Khrushchev sent in the tanks to crush a democratic, popular movement of workers' councils. So I knew this was going to happen and that the Communist Party wanted this to stop because they were losing whatever power they had left; it was the disintegration of the Communist Party. Which we saw happening with our own eyes, and this is why the PCF is almost down to zero, because it imploded. The Communist Party was absolutely a conservative and reactionary force.

Did you see France as no longer being a reactionary country?

That's what the mistake was. A terrible mistake. It took me years and years to cope with that. That all these tendencies within each human being are contradictory. We knew about the Paris Commune, we knew about the role of the Communists in the Popular Front, we knew that Jacques Duclos[4] had gone to the Nazi occupiers to ask them for permission to bring out again their party paper, *L'Humanité*. We knew all these things and that this was going to happen again. So you could have the near orgasmic joy of taking part in something much greater than yourself, in which … This is a paradox: being part of this mass movement gave you much more freedom than you ever dreamed of having as an individual; that you didn't renounce your freedom as an individual; you magnified it. This is an interesting social-historical paradox: that you're freer in a collective than you are as a separate human being.

Perhaps, but normality returned in a big way.

And you know why? It was because they were scared.

---

4   Jacques Duclos (1896–1975), historic leader of the PCF.

So it wasn't so much errors committed by the leaders ...

It's very complex. When you do what you're told to do, you are structured. There's a social structure you can rebel against and say, "I'm exploited, they're bastards, I want to kill them," you can do all that and you remain within the structure. When you destroy the structure you are put in a position of personal and social and sexual responsibility. You have to decide for yourself.

And that's what scared the shit out of everybody. There was no party left, there was no state left, there were no unions left, no teachers, no leaders to tell them what to do and how to do it. They had to become free human beings, and that's an important philosophical point that the German philosopher Max Stirner made, this is what that book was about: *The Ego and Its Own*, that if you become free you have much more responsibility, much more work to do, than if you're just a slave.

Etienne de La Boétie's voluntary servitude ...

In a nutshell, exactly. That's when the people were struck with vertigo and said, "We have to stop this, because freedom is too much."

A question I failed to ask before occurs to me: at the Odéon, were women as free to speak as the men?

They were, or rather they began to be. Nothing was done the first hour. It was a process. And definitely they began to speak. And then it happened as well in the newspapers. Do you know my paper, *Le Pavé?* I have one here for you. We ran it in a print run of 200,000 copies. Yes, they were beginning to speak. And homosexuals too were beginning to speak. "When we speak of freedom of sexuality, are we talking about all sexuality or just yours?" That's what they began to formulate.

You, who know America so well for having lived there, might have a good answer for this question. When I ask people about the lasting effect of May they talk about feminism, gay rights, etc., everything you said. But you know America, and you know we got

33

all that without May—though of course we had a variety of social movements that had been in action since the early '60s. I wonder if May wasn't just a way for you to catch up with us?

That's possible. Could be. But it's not that simple. There are two questions in your question. I would tend to agree, because when my friends Abbie Hoffman and Jerry Rubin and Phil Ochs came to Paris I put them up in my house, and they wanted to meet the anarchists. So we organized a meeting at the Jussieu science faculty and several hundred people came, curious to meet these guys. It was a disaster. Jerry Rubin—who ended up on Wall Street—was extremely arrogant and horrible. He said, "Why don't you guys speak English?" Fifty percent of the people were workers from Renault and they'd never been to a university. I mean it was imperialism, it was cultural imperialism. "We're the rockers. We're condescending. We'll teach you what revolution is about." And the people said "What??" It was really a clash of cultures and condescending cultural imperialism. That was very negative.

The second thing is, I don't quite agree with you because there's a history in America, from the Wobblies onwards, from people like the anarchists and Sacco and Vanzetti and all who'd already been through all this. Don't forget there was a lot of sexual revolution talk in those years. Like Emma Goldman, who wrote about it, who practiced sexual emancipation. So in fact it was a general international movement long before we were born and it so happened that thanks to people like Dylan and others, and Ginsberg, it was put into music and it was transmitted from individual to individual, not through the usual channels of political discourse, but through musical discourse and the joy of sex and getting stoned and the Beatles and the Rolling Stones and all the others. But what was lacking in America, and what we had in Europe was a certain basic knowledge of the historical process. We knew about the Paris Commune and we knew we had to avoid that bloodbath; we had to invent another way of doing things. But the American movement had more spontaneity, it had a wonderful, joyous childishness about it, in the American movement, until the Marxists and the Maoists destroyed everything.

Point taken about the movements in the US, but did you really need May to get to the movements I mentioned?

Yes. We really needed it. You can't compare the US and old Europe. The cultures and societies were different. Capitalism doesn't function on Wall Street as it does here, in London, or in Milan. It's not because we're all capitalist societies that they all work the same way. It doesn't work that way. There's a class-consciousness here that didn't exist in the US, except in the Wobblies and the anarchist circles around Emma Goldman, and some Socialists. But in the great movement of America they thought that capitalism was OK. At Woodstock people didn't understand when we did what we had to do to break down the walls and let the people in free, so the managers and exploiters wouldn't make a million bucks on the backs of the kids buying tickets, they didn't understand that.

You lived through all this and it looked like it was here, *le grand soir* …

No, I never thought of the *grand soir*. I thought it was a process.

OK, but you thought change was going to come out of this.

It did.

But it wasn't the big change you'd hoped for.

No, it was a micro change.

So millions of people are striking and demonstrating and occupying, and it only led to micro change. So can you have the hope that there'll be something even bigger that would bring about the rest of the change?

I certainly do, but then I have to tell you, it involves my own personal feelings, and though I don't like to talk about myself I have to explain this. There are several ways of seeing this. Many people think you have to be a militant, where you sacrifice your life, and become like many of my Trot friends, like the mathematician Gérard Bloch, who could have won a Nobel, he was so creative a mathematician. But he was also a Trotskyite leader, and I asked him why he didn't do more math, and he said, "No, I have to be an activist." And so day and night he was a militant, he was a zombie, he hardly ever saw his kids, he was a robot. "I'll only have time to write when they put me in prison." "Do you realize what you're saying? Living and to renounce being joyful, that's crazy." So that's one way of being an activist, to renounce the wonderful life where you know you'll die. Why don't you experience something deep and wonderful while it's still time. No, you have to be a militant, an organizer … It's very sacrificial, you sacrifice yourself for the revolution.

But there's another way of doing things, which for me worked better: it's to be extremely aware of and open to what's going on in the world. Always. What's happening in the social field, in the cultural field, to really feel part of everything and to divorce yourself from these processes that are continuously going on everywhere.

At one point it happened in '68. I'm 80 years old now so I don't expect to see it before I die, but it'll happen, maybe in the next century, but it's got to happen, that the energies coalesce in a certain programmed way and all of a sudden a small local process spreads, like the flu, like a virus, an anarchist virus, and all of a sudden there's a social event going on and it's not controlled by bureaucratic castrators, and then you drop what you're doing and join the fray and give it all you've got. And this is what I did. I gave up being an artist for over twenty years and got in there and gave it everything, all my energy, all my time, and I'm glad I did because I experienced some of the most intense, moving events and things I'd never have experienced had I continued to be an artist.

So May changed my life by putting me in contact with people I'd never have been in contact with and to realize that there is a thing called—I don't want to say network, it's got too capitalist a sound, "networking" and all that—a rhizome. Deleuze and Guattari would say they didn't write their books, the movement did. And it's true that it was a big rhizome that existed generations before us and will continue generations after us. And that's what the revolution is about. Rhizomic energies that radiate everywhere, and we have to find the right timing in which to participate and give it our all.

The best thing is to time what you want to do and to be like a jazz musician and listen to the other musicians, listen to what society is doing, and find the right movement to do your thing.

ဆာ   ၎

ALAIN KRIVINE

Born in 1941, Alain Krivine, founder of the Jeunesse Communiste Révolutionnaire, one of the most important political groups of the May events, has been active on the French left since the war in Algeria. I met him in his office in a building owned by the party of which he is currently a member, Nouveau Parti Anticapitaliste (NPA).

I come from an apolitical family, members of absolutely nothing. My mother, like so many bourgeois women of the time, didn't work: she stayed home and raised the children. My father was a dentist and both of them were on the left; sometimes they voted Socialist and sometimes they voted Communist, but more often PCF, because at the time being on the left meant voting Communist.

I had five brothers, two of them now dead, all of them older than me except for my twin. All were members of the Socialist Youth who moved on to the Communist Youth. So I was raised by left-wing parents and Communist brothers. I continued along that track, joining the Communist children's organization, and then the Union de la Jeunesse Républicaine de France, the ancestor of the Jeunesse Communiste. In 1957 I was sent to Moscow for the Youth Festival, thanks to my being the best salesman of the party paper. I was a Stalinist then, but things were already beginning to turn, since while I was there I met some Algerians from the FLN, and arranged meetings between Communists and people from the Algerian underground. The latter criticized the Communists for their vote granting special powers to the government during the war and their opposition to Algerian independence. So the party reprimanded me, and I thought they were right: I was already something of a *gauchiste*.[5]

When I got home, I was still a member of the Young Communists with a brother who was a Trotskyist, though he kept this from us, since at the time you joined Trotskyist groups in secrecy. I told him that I wanted to engage in underground activity in support of Algeria, but that I didn't want to have anything to do with Trotskyists. He asked me why I gave a damn about that and I told him they were all enemies. He introduced me to a professor who was a part of Jeune Résistance, which I secretly joined. So I was a member of the Union des Etudiants Communistes (UEC) at the Sorbonne while at the same time a clandestine member of Jeune Résistance, clandestine in regard to the PCF as well, which didn't want to directly support the FLN.

I soon found myself the leader of the Guevarist opposition within the UEC, and before long we were expelled from the UEC and the PC. After the expulsion we formed the Jeunesse Communiste Révolutionnaire (JCR), which would play an important role in May '68 and be banned in June '68. When the party was banned, I was arrested and then sent to do my military service, at which point we formed the Ligue Communiste, which was dissolved in '73 after a violent anti-fascist action, and then we created the Ligue Communiste Révolutionnaire (LCR) in order to be legalized. I was twice candidate for the presidency. And then five years ago we founded NPA.

Did your Jewish origins play any role in your activities?

Partially. I was never a believer, but I come from a family that was somewhat believing. My grandmother took me to temple when I was little. You know that among the Jews if there are 2,000 women you need thirteen men …

---

5   Literally "leftist," a *gauchiste* is someone to the left of the PCF.

Ten men ...

Ten men in order for services to begin. This is where my insolence and my impertinence come from. My grandmother was very Jewish, observing Yom Kippur, etc. My parents not at all, except for Yom Kippur, which they observed just to show they were Jews. But there were people in my family who were executed by the Nazis. That marked me some, but not a lot. I was always anti-religious. And something like the Manouchian Group[6] touched me mainly because they were foreigners, foreigners who were with the Communists and who died for France.

OK, so let's talk about the events. How did you and your group react in March to the events at Nanterre?

We had a connection there through Daniel Bensaïd, who was a professor at Nanterre. So we very quickly had a connection with the people there, but also through one of our comrades, Xavier Langlade, who was the one who planted the tiny bomb at American Express in protest against the Vietnam War that set off the events at Nanterre.

Didn't planting bombs run counter to your Marxist ideas?

A bomb ... It was a little thing intended to break windows. And anyway, we were all *gauchistes*, so we thought it was fine. So Langlade was arrested and Bensaïd served as our intermediary, a member of the leadership of the March 22 Movement. We were the Trotskyist wing and Cohn-Bendit was the anarchist wing. There were debates—sometimes violent ones. We followed events very closely, and the discussions revolved around anarchist self-organization, around delegates and their revocability, over the General Assemblies.

It seems to me that it was the anarchists who won the debates.

It's hard to say. On the whole yes, because every movement that came out of May had a spontaneous character.

---

6 Group of foreign Communist Resistance fighters, executed after a public trial in February 1944.

Every day at the Sorbonne—not at Nanterre, which was closed—there were General Assemblies with 2,000 people. There were all the street demos where crowds would ask, "Where should we go?" What a mess it was. But globally yes, it was all more Cohn-Bendit than Bensaïd, with all the assemblies and the lack of elected delegates. Whoever shouted loudest won, whoever had a mic, or whoever had stewards ...

When it all began in May you were working part-time, weren't you?

It's hard to explain. I was working part-time at Hachette publishing as secretary of the editorial committee, a job I got through my father-in-law, the journalist Gilles Martinet. So when everything began I was working there, and I left Hachette without even saying good-bye. I just upped and left. They even paid me for three months even though I was no longer coming to work, which was quite nice of them. But when I left I went right to the Sorbonne and there I stayed throughout the period.

You were there when the first disturbances occurred on May 3?

Oh yes. On May 3, when the cops occupied the Sorbonne, and I was also at the barricades of May 10 with Ernest Mandel,[7] who had come down from Belgium. There were barricades that were a joke: there was a side to all of it that was an imitation of the Paris Commune. Ridiculous barricades were put up, sometimes in an impasse where there was nothing behind it. We constructed barricades, we cut down trees, we played at being Communards of 1871. There were two things occurring at the same time, the new social movements and the old political ones, which met in May '68. There were artists, there was "make love not war" ... It was a mess. But it mattered even so.

So the night the barricades went up we took shelter in the Ecole Normale Supérieure (ENS) on rue d'Ulm, which was led by the Maoists, by Robert Linhart ... The people there took us in, even

---

7 Ernest Mandel (1923–1995), Belgian Trotskyist leader and theoretician.

if we were Trotskyists, they received us fraternally. They weren't involved in the fights, but they helped us out of solidarity. We also had the arrival en masse of the Lambertists, another Trotskyist sect, coming from a meeting at the Mutualité shouting "General Strike!" They saw there were nothing but students, so they left and went home to go to sleep. A couple of days later there was a general strike, but they didn't understand that it was the barricades that set off the strikes and not their workerist stupidity.

So I saw all this, I was there, rue Gay-Lussac, the trees cut down, the burning cars ...

The Latin Quarter was a middle-class neighborhood, not at all working-class, people with good salaries, but I saw people ... For example, there was a guy who asked, "Is that my car burning? No big deal." He didn't give a damn.

Did people talk about the Paris Commune?

No, it was rather something that was felt. The whole story of the barricades was nothing but a mess. Like all the nights of May '68. We always decided at the last minute what we were going to do. But on the Night of the Barricades the idea was that the police are occupying the Sorbonne so we're going to occupy the police. We're going to do it like our ancestors: we're going to put up barricades.

Now, people are wrong when they say that the women's movement came in May, it came after, but even so there were plenty of women at the barricades. They played a tremendous role, and the women's movement was born after May '68, because of May '68, but not in '68. In the film *Mourir à trente ans*, about the life of Recanati,[8] we see the role of the women, and it's entirely secondary, they're there to serve, to listen. It's not a normal role. There's no equality, there was not a single well-known woman in '68, there's Cohn-Bendit, Sauvageot, Geismar, me to a certain extent, but not a single woman.

---

8   *Half a Life* by Romain Goupil recounts the political life of Trotskyist militant Michel Recanati, who committed suicide in 1978.

At the General Assemblies ...

I was with the leadership, we met every single day at the offices of the Union Nationale des Etudiants de France (UNEF)[9] on rue Gay-Lussac. There was one person per organization and I represented the JCR.

Who else was there?

There was Geismar, Cohn-Bendit, Sauvageot, and others who were less well known. We were all there but frankly the political discussion was at level zero. We discussed what we were going to do that night or the next day and no further than that. When we spoke individually we recognized there were enormous cleavages, between Cohn-Bendit and the Maoists—between them it was virtually civil war—while for our part we were skeptical because, with our Marxist-Trotskyist education, we didn't know what it was, but we knew what it wasn't: we knew it wasn't a revolution. How far could it go? [dismissive noise] We pushed things, we pushed things ...

Towards what?

We had to push things as far as possible so there'd be a general strike, an insurrection.

So you thought it possible.

Oh no! We didn't believe in it. Firstly, because we saw that it was only the students, and then when the workers came—and I realized this later—they were there strictly physically and not politically. I remember the march on Renault during the general strike. We were at the Sorbonne, there was a GA with everyone braying, and I said OK, let's go to Renault, at which point everyone applauded. "We're going to see the workers!" And anytime a worker spoke it didn't matter, he could be a drunk, lumpen ... It was the token worker, a few stray workers, it was pitiful: the students were all excited. I propose we go visit a factory that was on strike, everyone

---

9 Principal student union, led during the May events by Jacques Sauvageot.

shouts "Bravo!" and a few thousand of us go there. When we would get there the workers would be happy to see us, but they distrusted us. They stayed behind their windows: it was the CGT that completely controlled everything. Afterwards there were common worker-student demos but we didn't have the same slogans: they had theirs, we had ours. There was never any real connection with them. There were many places where there were strike committees, but they were fake: they were really inter-union committees, I think there were real strike committees at Saclay,[10] and that wasn't even workers, it was mainly technicians.

May '68 was both a beginning and an end: it was a conglomeration of new and old traditions, of old groups like the PCF and the CGT which were very strong, and new groups like us and like Cohn-Bendit and the anarchists. It was the junction of two generations, the old and the new. This applies to the slogans and the forms of demonstration as well. In all cases we find both. That's why this was a beautiful transition. That's it, it was a transition.

When you spoke at the Sorbonne were you well received?

Yes, and that was the democratic side of the Sorbonne. Every political party had a stand in the courtyard. We had Che Guevara's mug and the red flag, and everyone tolerated everyone else. The only ones that weren't were when they came, the toughs, what were they called?

The *katangais*.

When they came we didn't know what to make of them. Were they on our side, weren't they? They were toughs, apolitical ... We were all against them when they arrived at the Sorbonne. Apart from that, at the Sorbonne there was every political group, people who were from our party, others, many of whom would later play an important role, like Marc Kravetz.[11] There were the GAs,

---

10   Site outside Paris of both a university and a major research center.

11   Marc Kravetz (1942–), militant of the far left in the 1960s and 1970s, and later a highly regarded journalist.

everyone listened quietly ... As far as I remember it was a great democracy. And then there were the artists who met, people like Michel Piccoli, who did their thing, but there was no connection between us, I mean, I had no connections: they didn't come see us and we didn't go see them, but we respected them.

Who did you spend your days with?

Well, every day I was at the Sorbonne, there were the GAs, the meetings of the UNEF, the JCR stand where I would sit and discuss issues with people. This went on all day and I never slept in my own home.

You didn't see much of your family during all this.

Very little. I was married and my wife and I had an apartment in the Latin Quarter, a little place that had been given me, but during the time I hardly slept there ... I was at the Sorbonne all the time and seldom saw my family We were totally caught up in what we were doing, devoured by it: there were demos every day and every evening we met at Denfert-Rochereau to decide where we were going next. What a mess ...

But at the time did you think it was a mess? It must have been exciting.

Oh yes, it was exciting, but at the same time we knew that the conditions weren't in place. We led the thing more or less, but with Mandel we knew ... I mean, we knew the conditions weren't right. We watched it without believing in it too much. Cohn-Bendit, I knew him then and again at the European parliament, I didn't take him too seriously and he was always on the radio—there was no TV so we all listened to the radio—and he was everywhere, at the doors of the Sorbonne, everywhere.

Cohn-Bendit amused you?

Yes, but at the same time I took him seriously. "*Nous sommes tous des juifs allemands*" (We are all German Jews),[12] I found that fantastic.

---

12   One of the most famous chants of the demonstrators in May, in defense of Cohn-Bendit, attacked by the Communists as "a German anarchist."

But I didn't believe in it too much. It was the students who shouted that, not the workers. I could feel there was no connection. We marched with the workers but there was no connection.

So physically you occupied the same space ...

The same space, and the workers saw that with the students the demos would be rough, and they thought that was great; it was different from the union bureaucrats, and they loved it. Fighting the cops, not allowing themselves to be had, that was good. But no more than that. And when power was vacant, when de Gaulle had left the country and hundreds of thousands of workers marched chanting "Power to the People," everyone laughed. I knew it was ridiculous. Power to who? Parliament was empty, the building was empty and it was guarded by three cops. And people were shouting power to the workers, power to the workers. It was all very nice, but there were no committees, the PCF didn't want power, there was the meeting with Mendès-France at Charléty, I was invited, and then there was a meeting with Mendès-France and Mitterrand that I was invited to and I refused to go.

Why?

Because I knew it was ridiculous. For me Mendès-France and Mitterrand were shit. I went to Charléty because we were part of the movement, but none of us thought we were an alternative because we were too small. Mendès-France and Mitterrand could be an alternative, but for us it was a bad one. There were small groups among the students and the workers, but there was really nothing. We had our token worker who we'd bring out. We had maybe twenty workers in all. There were some of us who spoke about and wrote about Soviets, but I don't even bother mentioning it, because we had almost no influence. Among the students yes, but not among the workers. Even if in Saint-Nazaire there were strikes that were pretty radical, I know that elsewhere they were set off by workers who were especially radical, like SAVIEM,[13] but we had nothing to do with it.

---

13 Truck manufacturing plant in Boulogne-Billancourt, part of the Renault group.

But when you watch films of you at the time, you seem to really be in the events, to really believe in it.

Well, yeah, I believed, and I was totally in it, but there was always this tiny doubt that this wasn't the socialist revolution. That's why when others said it was I had no trouble saying no. Even though I was *gauchiste* at the time I didn't see the working-class following us. I remember when a year later I ran for president and we went to the Renault factory I was greeted with boos and catcalls. And they were right! I was there, standing on a car, surrounded by comrades and the workers insulted me, and they were right to do so.

But what did you think at the time?

That I provoked them, that they were Stalinists, and that I was right to be there. The PCF had 2,000 members there and we had nothing, maybe two or three. So there I was on the car, surrounded by the stewards, and the others chanted "Fascism Will Not Pass."

But I saw in *Mourir à trente ans* there was a scene of a huge meeting...

Sure, students and professors. Later on, much later, some workers started coming, but back then there was nothing. We would take the ones we had and show them off, but it was ridiculous.

What kind of effect did the general strike of May 13 have on you?

It was fantastic, but I still didn't believe.

Still?

Even when de Gaulle left to go to Germany, and then when he called for elections and the PCF accepted them, I didn't believe at the time and I still don't even now. Everyone said *élections piège à cons* [elections, a fool's game; literally, a trap for idiots], and at that time the elections were truly a trap. We never should have accepted them: by doing it we had the movement enter the parliamentary road when it was the extra-parliamentary road that was positive.

When you started to fight against the war in Algeria there were few of you; the JCR too was small. Suddenly, you're in front of hundreds of thousands of people. How was that?

Well, remember that I began with the Communists, and we distributed tracts and newspapers, so I was used to having contact with people. But in a non-revolutionary period people don't read the tracts, they couldn't care less and throw them out or don't read them, but then when there's a great movement they take the tracts and read them. That's how I describe a revolutionary period.

Would you say there was a theatrical aspect to it all?

No, we thought there was an extraordinary movement: I'd never seen anything like that in my whole life except in books, so I was enthusiastic. We saw people cutting down trees and our group, a few hundred, we would wonder, where's this going? We knew where it wasn't going, and that it wasn't a revolution; there was nothing there that we'd learned in the school of Marxism, the working-class, a party …

You didn't think it might leave the Marxist schemas behind?

No, hardly. It was revolt and not a revolution.

Let's talk about the Gaullist demo on the Champs-Elysées. Had you thought France was behind you?

I was shocked by the numbers. Not that there was a demo: I was surprised there hadn't already been one. And this demo changed people's attitudes. The guy who had said that it was alright that his car be set on fire now said to me, "I'm voting for the guy who protects my car". And this was normal: the working-class was defeated and so the middle-class voted for those who would protect them. It was normal: we'd failed, and now we were going to pay for it.

After Grenelle you must have been disenchanted.

No, that took a while. There was some delay in the workers returning to work … But there was no opposition within the PCF, that came a few years later, and it's only now that they're beginning to say they were wrong in May. In May they were out there singing the "Internationale," but the students, blech, the *gauchistes*, blech, Cohn-Bendit, blech ...

So how do you remain hopeful? You've carried on for decades.

True, but there are many who gave up. But me? I was always a Communist, I've believed since I was a child. I left Communism from the left because of the war in Algeria, I was never a theoretician. Then I was a clandestine member of the Fourth International ... for me it was my upbringing.

But the others ...

My brothers remained Trotskyists until their death, while the others, like Henri Weber,[14] left on tiptoes, never writing a resignation letter. Sauvageot, he's aged so much that I didn't even recognize him. At least he's stayed on the left. Geismar became a minister. And Cohn-Bendit, he's a first-class schemer ... At the European parliament he would still use the old *gauchiste* formulas ... It didn't surprise me; I was never his friend.

Was 1968 1905?

We put a book out calling it a dress rehearsal. I understand all the weaknesses of May '68—no party that was well implanted, no radical unions, no self-organization: I saw all that was lacking and that must be done. So on the one hand today things are better, since parties no longer play a role, the students all have jobs so they no longer are told when you see a worker you should embrace him, and people are more disgusted than they were in '68: they've had it up to here. But on the other hand, the working-class is stronger than before but more divided than before, what with part-time workers, the unemployed, those whose jobs are precarious; they all have different salaries and they don't have the feeling that they belong to the same class. The working-class is in a state of ruin and we haven't been able to replace it. And people no longer

---

14   Henri Weber (1944–), one of the original leaders of the JCR. Later joined the Socialist Party and was elected to the European parliament.

believe. They're disgusted, but they no longer believe. I still believe, but it's really tough, and many of our comrades in the NPA are discouraged and no longer believe either. I still go out selling the party paper on Sundays, and everyone knows me.

Didn't it frustrate you that the workers didn't listen to you?

Absolutely, especially since I came from the PCF, it really annoyed me. But already, when I was expelled from the PCF, that really did something to me. I was summoned to the Central Committee and there was the guy who said, "I officially announce that you're expelled." The PCF was my family, and I understood why they expelled me, but it really bothered me. The cell members were my friends, and at that time when you were expelled you were expelled: people no longer spoke to you. And it was perhaps because we knew the Communist Party, its nastiness, that allowed us to stick it out.

When the JCR was dissolved, what did you do?

Well, there was a press conference announcing we were banned, they arrested me, sent me to the army based in Germany, and I was proposed as a candidate for the presidency. All the leftist groups were banned—except the Lambertists. I found all of it entirely normal. We'd failed and now there was the repression and we were paying. I was arrested with my wife. I was living underground; we'd arranged to meet in front of my high school and the police were there—and poof! So I was sent to prison, but there's no reason to carry on about it: I wasn't tortured or anything. And then they sent me to the army after a month.

Do you have any idea why was there so little violence during May? I mean, there were beatings, but compared to events in France's past, the repression was relatively mild. The same goes for the student and the worker side of things.

That's what the police prefect said. He said to me, "Thanks to you everything went well." For our part, violence for violence's sake, we're against it. I know that our stewards protected an armory near the Gare de l'Est against anarchists, or *gauchistes*, or I don't know who that wanted to rob an armory. But they were crazy: the people weren't ready for that. We weren't against mass violence, but individual violence … It was ridiculous. So we posted 200, maybe 150 comrades in front of the armory and we fought to keep them from taking the weapons. It would have been madness. There were hundreds of wounded, there was the Night of the Barricades that set off the strikes, there were demos, but they never fired into the crowd. At the end there was Tautin.[15] But all in all, the movement, given its breadth, could have been much more violent. I think we played a role in this, I mean the stewards of the JCR. Baader we were against, though we were in solidarity, the Red Brigades … Someone told me there were 30,000 people involved in the Red Brigades, and there were even factory workers.

Did you ever have 30,000 members?

No, never. We never had as many as we have now. When we created the NPA we had 8,000 members, when we began the JCR we had 300, and at the end of '68 we had 800 or 900. Later we grew to 2,000. Today the NPA has less than 3,000.

What changed in you after May?

Personally, nothing. A little bit of regret that I didn't take more care of my children. It doesn't cause me any pain now because I have excellent relations with my daughters; they're grown and we have an excellent relationship. It's also true that I didn't take very much care of my wife either. She accepted it, but there was a distribution of tasks that was completely unequal. On the political level I regret nothing. We did stupid things, to be sure, but I remain every bit as much of a militant as before. What I'm happy about is that I knew—something I'll never see again—an enormous explosion. And that's what allows me to reject those who only remember May '68 for the sexual revolution. I remember

---

15   Gilles Tautin, high school Maoist who drowned on June 10, 1968, fleeing police at a demonstration at the Renault Flins factory.

the general strike. It's Trotsky who said—and it's the only thing I recall from him from memory—during a revolution, with every passing day people become unrecognizable. And that's exactly what I saw. I saw people talking to each other on the street, people you would pass every day and never say hello to and then everyone was talking to everyone. On the metro too everyone talked. It was fantastic. You never drove alone, you picked people up and took them, it was absurd to be alone. People became unrecognizable. I never saw it before and never saw it again.

And France ...

I think here we can talk about the sexual revolution. It permitted the women's movement later on, and the gay movement. There are assholes who demonstrate against it, but there's also the recognition of gays and gay marriage. All this is really important. May freed all this up, but later.

It was a social revolt, not a revolution. A cultural revolution that would later become, thanks to the social revolt, something that left its traces.

On the political level for decades no one dared put May '68 in question, not our parents, not the grandparents. It was Sarkozy who was the first to dare say it was shit. No one dared do this before him, even on the right. Now May is demonized.

And there was the revolt of the artists. That was the time when I knew so many artists and my address book was enormous, but now ... [shows me a slim address book]. I even hid at Piccoli's house in '68 when he was living with Juliette Gréco. We maintained close relations and this would serve us in good stead when we were banned again in 1973.

And your grandchildren?

They're a little politicized. "Grandpa, tell me about it ..."

But in every country there's forgetfulness. Memories remain for a few years, but if conditions change the memories fly out the window. There are those who say, "We have to make a '68 that wins," and I answer it's like pissing in the wind. You tell people this and they go "yeah, yeah …" So we have the impression there was no '68. And even those like me, who lived it, talk less and less about it. They have fond memories of it, but it's far from their concerns. When you fail there's an amnesia, and for the masses there's a disappointment that leads them to go over to the other side.

May '68 failed, so it failed. But you have to rebel, even if you fail.

$\wp$ ϖ

PRISCA BACHELET

Brought up in a milieu she described as "marginal," though receiving a Catholic education Prisca Bachelet spent her time as an adolescent reading anarchist books and attempting to enter anarchist circles. Along with a friend she attempted to meet the great anarchist Maurice Joyeux (grandfather by marriage of Wally Rosell, see below), who threw her out of his bookstore, le Chateau du Brouillard, saying "No minors! We have nothing but headaches with minors!"

At the Sorbonne she entered the world of the French left, learning about all those forces opposed to the PCF, "and God only knows, that was quite a task."

Active in the student union of the Sorbonne's school of letters, she was a militant opponent of the war in Algeria.

She joined the Communist UEC and was part of a left-wing, minority opposition within it, which was expelled en masse in 1965. The congress at which this occurred "was a really violent struggle, people shouting, fighting over the mic. For me the congresses of the UEC were comical." The expelled groups served as the nucleus for organizations like the Maoist Union de la Jeunesse Communiste Marxiste-Léniniste (the precursor to the Gauche Prolétarienne) and the Trotskyist JCR.

Having completed her studies, in 1966 she was assigned a teaching post near the Belgian border, "and even though I was in the provinces and far away, I remained very Parisian."

When her friend Régis Debray was arrested in Bolivia in 1967, Prisca was active in his support network, which led to broader activity in support of the Latin American left, along with her friends Serge July (future editor of the daily newspaper Libération*) and his wife Evelyne. "In France there was nothing, so we were all leaving for Latin America."*

But Prisca, unlike her friend Michèle Firk (who fought with guerrillas in Guatemala and participated in the kidnapping and killing of the American ambassador, killing herself before she could be captured) and Pierre Goldman, stayed in France, working in the cultural section of the town hall of Nanterre. She says of her early days there, "I'm sitting in my office at the town hall and thinking of revolution in Latin America."

While organizing a conference in February 1968 on workers and culture, she realized she didn't know enough about the working-class to truly speak of their interests, so she organized a discussion at the university between students and workers: "The militants in Nanterre would finally have their chance to go to the factories." While she was working at the town hall, the students, led by Daniel Cohn-Bendit, had driven PCF leader Pierre Juquin[16] from the campus and had confronted the minister of sport when he visited the campus. The stage was set for the events at the university on March 22, 1968, which would give the movement its name.

At that time I was living in Nanterre in an HLM [*habitation à loyer modéré*, a form of social housing] that the city had gotten me. On the evening of March 22 Evelyne July was there when it was decided to occupy the administrative tower. It was around 9:00, and she called me at home, where I was enjoying a peaceful evening, and she says to me, "Come on over. They want to occupy the university but they don't know what to do, and you've got experience." And in fact at the school of letters we from the Association of the Faculty of Letters had attempted an occupation

---

16   Pierre Juquin (1930–), graduate of the Ecole Normale Supérieure, member of the Central Committee of the PCF at the time of the events.

in February 1964. I went over, and what do I see but Dany who was—I can't really say presiding—calling on people to speak. I didn't know Dany, so when I saw things that I thought needed to be pointed out, I said I wanted to talk to him in private. He said no, take the floor. I said I wasn't a student and he said no problem, take the floor. This was something that really struck me.

At Nanterre there was a joyful mixing of groups and people. The JCR had carried out an action against American Express. The rumor had spread that those arrested at the demo would be blacklisted from taking their exams. The dean denied this, but the young people were persuaded that there was this blacklist. So they occupied to see if they could get their hands on this list. It was like the *armoire de fer* of Louis XVI:[17] somewhere there was an archive that had to be found. Dany was playing with the keys and he said, "If we find the right key it's a sign that we were right to do this." This was so far away from the imperturbable seriousness of the unions and the opposition Communists I'd known. There was such spontaneity ... Seeing that everything seemed to be going well, I told Evelyne, "I'm going home to go to sleep," so I didn't see what happened after that and wasn't part of the famous photo of the room being occupied.

I went back home and the next morning called a friend and I told him, "I was at a meeting last night and it was either the end of the student movement as we know it"—and I had a very vague idea of what it could be, I'd seen what had gone on on American campuses and it seemed to me a bit wild—"or it's some hippie thing, or it's the end of political activism as we've practiced it, or it's the beginning of something really extraordinary." So that was March 22.

Between March and May ...

It never let up. There was the *université critique*. I went there whenever I had a free moment, and we had a great time. It has

---

17 Reference to the hiding place in the apartments of Louis XVI of compromising documents, discovered and revealed in 1792.

to be said that the Maoists and the Trotskyists at Nanterre were very different from the national varieties. It was far more mixed there, people were good friends. The Comités Vietnam de Base (CVB)[18] wanted to put up posters and while I was in the cafeteria I heard the bigwigs of the CGT who said, "Damn, they're gonna go out and hang up posters again, we have to take care of this." I knew where the CGT was going to be lying in wait for them, so I warned the Maoists and they changed their route for putting up posters.

So even before the events began, the CGT was already opposed to them?

Opposed to things they considered radical about Vietnam and any attempt to enter their factories. You know it's the history of humanity, all these fights over territory ... So that's the kind of stuff I was involved in until May '68.

And on May 3, the day of the disciplinary council, I'm someone quite distant from the students: I have a job that keeps me busy eight hours a day ... In fact, everything was going swimmingly: I had three lovers, I finally had money, I was no longer a teacher, which was an enormous relief, I had my apartment that I'd set up to my liking, I'd signed up for driving lessons; it was not at all a matter of personal revolt! I was in a state of political despair, but this is something I've grown used to, so life was beautiful.

I was at my HLM the day of the disciplinary council. Though I knew that it would be taking place, it really wasn't my main concern when Serge called me and said we're going to the Latin Quarter. I called a taxi and the driver asked me, "Where are we going?" I could only answer, "I have no idea." Once we reached place Saint-Michel I saw all the agitation and I told him to let me off there. I saw there were brawls going on everywhere. I reached place Maubert and suddenly I saw Michel Blutel, who I'd known for years, who was asthmatic and not at all sturdy, in the process of tossing a paving stone at the cops. I said to myself, Oh-la-la! It's begun! Instead of fleeing, as was usually the case, there was

---

18   The Maoist-led anti-Vietnam War committees.

something that'll never be explained, despite all the possible explanations about revolutionary subjectivity and Sartre and all ... It was simply that one day people were no longer afraid.

This was on May 3, the day of the famous photo of girls' shoes ...

What's that? I don't know it.

There's a photo where you can see the street filled with girls' shoes, since they'd lost them when they ran. The tear gas, all of that ....

Did you play hooky from work?

Sometimes I went to work, sometimes I didn't. Finally, from the Night of the Barricades on, I no longer went in.

Was there discussion about where to go in Paris?

There was the occupation of the Sorbonne by the cops and a grand tactical and theoretical discussion about what kind of demo we should have. The UJCML began to show its nose again and they didn't stop saying we have to have demos in the working-class neighborhoods. And the JCR said, "No, we have to stay in the Latin Quarter." The main debate was, do we try to take over the Sorbonne, or do we remain in the Latin Quarter ... Now this caused me enormous problems: I have always been workerist and I'll die workerist, and I said, "Absolutely, we need other people to join us so we can come to a meeting of the minds with them." So on one hand I was pulled towards the desire to go to the masses, and on the other hand I felt a strong drive for us to stay in the Latin Quarter and take over the Sorbonne, a subjective, territorialist, archaic feeling. This brought back memories of the confrontations with the fascists during the war in Algeria, where there too it was a struggle over territory. I would discuss it with Félix [Guattari], and he thought it was perhaps one of the archaisms necessary for revolutionaries. It's not as simple as all that, that territory equals reaction. There's an element of not wanting to be driven out of the place you want to be in.

The Syndicat National de l'Enseignement Supérieur (SNESUP) had joined in the fight, as well as the UNEF, all alongside the

March 22 Movement. The Comités d'Action Lycéen (CAL) [High School Action Committees] were created, which provided reinforcements for March 22, but March 22 had no legitimacy in the eyes of the public yet.

Did you feel that you were part of it?

Oh, I felt completely part of March 22. The journalists ran after us and we had our line that "We don't speak to journalists." While the others talked to everyone … And there was the enormous role of TV, with Dany and Geismar[19] appearing on it regularly. Dany's style was great for mobilizing people, but it had a bad side, because his insolence, his humor … It eventually reached a point that that was all people wanted to see.

At around this time Serge and I and a couple of others contacted someone from our solidarity network who told us, "We're following the events and if you want to continue to work with us you have to stop taking part in street demos. There's no way you can be swept up by the police." They told us we had to choose, so we discussed the options and decided there was no way we were going to miss taking part in history. We chose May '68.

We organized ever greater numbers of demos with ever greater numbers of participants, and we went further and further from the Latin Quarter. I heard somewhere that we weren't interested in prisoners, but that's just not true. We marched past La Santé Prison where the inmates hung banners out in support of us and we swore solidarity between the guys in their cells and us on the street.

Nanterre was only Nanterre: it was one university among others. But as it grew SNESUP, UNEF, the JCR, the Maoists, the Lambertists, everyone was coming on board and wanted to lead the thing.

Now for the first Night of the Barricades. Every time we got back to the Latin Quarter there was an order to disperse. The cops would give the order and then the leaders would say, OK, let's stop.

19   Alain Geismar (1939–), leader of the SNESUP, the union of professors.

So there were open meetings every night in various places to decide what to do, and we from March 22 were increasingly peeved: we had the impression the people's energy was being frittered away. One day the order was given to disperse and I hollered at Geismar and the other leaders, calling them every name in the book, telling them that it wasn't acceptable, that they had no respect for the will of the demonstrators, that we all wanted to stay in the Latin Quarter and they weren't going to drag us around for twenty years, that they had no idea what they wanted to accomplish ... We attacked them really violently right there on the street.

So Geismar came to a meeting of March 22, did his self-criticism as a union leader for having given the order to disperse, declared that he was resigning from SNESUP, though we told him it was perhaps better that he stay there.

Now I who had experience as a union leader, a little, all of this touched me. I saw the contradictions he was living. And the SNESUP was of enormous assistance to us, helping us to run off things on their mimeo machine ... They provided us the means to run off the tracts, and the place for us to write them, the four or five members on the tract commission.

How many were you in March 22?

The number Jean-Pierre Duteuil gives is 142. But before the barricades, more and more people came every day, until we were finally in the hundreds.

When we met we discussed what was to be done, strategy and tactics, we were all for self-organization, rank-and-file action. The Comités de Base were beginning to be created and the day of the Night of the Barricades we had a demo like usual—that is, we covered half of Paris.

So to return to the Night of the Barricades: we're there at the Luxembourg Gardens and we know there'll be the order to disperse. Everyone came over to talk to Dany, Jean-Pierre, Alain, and maybe Maurice Najman[20] for the CAL and gave their opinion

---

20 Maurice Najman (1948–1999), founder of the CAL, later a journalist.

on what to do next. Krivine was there too, and they were saying we have to do this, we have to do that, and we pushed away all the people who were talking and said that only those part of March 22 from the beginning will decide. They discussed and they decided we're going to stay. Not that we're going to put up barricades, just we won't disperse and we'll stay where we are. The cops were at the other end of Boul' Mich' by Saint-Jacques, and we were on Gay-Lussac, probably because there was more room there than on Boul' Mich'. Whatever the case, we'd decided we were staying right where we were. Things were beginning to drag on. Time is long when you're face to face with the cops.

Did you have a foreboding that something was going to happen?

Things were very tense because it was the end of a long day. We felt that if the order was given to disperse things would get rough. At first we stayed, almost as if it was a sit-in. We moved, I don't remember how, to a bookstore that had remained open. The tension rose, on both sides. I roamed around and I saw people were beginning to tear up paving stones. I went back to find Dany and Alain at the bookstore where I'd left them, and I thought, well, it's better people tear up paving stones than that they stand around frightened, feeling the tension. Word then circulated that Geismar said to tear up the paving stones. As far as I know, though, Alain never said any such thing. At which point the barricades started going up. Now I don't know which minister of the interior spoke of a guerilla strategy ... As if these people who were running in all directions were experts in urban guerrilla warfare! So the barricades went up and there you were seeking projectiles just in case, with a paving stone in your hand ...

And you, you had paving stones?

I was incapable of tearing up stones, so I was the liaison agent, running all over the neighborhood ... to inform people of what was going on.

We were there for some time, with the barricades, and there was a kind of incident. There was a telephone in the bookstore and

Dany and the others were in communication with the minister of education or someone like that, and there were skirmishes going on all around. I even saw the students bring a wounded cop back to his camp. Honestly, we weren't savages, we weren't battle-hardened.

You stayed there all that night?

The cops attacked after sending up the rockets—it was either one or three—that was the signal to disperse, since though the call was made over a megaphone no one could hear it because they were so far away. So they attacked and—it must have been 2:00 in the morning or something like that—I have the impression it was a very long night—And what was terrific was that bakers opened their shops and brought us bread—people brought us food, and lemons to counteract the tear gas—they brought us things to drink—we had such fabulous support from the neighborhood.

Despite the disruption of their lives.

They knew we were young people ... It shows up in films about the period, where the parents say, "I would have liked to do this or that ..."

Did you have the feeling you were inserting yourself into French history?

I never asked myself the question. I thought we were in 1905. France wasn't our frame of reference; for me it was 1905 in relation to 1917.

So you knew it was a dress rehearsal ...

At the end. On the Night of the Barricades all I could think about was what was going to happen in the next few hours, what would become of us. We were in no way cold leaders contemplating things. In any case, we refused to be leaders: it's in this sense that May was anarchist. The idea at all times was not to short-circuit the base, not to cut them off; it was to respect the people, our friends, the ones who were there: they're the ones who speak, they're the ones who do. No one should think for them. This was my profound feeling. And I think the others who were close thought the same way. Which doesn't prevent you from thinking about strategy and tactics, because at a certain moment it's necessary.

And the workers in all this?

I went to meetings of the CGT, and guys kept coming in all excited: this factory's on strike, that factory's on strike. People came from small factories to tell us they didn't even have any union delegates and they're on strike and want to vote on it. The general strike was in process of forming. One of the CGT leaders said, "The situation is serious, more serious than in 1958, but we have allies; the Socialists are with us." I was stunned! I, who had visions of 1936 and 1917, the workers throwing themselves into the action, and now, this: it was a cold shower. It's not that they were hostile; it was that they were afraid, afraid of responsibility. What you have to do is to interview the people who put the brakes on the movement. That's something that would be interesting.[21]

With all that, the enthusiasm, the hope ... what did you feel on May 30?

My big disappointment was that we didn't seize the Ministry of Justice. It was empty. The place was empty and barely protected; we could have just gone in and said, "We're occupying the Ministry of Justice." (Here again we have the PCF: a friend in the Ardennes told me it was the PC that prevented the people from seizing the prefecture there. We later learned there were almost no CRS there, since they'd sent them all here.) The real fear was the army. The maneuvers that were going on every day ... Mitterrand called Geismar every day to find out what was going on. I said that if Mitterrand wants to hear from the spokesman of the movement, then let him come to the assemblies of the March 22 Movement.

---

21 See the interview with Guy Texier and the workers from Saint-Nazaire and Nantes below.

There was Flins ... You should write that the head of the Committee for Military Security for Flins was a woman. That's for the people who go around saying that all we did was butter bread ...

The March 22 Movement was dissolved in June, as were most of the other *gauchiste* groups.

When we were dissolved we didn't accept it, and the JCR went underground. I remember a meeting at the Mutualité where we from March 22 presented ourselves publicly: let's see if they arrest us, and if they put us in jail, they'll put us on trial. As Jean-Pierre [Duteuil] said to his son: if you want to be a revolutionary, expect at least five years of prison.

We felt the thing was fizzling out. There was the famous return to work at Wonder. For me I thought (1) even revolutionary armies need to go on leave, and (2) everyone was so tired and things were bad among us: when people are exhausted old personal things come out, lovers' quarrels and all that ...

There were some who thought we were the majority: this was something I never thought. I talked to you before about 1905, well, here I thought it's time to rest; we lost the battle but we didn't lose the war.

It was more things were beginning to decompose, voices on the right were beginning to be raised again, people were losing hope. This was more important than any demo and Malraux and his puppets.

So let me ask you then: you lost the battle, but you didn't win the war.

No, and we're losing it even more now. But we lost *a* war, not *the* war.

What happened afterwards for you?

I resigned from my post at the town hall of Nanterre in June and asked to return to teaching, and after doing little jobs here and there, moving from one friend's house to another, I knew that wherever I worked I'd find things I could say or could do. Eventually I worked at the Ecole Normale des Instituteurs, thus transforming school for the children of the people. What joy! And many of us worked at our workplaces at transforming things; we acted as if we'd seized power and were post-revolution. We were constantly doing work with the rank and file, assemblies and all that. But while we were doing this the Socialist Party reconstituted itself, the right re-mobilized, working like crazy while we didn't, and while we assumed intellectual hegemony, we didn't notice that the bosses were reorganizing and modernizing, that there was new management ... We missed the central axes, which leaves us in the situation we're in.

ℰ   ℛ

HENRI SIMON

Born in the countryside outside Paris, in the Brie, in 1922, as a young man around the time of the Popular Front, Henri Simon was sympathetic to the PCF. For young Henri, living in a poor, rural milieu, "the PC represented a kind of liberation in the face of the flagrant social injustices everywhere." After the war Simon joined the CGT, but never the PCF. As he says, "they never proposed I join. Perhaps they already saw me as a black sheep."

A friend introduced him to Socialisme ou Barbarie, which he was attracted to for its critique of the Soviet Union and the fact that "within France they tried to detect the tendency in France towards autonomy. In all struggles there's something that attempts to escape legal and union shackles, and this has always been a constant for me, this idea of autonomy."

Hired at the government insurance company, Assurance Générale, he defended those workers the unions wouldn't, "people who do stupid things, and the unions didn't defend them. And we defended them."

SouB split in 1958, in part over the question of whether de Gaulle represented fascism. "For our small fraction it was obvious he wasn't fascism, but the idea of the others was that de Gaulle was a fascist—which they quickly dropped afterwards—and that it was necessary for the workers to be present, so they had to be organized in a very formal manner. We refused this and were pushed out the door." He would later form Informations et Correspondances Ouvrières (ICO). For Henri Simon, de Gaulle's role was a complex one. "It was de Gaulle's ambiguity that allowed him to do that. Because at once he had the confidence of the modernizers of capitalism, and he had the confidence of the old; he was an old-fashioned general, so he could do something coherent and advance. It was his ambiguity that allowed him to do what he did."

We were joined for the interview by Lola Miesseroff, who was preparing a history of the French far left.

France is modernizing. It's the mid-'60s. Do you see things bubbling beneath the surface?

Not really. There are groups like the Trotskyists for whom the revolution is just around the corner, apropos no matter what. There were big strikes, miners strikes in '62, but there was no increase in struggles before '68, as some have maintained. That's false. There was neither more nor less than in other periods. Only those who want to say they predicted it can, a posteriori, say they saw it coming. A week before no one thought of it.

What were you doing at the time, at the beginning of May, or even before that, in March at Nanterre?

We had contacts with Cohn-Bendit, who was in Noir et Rouge, a group we were in close contact with. We knew what was going on, but nevertheless, before March 22 the struggle was restricted, curiously, to the fight against the war in Vietnam. The big demos that preceded '68 and even during '68 were around the war in Vietnam. Curiously, since France wasn't involved; it was an American war.

As for me, there was always a separation. My activity at work was my work at work, that is to push people into doing things themselves, to express themselves, to gain their autonomy. That was the axis. On the other hand, I never spoke at my enterprise of my theoretical work. To such a point that during the events someone at work asked me if I knew ICO!

Why?

Because I thought that to declare a political position, even without spreading it, sets you apart, because you go beyond the workers, and the workers' response to political engagement is a certain recoil. It wasn't because I wanted to keep it a secret or to be clandestine; it was because I thought it useless, and even more, harmful to autonomous activity, so I kept it all separate. I never sought to put forth my autonomist ideas theoretically; I always did so practically.

Lola: And to have done so would have been contrary to the very idea of autonomy.

Henri: Absolutely. When a guy came to me and said my boss is busting my balls, will you take care of it? I'd say to him, "You come with me and it's you that will talk." Things like that.

So between March 22 and May 3, what did you do?

The contact wasn't direct. But the students came to see us at ICO and laid out their activities. Which earned us a visit from the Situationists—within the March 22 Movement were the Enragés—to contradict what we'd been told, because inside March 22 there was a conflict between the Enragés and the others. We invited them and we listened to what they had to say. We didn't hear them out in order to participate, but simply in order to be informed of what was going on. But I have to say that at that time these events had absolutely no impact on workplaces. It remained exterior, a student thing, and this separation between workers and students persisted throughout May '68.

Things begin at the Sorbonne, there was the tearing up of paving stones, the big demos ... What did you think?

We thought none of it could have any impact on working-class activity. We thought it was a student thing, it was interesting, but ... A thing that struck me, after what happened on rue Gay-Lussac, which was a Friday, there was no spontaneous reaction from the workers to it. Anywhere. Nothing, absolutely nothing. Monday, May 13 arrives, the conjoined demonstration, students and unions, but spontaneously there was nothing. The radio kept us informed of what was happening. There was nothing. From the very beginning there was a kind of command structure of the student and workers' unions that jointly organized May 13.

So for you the fact that it was a student movement made it interesting and nothing more.

Yes. It really struck me that there was no reaction for two days and everyone could see and know what was happening.

The worker-student demo was on Monday, three days later, bringing everyone together ...

That's what was said, but where I worked I saw that most people didn't go to the demonstration. And there was a total dichotomy between the student and worker fractions. The demonstration as organized beforehand by the worker and student organizations would place the workers ahead under the union banners and the students behind. Everyone was supposed to gather at boulevard Magenta and the demo would start from place de la République. The leadership of the students decided to short-circuit the union demo and to go to the head of the march. They ran down rue de Faubourg Saint-Denis and they reached the bank of the River Seine, just where the workers' demo entered. In this way March 22 and *gauchistes* of all kinds could cross the river and take the lead of the demo, because the idea of the people from March 22 was to try to organize a worker-student assembly on the Champ-de-Mars. Having arrived at the head at place Denfert-Rochereau, all this part of the demo turned to the right towards the Champ-de-Mars, leaving only some militants on place Denfert-Rochereau to advise the workers to follow the students. Then, when the workers behind the union banners arrived, the unions shouted that it was time to break up and to go home towards the left, while those of March 22, having remained on the place, tried to shout "Don't go, go to the right and head to the Champs-de-Mars and the workers and students will discuss things together." I must say that here there appeared a certain pretension on the part of the students to lead things. We had relations with March 22 and they never asked advice on strategy.

When you say "we," who was "we?"

The groups like ICO and Rouge et Noir. We were all workers of one kind or another, and they could have told us we plan to do this or that, will it work? But they said nothing. When we passed there, I told a friend who was in Rouge et Noir, you continue and I'm staying here, because it's here where things will be decided. And in fact, Cohn-Bendit arrived with a megaphone, climbed the lion, the big statue in the middle of the plaza, and began to shout at the worker section that was arriving, "Don't go home." A minute later a sound truck from the PC came playing loud music and Cohn-Bendit was stuck there like a fool and had to climb down. He tried to enter the ranks of the workers with his megaphone—I followed him at this moment—to tell them to stay, when the CGT stewards surrounded us, and at first there was a certain violence, there were some who wanted to hit his megaphone, and there were those who wanted to allow him to speak. So there was already a certain reaction against the union violence. Few followed to the Champ-de-Mars, not even I.

Had they asked us, for example, the simplest answer would have been to print up thousands of tracts and mix in with the crowd and distribute them. That's all.

And what did you do so that people would act more freely and autonomously?

At a demo like that it was impossible. In general, it was impossible, there was nothing to do. After May 13 the government ceded by reopening the Sorbonne and it was occupied. This, in my opinion, was a sign of weakness on the part of the government. A power that cedes before an imposing demonstration, this is a sign of weakness. I think that was the catalyst to say, let's take advantage of this weakness, because the strikes started almost immediately after the occupation of the Sorbonne, and the next week was the general strike.

During all this, what did you see as a possible result?

None. Other than saying there was something that was beginning that should be pushed as far as possible, but that was that. We should push it to see what would develop ...

Lola: Push it towards what?

Henri: Towards a general strike, which is what ended up happening. I was involved at work, in discussions, etc., and I went to the Sorbonne, but the occupation happened, I think, spontaneously. The feeling was that with this sign of weakness we could take advantage of it.

What were you doing at your workplace?

What was happening was that little by little we had news of what was going on and we discussed the events. And on the Monday we of ICO wrote a flyer—which we were much attacked for afterwards, but for us it was a test—that said the moment has come and we have to take the enterprise in hand and see what we're going to do. We didn't distribute it, we were too well known, we risked huge problems and we had people from March 22 do it for us. So on that Monday morning, the unions found themselves forced to call a GA. I don't know if it was the tract that pushed them to it ... In the face of the spontaneous rise of the struggles the CGT immediately put itself in the position of taking the lead in order to control matters. This was clear. They called the GA and all we could do was impose a workers' strike committee that wasn't just inter-union. Nevertheless, they succeeded in taking control of the strike committee, which met continuously and where everyone could speak: it was really open.

At the same time the CGT everywhere blocked any contact with the outside. They posted guards at the door to prevent this from happening.

What was spoken about at the assemblies where you worked?

It was very concrete things, like food. There was something funny that happened one day: a gardener came to the door to take care of privets we had in the office: some had died, and he had come to replace them. There was a debate over whether we allow him to enter and change the plants. That kind of stupidity.

Lola: So he wasn't on strike.

So people didn't see further than that? There were no big demands?

Henri: The comical part of the story, if I can call it that, is that when the strike began there were no demands, and this was the case everywhere. People met with the boss—you had to present something to him—and they elaborated a list of demands based on what people told them. So that could go from personal things happening to them with their jobs, to more general things, like salaries. This explains why the Grenelle Accords took hold so quickly: they satisfied a certain number of things. At the beginning there were no demands. People went on strike because others had gone on strike.

And what did you say at assemblies?

I said we had to maintain the struggle, and criticized the fact that there were negotiations. At a certain moment the CFDT tossed out the idea of self-management. I remember speaking up saying that this was self-management in their interest. There was a kind of committee formed to study self-management. I attended to see what they were talking about, and the committee was made up only of middle managers, not a single base-level employee, which meant they didn't give a damn about it.

Union organization was such that there were divisions within each union: there was the union of the employees, the supervisors, and the middle managers. And it was the middle managers who were interested in self-management; in the end it was technocratic self-management they wanted. I listened to what was being spoken about and I said: under another system insurance is pointless. The problem is what we should do with the offices? Should we convert them into hospitals? At that moment it was all over.

Even so, there were strikes and demos everywhere, there was the workers-student connection. But this still wasn't what you were waiting for?

I was waiting for nothing. And I was waiting for everything. I had no preconceived ideas. Things for me had to evolve, and if they didn't ... And you talk about demos, well, there's no doubt there were demos, but few strikers went to the demos. Very few. It was mainly students and a few people who were workers who went on their own, but not otherwise.

When you went to the demos, did you give out your flyers?

The characteristic of the demos in '68 was that there were no flags, no songs, and no distribution of tracts.

But there were the slogans like "It's Only a Beginning! Continue the Struggle."

No. You know, the crowd was silent. In the Latin Quarter I had the feeling we were at a funeral.

It was very different from the demos I'd known. It really struck me. There was a crowd, indistinct, where you couldn't distinguish anything. It would have been inappropriate to distribute tracts.

And you found that good or bad?

It was how it was. There was great confusion. There was a big demo that set off from the Gare de Lyon, that went down rue Réaumur to get to the Stock Exchange. There was a little commando that decided to set it on fire. All they were able to set aflame was the phone booth at the entrance, and that was all. There was the idea—which wasn't followed—that we'll occupy the Stock Exchange. They'd occupied the Odéon, so why not the Stock Exchange? Which would have been much more symbolic than setting a phone booth on fire. It could have been not only symbolic, but polarizing. In any case it wasn't done. I saw Geismar, who'd climbed the fence of the Stock Exchange, surrounded by his people, and he asked—and I saw this with my own eyes—what do we do now? Which shows that even the generals didn't know what to do with the moment. The demo set off again and reached place Vendôme, and there were some who wanted to occupy the Ministry of Justice, but I heard—I don't know if it's true—that Michel Rocard[22] dissuaded them. In any event, the demo set off again, it went along the quais, and reached the Latin Quarter. The cops had left a bridge open so the demo walked into a trap, and the cops tossed tear gas grenades at the demonstrators. The air was unbreathable. My children had a little flat at the time, and about a dozen of us found ourselves in a 20 square meter apartment where we passed the night waiting for the gas to disperse. So you see it was a demo that was headed nowhere and found itself in a trap.

But people I've spoken to who were involved in March 22 found this good, that they didn't know precisely where they were going.

That's obvious. But at the same time it allowed all kinds of manipulation on the part of the authorities.

How did the vote go at your place on the Grenelle Accords?

The CGT played a very ambiguous role. The vote on the return to work was a fraud. At my enterprise they announced at 11:00 that there would be a vote at 2:00 on an agreement they'd reached with the bosses. That left us as the opposition, since there were quite a few of us, practically unable to write and produce a tract, since we had nothing at hand: they had all the means. All we could do was distribute blank pages saying that this meant abstention. Despite it all, one third of the vote opposed the agreement, which granted a few little things here and there, trifles, if you will. A pay raise, maybe it was 5 percent in application of Grenelle.

---

22   Michel Rocard (1930–2016) was leader of the independent leftist Parti Socialiste Unifié in May; he later joined the Socialist Party and was prime minister from 1988 to 1991.

So there was no assembly to discuss it?

Absolutely not! Nothing. A fake! At 11:00 they announced a vote at 2:00!

Even so, if one third said no, two thirds said yes. They'd had enough?

Hard to say. People returned, bowing before reality, but there was a secondary episode: our place was a government office under the control of the Ministry of Finance. The agreement called for payment for the time we were on strike. But the ministry rejected the agreement, saying there was no way the hours on strike would be paid for. So a new strike committee was formed by the unions, and in this committee I proposed we try to create self-organization in every service, which would decide what to do. When the unions learned this was being done, they blocked it all. There was a big demo and it ended with another agreement which reached the same results with circumvolutions, and the movement died. There were ideas that were germinating, but they couldn't flower because the unions immediately blocked them.

How did you view the demo on the Champs-Elysées?

They played *la France profonde* against industrial, active, wage-earning France. They played on fear. And there were rumors, I don't know if you heard them, that it was the same people who simply went from the head of the march around to the back. It's quite possible.

Lola: But either way, there were a lot of people.

Henri: Oh yes, there were a lot of people.

During the events, did you think France was behind Paris?

I never thought that, it never even crossed my mind. You move forward, period. I never posed the political question.

Lola: Even so, the strike was all over France.

Henri: You have to look at France's social situation. At the time there were still at least 30 percent peasants. It was rapidly evolving, but there was still a large fraction tied to traditional property. The Gaullists must have mobilized people who relied on the countryside.

Lola: And there were the small shopkeepers as well. You never heard or saw them during May, but they were there.

Henri: And it was a measure of the fear that was felt, because a movement like May '68, for the middle-class, was the revolution. They didn't know where it was going. We didn't, nor did they. They fantasized about it, that's certain.

What did you think about the return to work?

It's difficult to measure the effect because the unions pushed and pushed for the return. There were places, like Sochaux, where it went badly. They'd taken possession of the city of Montbéliard, where the factory was, and there were terrible confrontations where the workers took CRS prisoners and they're said to have thrown one into an acid bath.

Lola: Do you believe that?

Henri: I don't know a thing, but there was one person killed. The whole region was like that. Many of the workers come from a rural milieu and they all have hunting rifles. There was a brief period where there was a kind of localized insurrection and the cops retreated. It was the social democrats who intervened who settled the situation. But for a brief period, and it was the only moment in '68 when there was a kind of autonomization of the movement on a local level. It was at the moment of the return. This was the place where there were real possibilities.

It has to be said that the authorities were very skillful. The prefect Grimaud did everything possible to avoid incidents, contrary to de Gaulle, who wanted to fire into the crowd.

Why was there so little violence in France compared to many other countries?

First there was the deliberate policy of the government to avoid too violent a repression. It was limited to tear gas. For the confrontations, there was a limit beyond which violence didn't go.

There's another reason, and that was the union control that existed in France and not in a country like Italy. There was a mix of union and student movements in Italy, so there was no union that could interpose itself as the CGT did here. In France the unions fully played the role of keeping things in check. The fact is there were no Action Committees inside the factories, they were only outside the factories.

What happened to you afterwards?

And as for me, in '71 I found myself fired, because without our really being aware of it the relation of forces had changed and repression was unfurling everywhere. We had held prisoner a labor-management committee over the management of the company and over salary issues. I was fired after this. I looked back afterwards and the number of militants who found themselves fired under the same conditions was frightening. Things were taken in hand, which was inevitable, because when a movement ends the relations of force collapse. The militants in place don't always see this and think things can go forward. You don't see that the others are in the process of reinforcing their power.

Lola: And like the young dopes we were, we thought that things would continue to progress. So what was your analysis of '68?

Henri: It was a great confusion. I think that a transformation of mores had been going on for some time because of transformations in the system, and that in the end '68 was a mark of that, but it didn't cause the change. May '68 smashed forms of control and brought others, it modernized the system. And the restructuring of the capitalist system was happening.

You can't underestimate the conformism of the time. I have photos of myself speaking at assemblies during May. I'm surrounded by union leaders, and all of them are wearing jackets and ties. I'm the only one not wearing a tie.

CHAPTER THREE

Students in Paris

For me it was something like the famous cartoon in the
New Yorker where there's a typical New Yorker's vision of
America, where New York is gigantic and the rest of the
country is a little spot. As a Parisian I had the same impression.
Ahhh, things are going on elsewhere, that's nice. We were polite.
—Jean-Pierre Fournier

SUZANNE BORDE

Though much attention is focused on the factories and schools, the neighborhood Action Committees were an important element of May. Suzanne Borde was a member of the Comité d'Action of the third and fourth arrondissements, along with Pauline Steiner, whose interview follows below. When I asked Suzanne what she did after May, she said, "I taught chemistry and physics until 1976, and then went to work at the CRS as an astrophysicist. I had my daughter in 1971. I made new friends and worked hard at keeping the old ones. I knitted sweaters. I bicycled and grew flowers. I learned Italian and Russian. One can do many things in life, and I continue to do them!"

I was 24 in May '68 and I had absolutely no political life before the events. I had the education of the average Catholic Frenchwoman. I pursued it until I was 18, when I realized it was all shit and I dropped it. So politically, nothing.

I arrived in Paris with my boyfriend in '67 from Grenoble, right on time, and attended Jussieu. When things started at Nanterre I heard about it and was interested, vaguely, but it only really began to matter to me in early May when a group of people entered the lecture hall and said, "We're on strike. Those who want to leave should leave." And the professor said, "OK, those who want to can go." And me, not in the least political, I stayed in the lecture hall. There were ten of us, and I was sick until the end of the class. "Why didn't I leave?" As soon as the class ended I ran outside and said, "I want to participate, give me flyers, I'll distribute them." And I did. I had no idea what I was distributing.

No one was surprised that the professor told you you could leave?

No, it seemed totally normal. There were the ten of us who remained in the huge lecture hall, but that day was the catalyst, and I began to live May '68. That evening I went home to the *chambre de bonne* I shared with my boyfriend, and I told him what had gone on at school. I said to him, "Let's go," and he said, "No, mass movements don't interest me." So I went on my own and took a place at the back of the demo. The cops had released tear gas and I cried and cried, both from the tear gas and my rage at my boyfriend. I had to be there because I had to live it. So that was how May '68 began for me.

Within a week I realized that what was going on at school didn't interest me. The school was occupied and I continued to go there, but now as a militant, not as a student attending classes. I gave out tracts—I read them so I could see what I was distributing—but I realizd it didn't interest me, this way of seeing. And it was then that I heard of the Comités d'Action (CA) in the neighborhoods. To tell you just how far I was from any kind of politics, when I went in search of the CA, along my way was the office of the PCF in the fourth arrondissement, and I went in and asked them, "Where's the committee?" as if they would tell me that. They were nice about it, they took my name and address, but that was my sole dealing with the PCF.

I found the CA and found my way of being active, in the CA in the third and fourth arrondissements.

You didn't go to the Sorbonne for the GAs?

Sure, but not for the GAs; it was more to show my solidarity. I occupied for a while. But the blah-blah-blah political element of May '68 wasn't for me. For me it was the CA in the third and fourth, talking with people, meeting with them at the marketplace. We distributed flyers we'd written during the week, and with a friend we hung up posters every night; we wrote on the walls …

What attracted you to the CA?

It was the permanent discussions, where everyone expressed their thoughts about what was going on. How we saw life. And this completely changed me, changed my way of thinking. Until then I had no political consciousness or any idea of what my life would be. Now I was living with a boy without being married to him, which was a great change from my well-bred life, but aside from that I had no idea of anything … And to meet all those people! It little by little opened my mind.

78

And I even changed physically. When I arrived in Paris I was the type of girl who wore a nice pleated skirt. Not that I actually wore one, but I was the type to wear one. A young, proper girl with long hair and a bow. And then suddenly, I went to have all my hair cut off and out of some fabric I found I made myself a skirt—red, that only reached to here—and I wrote along the bottom, in black marker, "Indecency is not in the clothing but in the gaze." You had to spin me around to read the whole thing.

Everything changed, my way of thinking, everything. I would send all our newspapers to my family, so many that my father reminded me that he had sung the "Internationale" well before I did, in 1936. My favorite expression at the time was *"La Vie, Vite"* (Life, Quickly)! I wanted to change the usual way of life.

Had you been unhappy before?

Not in the least. I had a happy childhood.

So what were you rebelling against?

Until then I'd rebelled for the first time in '62 against my parents, I was 18 and had passed my bac. I'd met a guy—the one I'd move to Paris with—and we had flirted, OK? And it was a question of going further. My parents got wind of this and they carried on about this boy who was corrupting their daughter. I rebelled against this, saying it was my life. My parents reacted well, but they said if you want to live your life that's fine, but then you have to work. So I became an elementary school teacher, continuing my studies at the same time, and keeping the boyfriend. So this was my first rebellion against the established order. So May '68 showed me I was on the right road. As a teacher it led me to have a different relationship with the children, and I saw that the way the school functioned wasn't right at all. All of this was made concrete by May. May showed me the way I should live. This was what was true and right for me.

Were you inspired by any of the leaders?

No, only the people on the CA. That was my world, and among ourselves we discussed things, everyone gave his or her opinion.

There were some there who were older, who'd lived the campaign against the Algerian War, who had even been in the Resistance, and these people gave me a lot in their way of thinking, and of saying things.

And even though you had no political formation, you felt strong enough to talk to people on the street?

It seemed natural to me, given the circumstances. I always loved to communicate, so it was not a problem. Though I was a well-behaved little girl, I was never one to bite my tongue. And even within the CA, where there were people with a deeper background than I, they listened to me. But I was impressed by them, people who had well-thought-out ideas. I didn't always follow them, but I contradicted them when I wasn't in agreement. And from this I developed my own voice.

When you spoke to the people on the street, did you use the familiar *tu* form with them?

No, no, no. The young yes, but not those older. It wasn't the French Revolution. And I didn't call them comrade.

Were you at all inspired by events in the French past, like the Commune?

Oh yes, and I started reading about the Commune immediately. Others spoke about it and I knew absolutely nothing about it, so I started reading up on it. It was an example, especially Louise Michel, who was a teacher. What attracted me in the Commune was the relations among the people. What pleased me in the Commune and in May '68 was the way of speaking. Even now my grandchildren say, "Stop grandma, you talk too much."

Did you think that, like the Communards, what you were doing was doomed to failure?

No, and anyway, it wasn't a failure. For me, in my life, May gave an impulse for changing schools, for women, for homosexuals: it opened eyes to all this. Perhaps this was only in my milieu, but I never viewed May as a failure, and it's precisely for that reason that I wanted to continue. And this time for good.

Where did your CA meet?

We met at different people's houses, and we'd spend the evening doing silk-screen posters; we found a way to improvise and get it done. One of us had a huge apartment where we used to make them, and we spent the nights putting them up. We were arrested several times while posting them. We'd spend the night at the commissariat, and I remember there was one night when the bucket and broom I used to plaster them up were stolen, so I went back to the commissariat and made a formal complaint.

Did you have a place you went to regularly to meet with people in the neighborhood?

At that time, every Sunday, on avenue de Bretagne, there was a market with little tables where people sold their produce. We found a place near a blank wall, and we pasted up paper and told people to write on it whatever they wanted. We also wrote what we thought, and then there were discussions with the people. And of course, every time we did so the police came and chased us off. But most of the time they weren't aggressive about it, and we knew that we were going to spend much of our Sunday afternoon at the commissariat. We were prepared for it, so we brought oranges, and sandwiches for lunch. The cops came to know us, and they'd tell me, "No point in talking to you, we'll get nothing out of it." We knew them, they knew us and it was usually OK, except one time they sent the CRS and then it was pretty violent. We responded violently and they had to carry me to the paddy wagon.

Why'd they send the CRS after you?

Who knows. Maybe they'd gotten word from higher up that our presence had gone on long enough, though the people at the market had no complaints. And the cafe that was there certainly had no complaints, since we went to drink there every Sunday.

What did people write on the walls?

I can't remember what they wrote, but we expressed our desire to change life.

It was more change life than change society?

It was change life. Some of us did want to change society, but we weren't aggressive about it. And our main idea was to change life, change our lives, open yourself to others, let's talk …

Did the people in the market write as well?

Looking back, I'd have to say only a little. But at the time I thought we were having a real impact. But mostly they continued to buy their vegetables, though some talked with us, some joined us.

Did you dress and look differently from the people shopping?

Yes. For my part I looked like a real hippie, with my long skirt.

Dressing like that, did you set yourself off from the others? Did you alienate them?

I dressed that way because it was natural, and though I differentiated myself from them, I didn't alienate them. But it's true they didn't dress like us. My grandmother called me "The Slob."

When it was at its height, what was the largest number in the CA?

About forty. Maybe fifty. We were two arrondissements, it was the right amount, it was lively, and though we spoke before about the Commune, I was also exposed to anarchists, and if I were to define myself it would be as an anarchist. But not a political anarchist.

Though I avoided the Sorbonne, we went to every demo as a group. We had banners that said we were the CA of the third and fourth arrondissements, and they were always centered around changing life rather than eliminating de Gaulle.

I only approached the barricades once, but I didn't participate in the Night of the Barricades. It scared me and I quickly beat it out of there. And for many years I was afraid of the police and the CRS. When I'd see them I'd freeze. After all, I'd been arrested several times. I was once arrested with Marguerite Duras. At the end of a demo we found ourselves together in a paddy wagon and we were taken in, photographed, put on file.

For someone who wasn't at the barricades or who didn't go to the Sorbonne, you were certainly arrested a lot.

Several times. It's because I didn't run fast enough. It was because of my long skirts and sandals.

You had good relations with the people in your neighborhood?

Excellent.

Did you feel like they agreed with you?

My idea then and now was that my life should be an example to others. I was always someone who was pleasant to others, open, while having my own ideas. The people in the neighborhood I spoke to might not have shared my ideas, but they accepted me. I was a teacher and I was accepted as a teacher in a long skirt …

The life I wanted to change was first off mine. To set an example. I didn't want to force people to live like me; all I wanted them to do was to be open-minded and accept all ways of living.

And when there was that pro-de Gaulle demo in late May I didn't think we'd failed, I just said to myself, there are assholes and there'll always be assholes. What was important was to talk to people one on one.

The Action Committee continued to exist, right?

Yes, and everyone had the same enthusiasm, wanted to meet, to discuss. To find a way to remain active. We kept putting up posters, demos or not. And we continued all the way through '69. And then, when I decided to leave for a commune it was with people from the CA. At the beginning, after May '68, the following winter, several of us—six of us—went to Switzerland. We were really happy living together, and when the time came to return to Paris it was raining cats and dogs and we didn't feel like leaving. Then the sun came out and we decided that was it, we're staying. So those who had jobs quit and we said we're going to live together in the south. We came back to Paris and told everyone what we were going to do and said, "Let those who love us follow us." And in summer '69 we left to live near Montpellier and built our own house. I met a guy, we fell in love, and I told him to come join us. But we weren't a couple! We were so little a couple that we quickly decided to have a child, who was born in 1971. Then the commune fell apart. We had no idea what to do next, so we decided to educate our child differently, and formed a second commune that lasted through the '70s, raising our children differently. They didn't go to school. We all had jobs—I was a teacher—and the commune was so large that we had four buildings. There was the mill, where we brought the children together, there was an organic farm, there was a building for women who didn't want to live with men, and then there was a building for couples with children. It was here that I lived what I'd dreamed of living.

All this was a direct result of '68. My daughter was born in 1971 and lived on a commune till 1979, so she's truly a child of May '68.

This second commune ended in failure also, when many of the parents panicked when their children reached age six. Until then they're in the nursery and it's not a problem, but at six you have to go to school, so some of the parents pulled their kids out. Then there were other problems, with people wanting to pull out their shares and live differently. We couldn't find replacements for them and it ended badly and sordidly, with me the only one who really wanted to continue.

May '68 didn't result in anything concrete then.

Sure it did. It completely changed the way I live.

But in France …

In general, yes. It made it possible to change the way children were educated, leading many teachers to reflect and to teach differently. Experimental schools opened, and my two grandchildren went to experimental elementary schools that aren't even private. But it had no consequences on political life and failed to change anything real.

Without May '68 what would you have been? Would you have remained the person you were on May 2 had there been no events beginning May 3?

I think everything was germinating within me, and I wouldn't have been very different from what I am now. I might have remained a teacher, but I left teaching—or rather teaching left me—in 1976 because I had a way of teaching and saw to it that everyone passed their bac one way or another by giving them the grades they needed to get it if they were close to the score. Later I joined the CNRS as an astrophysicist, which I studied while I was working as a teacher, since I loved to learn. And this would not have been different. Perhaps I'd have married, which I never did.

So for you, in the end May '68 wasn't a mass movement, it was a way to change yourself.

Exactly.

ℴ ⇣

ISABELLE SAINT-SAËNS

Isabelle Saint-Saëns, who was 20 in 1968, came from a family both political and artistic. Her father, a professor at the Ecole des Beaux-Arts, was a member of the PCF, though opposed to many of the party's positions. "From 1945 to 1970 he was part of a group within the party that was critical of its line, people who naively believed they could change the party by criticizing it from within." He was among the signatories of the Manifesto of the 121, which called on those called to service in Algeria to refuse service or desert. He would leave the party in 1968, after the invasion of Czechoslovakia. From this Isabelle admits that her parents' experience taught her that "political parties and their bureaucracies were something I saw that had to be fought against, something I'd also learned from my mother, who was in the Resistance in the south and had been deported to Ravensbruck, had met Spanish women who were able to testify to the way the Communists acted during the civil war." Both her parents would support the revolt of May.

Why did you go to Nanterre?

This was purely a matter of chance. At the time we were dispatched to schools based on where we lived. I lived in the eighteenth, in Montmartre, so I was sent to Nanterre. I never contested this and asked to go to Paris. All my friends were there, some of them a year ahead of me, since I'd done a year of preparatory class in science. So even if it wasn't mandatory—and we'd have to check to see if I'm right—all my friends were there.

Now things actually began in Nanterre in '67 …

That's true, but there was also the fact that there was a general effervescence that was particular to Nanterre, while at the same time there was an opening on to the world. At Nanterre, for all the far-left parties, even the Communists, one of the main subjects of mobilization was the war in Vietnam, be it in the CVB, that is, the Maoists, or the Comités Vietnam (CVN), that is, the Trotskyists. As for me, opposed as I was to groups, I had friends in both. So I followed what went on in the CVB because I had a close friend there, but I was closer to the CVN because there was an openness about it and less dogmatism than with the Maoists. I was also a sympathizer for about a year of the JCR, and at the end of that year they told me I could join, but I chose not to. I enjoyed all the discussions that were going on at Nanterre, between the anars, the Maoists, and the Trotskyists.

What were the first actions there? In '67 …

There was a first occupation, a first strike, in November '67 to demand that the boys could visit the girls' dorms and vice versa. Even though I didn't live in the Cité Universitaire, it was a convenient place to hold meetings on evenings and weekends. As for the strike, there were posters everywhere, there were picket lines everywhere, we discussed non-stop.

One of the things that mobilized us originally was when Malraux as minister of culture wanted to fire Henri Langlois, the director of the Cinématheque. There were a bunch of us from Nanterre who went to support him. Here's a tract that that we distributed in Nanterre. I don't know if it was Truffaut or Godard who wrote it, but it's magnificent. Look, I even scribbled "The NLF Will Win" on it! There wasn't just one demo, there were many, and then later, when the Cannes Festival was interrupted, there were even people from Nanterre who went there.

And then there was March 22, 1968.

On March 20 there was an action against the Vietnam War organized by the JCR in front of American Express, near the Opéra. It was very well organized and there were about 200 of us. We took the metro and when we got off—maybe at Opéra—we passed in front of American Express and some people tossed things at it. No one was arrested at the time and the next day—or maybe two days later—Xavier Langlade, one of the organizers, was arrested. He was a wonderful man who died a few years ago. So immediately the decision was taken to occupy the faculty council room of Nanterre. The school had a lively cultural life, and that evening there was a concert of classical music and we went there to speak. We entered the hall and said, "Free our comrades. The NLF will win."[1] And then we took the elevators that were normally reserved and we climbed to the seventh or eighth floor—it's an image I still carry with me—and all night we occupied the room of the faculty council.

How was the decision taken to do that?

It was just like that. It was decided to do something, and that we needed to hold discussions, which is just what we did all night.

---

1   The concert that night was not in the same building as the occupation, which was in the administration building.

We weren't going to be satisfied with demanding freedom for our comrades, we were going to launch a movement. We discussed society, the struggles of the working-class—because one of the things that mobilized us was support for the workers' strikes, the strikes in Rouen ... And as I said, there was an opening onto the international situation, the US, the war, and there were people among us who were older who could talk about the war in Algeria. These were people who came to see what was going on in Nanterre, because they'd heard there was a group of young people there doing funny things.

There were 142 of us there.

Cohn-Bendit was there of course. Was he already known?

He was already known. And he didn't assume the posture of a leader, like among the Maoists and even some Trotskyists. He was simply someone who knew how to talk and didn't abuse it. He didn't say, "Me, I know" or "I will subjugate you through my amazing words." He was also someone amazingly cultivated with an incredible family story: his parents were German political refugees, friends of Hannah Arendt's ... He served as a connector so things would gel between people from different groups. Dany managed to crystalize everything, and it's true that he later perhaps assumed too much, though this was perhaps something owed to the press, which had a terrible need for a leader. Now objectively he had the role of leader, because he knew how to bring people together, like at the moment of the inauguration of the pool, when the minister made a big speech about the role of sport in allowing people to fulfill their potential and Dany said this was the kind of speech we could hear in Nazi propaganda. When he did this he was threatened with expulsion. And this was well before March 22.

We occupied the school and we remained until the end of April, early May. That is, we were there and there were no more classes, and there were many professors who supported us, Henri Lefebvre, the philosopher, was with us, and Baudrillard and Lyotard were completely on our side and took part in meetings. Something else that was important was the Situationist pamphlet *De la Misère dans le milieu étudiant* ...

So the school is closed and a day or two later—this is how I remember it, and since this is my story we'll stick with that—there's a meeting at the Sorbonne about the students expelled from Nanterre. But not only to support us, but to do something. The people there were from Sorbonne Letters, including people like Marc Kravetz, people a little older than us who'd been active during the war in Algeria but who closely followed what was going on. And then the police came in and arrested everyone—I wasn't there, to my great regret.

This was before May 3?

Probably. Anyway, once we no longer had Nanterre as our rear base—as the Maoist assholes called it—we met at the Sorbonne and at the offices of SNESUP on rue Monsieur le Prince. And I remember that around this time the group around Guattari and Geismar came in and said we absolutely have to work with you.

There were nine students summoned before the disciplinary council, at the Sorbonne where there was a great assembly that turned into a demo. After that there were demos every day.

Were you there on the first day, when people started tearing up the paving stones?

Oh yes, but not in the front line: I was never very brave. At least not to the point of throwing paving stones.

From that point on I almost never slept at home, and my father often slept at Arts Decos. My mother also participated in the events. We came home in the morning and then went right back out again. While we were occupying Nanterre my mother would ask, "When's this gonna end? It's almost time for final exams."

And did they happen?

They weren't held. No tests took place in Paris and maybe even in France. There were certain Maoist leaders, people who've evolved greatly since, people at ENS (Ecole Normale Supérieure), who forbade their members from participating in the petit bourgeois barricades. The Maoist leaders were real bureaucrats who sent their members to go work in factories while they remained comfortably in their schools. For example, in September '68 when the tests were finally held, Blandine Kriegel[2] and her husband took them and said, "Well, the degree could someday be useful." At the same time there were people, including Maoists, who boycotted the *agrégation* and who never took it or took it many years later. They had this "We have the correct idea" side to them, all that Maoist stupidity.

Did you see beyond the "critical university"? Were you looking to change society?

There were immediate demands concerning the university and factories, but I don't think we saw as far as changing society. That's why I was surprised when I went to Italy in June, where I had a lot of friends. I went to Venice to the lecture hall of the university, which was packed to the rafters with students and workers. Maybe I was the wrong person to send to talk about what was happening in Paris, but I found myself stumped, since the Italian comrades had a theoretical analysis of the situation in Italy and Europe that was far more advanced than ours. There was another difference between Italy and France, which was that they were much more used to rank-and-file activities, to squats, to local actions, the circulation of ideas …

What are your memories of May 10, the Night of the Barricades?

I spent all my time running from rue d'Ulm to place de la Contrescarpe. There was a moment—it began joyously and then became tense and violent. I was on rue d'Ulm and people said there's the Foyer Liban and there were people who sheltered us

---

2 Blandine Kriegel (1943–) was a Maoist at the time of the events who did, indeed, get a graduate degree in 1968. She ceased all political activity and broke with the left within a couple of years and concentrated on her work as a philosopher.

there till the morning. There were about ten of us in a tiny studio. It was all pretty impressive, with the cars burning.

Were you afraid?

Of course!

There are some who weren't, saying this was finally the moment to fight the cops.

No, that's not my thing. Like everyone else, I thought they were bastards and said they all should be killed, but ...

Monday May 13 was the monster demo ...

That was really impressive. We marched as far as the Invalides and afterwards we went back to the Sorbonne, which was now open, and I saw a guy there playing the piano in the entryway and everyone was talking among themselves.

When we marched with the workers we felt united with them, but it remained theoretical as well. For me, in any case, that was how it was, even if at Nanterre we'd had some liaison with the workers. It never occurred to me to go work in factories, and for distributing tracts I would go to Citroën on Quai Javel or Renault at Billancourt. But you have to bear in mind the power of the PCF and the CGT, and their line, which was Stalinist, reactionary ... They had a vision of the economic and international reality that at the time could still be sustained, given the power of the working-class and their leaders, and then we came along to shake all this up.

At the Sorbonne ...

We occupied and we discussed. I didn't occupy it, but we met there, but also other places. And I believed in it, but we began to be disenchanted, and the last demo I took part in was that at the Bastille after de Gaulle's return from Baden-Baden. It was transmitted—I have no idea how—and it was clear that the state was back in force. I remember we crossed Paris, and it was the night the Stock Exchange was set on fire, but we were stopped by the cops at place de la République, so I wasn't there for the fire.

But let's go back to the demo on the Champs-Elysées. Was it real or did you think it was fake …?

I thought that things were no longer going well. The government was taking things in hand after a moment of hesitation, which could then give confidence to those who were either against or not for us that we had once again the assertion of authority, repression. I don't know if you have the pictures of it in your head, but there was a huge mass on the Champs-Elysées, and on the front line there was Malraux held up by the others. I felt like it was the return of the living dead. Malraux was being held up by two ministers, one on each side. I remember a meeting at Beaux-Arts after this demo and de Gaulle's speech from Baden-Baden, and we from March 22, Geismar and July among them, were writing a tract that began with "The Bourgeoisie Is Scared, Power at Bay Provokes." I remember a friend and I broke out in laughter. We thought the bourgeoisie no longer had its back against the wall, perhaps it had once been, but it no longer was.

You laughed, but did you think that those who wrote the tract were serious?

Absolutely! There was auto-persuasion. Geismar and July weren't yet Maoists, but there was a kind of incantatory power to the words. Later that year July and a group of his friends went to Cuba and they went to see Castro and they brought with them a book that they told him he had to read: *Vers la guerre civile* [Towards Civil War], in which there's a chapter "Vietnam: Geometric Place of our Most Profound Joy"! We were truly carried away by the struggle of our Vietnamese comrades, by the Vietnamese army, but with the thousands and thousands being killed under American bombs, how could they say, "Our most profound joy"? This was the beginning of all those military incantations that later led the Gauche Prolétarienne (GP) to say, "We're the new partisans." What monstrous stupidity! Now one of the most effective slogans of the twentieth century was "CRS SS." Which is totally idiotic. After all, if you know history the SS has to do with extermination, it's got nothing to do with the violence—even extreme—of the CRS. So to say "CRS SS," however brilliant it was as a find—it's short, punchy, it rhymes—in looking at events by placing the past over the present you understand neither the one nor the other.

Though things continued into mid-June, when did you feel like it was all over?

If there's a moment that incarnated that, I don't remember the date, but it was when we decided to go to Flins. I remember we first went to Nanterre and ate couscous in a restaurant in the slum there. People had been going to Flins all day, and then we set off and like total asses we decided to go by car. There we were, me, Serge July, Geismar, maybe Prisca; we took the Saint-Cloud tunnel and there, because people had been heading to Flins for a few hours, we were arrested and spent twenty-four hours at the police station. They were stopping every car going west.

What law had you violated?

I have no idea. They held us for twenty-four hours—the maximum allowed—for an identity control. There were tons of people at the commissariat, we were singing in the cells. The girls were in one cell, the boys in another, and in our cell was Jean-Edern Hallier[3] with his fiancée of the moment, they'd taken his sumptuous convertible and like us he was arrested. We were chanting "CRS SS" and he told us, "Be quiet, you're going to get them worked up!" Then he used his pull and got himself released well before us.

But being arrested, why I felt it was the end, it was that in Flins it was really really violent, it was there that Gilles Tautin died. We didn't succeed in making the connection with the workers. Later on people from the GP would work in the factory, but for me that was the moment when we couldn't do any more.

What did you feel after all the demos, the occupation, and then suddenly it's over?

---

3   Jean-Edern Hallier (1936–1997), writer and journalist, famous as a provocateur and bon vivant.

We thought it would start up again. I stayed at Nanterre, but for ten years I was depressed—though it was more general and not really because of the failure of May—I drank, and that doesn't help things. I stayed at Nanterre, where not much was left, and then I began to work. I was involved in feminism, in work with the peasantry ... There were those who stayed more active than I, but for me it was different.

But it wasn't all over, there were interesting things going on in the '70s that could have saved us: feminism, gay rights, prisoners, mental health, high school students, movements not at all bureaucratic. But which weren't strong enough to keep things moving after the '80s and the arrival of Mitterrand.

Is one way of looking at May is that it influenced those who were influenceable?

Probably. It didn't profoundly change the structure of society. Not that there weren't impressive things in the '70s; there was Lip, the movement around immigrant housing, that lasted from '75 to '81. But that wasn't enough. It was like there was a lead weight that descended on us, with little things, like ACT UP.

What changed in you?

I think I kept—it was buried but later came out—the taste for discussion, for listening, openness to the international. Throughout the '70s I did Latin American support work, and collective action. But it took time for all of this to come out again, the mid-'90s in fact.

After all this, do you think another world is possible?

You have to believe it, but ... The world of '68 wasn't the world of 2000, and the world of 2000 isn't the world of today. If you look at what's happening to refugees today, you see history being made against them and against us. Every day we have to endure new deaths ... Things close up anew every day.

INTERLUDE:
SONIA FAYMAN—A DUTIFUL
DAUGHTER IN MAY

*Sonia Fayman was a student at Nanterre. She was torn between filial
duty and her political engagement.*

*Like so many of the people interviewed, she had a family history
of involvement with the Resistance, in this case the Jewish Resistance
movement: "My political understanding of the world was given me by
my father, who was in the Resistance, who was deported, who came
back from the concentration camps. He spoke a great deal with my
brother, my sister, and me about this period of his life. But it wasn't
really politics, it was more humanism, and from my childhood I felt an
awareness of the unhappiness in the world." Unlike the other Jews I
interviewed, Sonia's political upbringing was specifically Jewish.*

It was on March 22 that we occupied the office of the rector. It
was my mother's birthday and the whole family had planned to go
out for dinner to a restaurant. So what I did was I cut the apple in
two: I went for dinner with the family and then they then took me
to Nanterre so I could occupy the school. And afterwards, when
things exploded in May, they formed a support committee for the
students. They even had a sit-in so the cops wouldn't arrest or
beat us.

I have memories of boulevard Saint-Michel, the tearing up of
the paving stones. Wait, no, I wasn't there for the first demos. My
parents were worried, and since I was a good daughter and didn't
want to frighten them, they asked me to stay home. Or maybe I
went after the first and then stayed home. But after a few days I
got their permission, telling them that it just wasn't possible not
to participate; there was something important happening and I
had to be there. And that was when they formed their support
group. I was there the day we were a million parading through
the streets, on May 13, the day the workers joined us. I didn't put
myself in the front lines since I was afraid of the cops, and when

the cops fired tear gas I'd take off, even hiding in apartments in the neighborhood.

ℰ   ℛ

JEAN-PIERRE FOURNIER

Jean-Pierre Fournier lives in Paris and was still working in education when we met to discuss his activities during May. Along with his functions as a school administrator, he is also a volunteer for Education sans Frontières. As we spoke he moved around his apartment, handing me books and newspapers he'd saved from May to illustrate his points, which he then told me to keep, telling me they'd be of more use to me than to him.

I was 16 in '68 and a high school student at Lycée Condorcet, one of the good high schools, one for the children of the bourgeoisie, though it didn't look so to the students. At the time the bac was only 5 to 10 percent of the population. It was a boy's high school, a very peaceful high school, but within which there was a real political life, as among the students were militants of Voix Ouvrière (VO),[4] the JCR, and a group of two or three Young Communists, of which I was one. On the other side there was the far right, principally Action Française, however anachronistic that might seem. Not Occident, because at Condorcet the extreme right was more traditional. The students were the children and grandchildren of the neighborhood, largely petit bourgeois shopkeepers. There were clashes, including physical ones at the exits, even among people who rubbed shoulders in class, but also grand political discussions. Personally, I was sensitive to the call of the *gauchistes*, but in the beginning with the typical Stalinist attitude of refusal and slander. You have to see that the PCF at the time

---

4 A famously austere Trotskyist group. For a more extensive portrait of VO, see the interview with José and Hélène Chatroussat below.

was a very Stalinist party, both in form and content, distributing insults with great rigidity, sanctifying the USSR. Reading what they wrote at the time in the press, it was totally monolithic; the tone was, how should I put it? Contemptuous, and condescending, while also of an ignorance so profound that it's hard to imagine.

Given all this, is it safe to say that for you the working-class was the revolutionary class?

Yes, completely. This class, whose concrete reality I was totally ignorant of, was *the* great reference. I had gone to one or two demos in '67 in defense of Social Security, if I remember correctly, traditional, union demonstrations. I was there, discreet and admiring. In the same way I went to demonstrations—was it in '67 or '68?—against the banning of *La Réligieuse*.[5] Today, when I think of it, how antediluvian it was, just as I spoke of the rigidity of the PCF, there was also the rigidity in the forms of Gaullist power that are hard to imagine today.

Let me add that I was very young, I was very much in the grips of my family, that I didn't go out much, had little social life. And that, for example, I didn't know Paris, though I lived in the seventeenth arrondissement.

Did your parents know you were a Young Communist?

No. I didn't hide it, my mother knew I read *l'Huma*, but it wasn't something I talked about. As long as things remained on the level of discussion everything was fine at home. My parents were separated, and my father's ideas weren't far off from mine. It wasn't a problem as long as I lived my life as a student.

Were you aware of all that was going on at Nanterre?

I didn't know about it then at all. Not at all. I didn't at all follow that, but where I did begin to take an interest was the demo against American Express, presented as an action against the

---

5   Film by Jacques Rivette based on Diderot's novel and which faced harsh battles with the censor, resulting in its being banned and then finally released after a court battle.

Vietnam War. A friend in the JCR told me come along, there's something going on tonight. I was short and skinny and I had a classic backpack—not like the ones of today—that of a little boy of the '60s, really heavy, filled with books, and American Express wasn't far from Condorcet, two stops away, so I went with the group. Seeing these big people a little older than me running and throwing rocks at the windows was really exciting.

I didn't throw stones; I was just there, I ran with the others; everyone else seemed to know what they were doing and where they were going, and I was really impressed ...

I'd simply been brought there by a friend who wasn't all that old, and that's that.

Then I went home and had dinner. This was my first glimpse of what would be May '68.

But as for events like the occupation of Nanterre, I'm just like Fabrice at Waterloo. I didn't understand what was going on. I was involved, I was for it, I read about what was going on in the papers, I knew Daniel Cohn-Bendit's name, but only through the press—I read *Le Monde*—but it wasn't something I lived personally. I saw things bubbling up, but no more than that.

And on May 3 ...

At that moment I lived it, and through it I saw the impact of an event and how it could change people. I was in a class, in my final year, and there were students who were still dressed like adults, that is, with white shirts and ties, suits. They were high school students who spoke as if they were notary's clerks or office heads ten years later. They used the *tu* form, but grudgingly. It was incredible. The first school day after the big demo everyone said we have to do something, and the entire class, except a few in ties, met in a nearby square in front of the Church of the Trinity. Kids who had been not in the least concerned with politics except for one or two hippie non-conformists: but if they were non-conformist they were also non-political, they had long hair, they were cutups, but not protestors. So the entire class says, there's nothing to be done but make the revolution. Things had completely tipped over. This truly impressed me. Afterwards I would come to think that there were moments when there could be sudden leaps, when nothing could be foreseen, which weren't in the natural course of events, the current of ideas. Inversions of tendency that were absolutely unpredictable.

Was Condorcet occupied?

Yeah, I guess. Half-heartedly. There was nothing organized. The administration never even thought to lock the doors, there were perhaps even classes that continued. It was a time when a high school like that one, a bourgeois high school, as stiff and rigid as it was—where a student could be sent before the disciplinary council for having long hair—was also extremely liberal, it was "cool." We were all from the same world. From the point of view of security, we entered and left as we pleased. But at the same time there were all kinds of disciplinary sanctions, though there was never any strict surveillance. The people in the school's administration didn't have much to do.

At the high school there were meetings, discussions. The most active of the *gauchistes* (and this doesn't include me) went to the Latin Quarter for demos, while militants of VO went to factories. They asked me to join them, feeling I was changing—but no. I was still attached to the PCF.

And what was written in *L'Humanité* at the time didn't shock you?

Yes. For me, this was a break. I remember a small demo in the neighborhood that passed in front of the high school. There were people from the school, Young Communists, who were there. So they came and they began to chant the Communist slogans of May '68, they chanted, "Democratic reform of the university." They were the only ones to chant it: no one else picked it up. Nor did I. I picked up the ones of the period. So it was then that I said, "No!" I continued to read *L'Huma*, but the break had been made. I learned, or rather the head of the Young Communists told me, in late May or early June, that I was expelled. I'd been expelled because I had shown too much sympathy for the *gauchistes* and I was expelled, a decision of Pierre Juquin's.

Did you ever make it to the Sorbonne?

I went there, and I have a very clear memory of it. There were tables of newspapers—and I was already papervore: I devoured it with delight. There I discovered that the *gauchistes* weren't just the three or four friends at high school; there were many of them, all with their stewards. I remember Maoists that I discovered at the time, they were then UJCML. I saw them, so exalted, so numerous, so dynamic, with the wind in their sails. And afterwards—I'm now leaping a few months ahead—when I was a student at Louis le Grand—that was one of their bastions—I bought their paper, and it was truly impressive. We saw people who believed and were in it up to their necks. On the other hand, I recall the sad impression made by the anarchists, who I would later join for a couple of years in the Confédération Nationale du Travail (CNT).[6] They were like grandpas, old people, with newspapers out of date in their form and content. And they didn't have that manner of the leftists of the period, that way of grabbing you by your lapels and saying, "Did you know that ..." and starting a discussion.

Did you go to the GAs?

No, I nicely and properly would go home. My mother was a worrywart and she blackmailed me terribly, an emotional blackmail. She got sick—a marvelous period to become ill—and her son had to take care of her morning and evening. I wasn't completely fooled: I knew it was a way to keep me at home. "Mama's sick."

You read a lot, you were intelligent, you have a theoretical foundation. How did you see things?

I saw things not as a repeat of the Commune, but rather as a repeat—no, let me say as something completely original, as a part

---

6 Anarcho-syndicalist union founded in 1946.

of the flow of history, but original in that it was tied to the Vietnam War, and also to what I'd lived during the war in Algeria. When I was little we'd play Algerian War in the schoolyard and the group I was with played the part of the Algerians. Behind all that was the Resistance, which my parents had been a part of. Aside from all this, the imaginary was that of the Russian Revolution, perhaps. That of 1917. Something like that, but it wasn't too clear. My mother was Jewish and there was something tied to that as well, which was why she tolerated my activity as long as it didn't take me too far from home. She connected it to the USSR.

But the Commune? No. I discovered it much later when I joined VO. And I also discovered the history of the working-class movement, but back then the words "workers" and "working-class movement" were just labels and flags that were part of a glorious past we were the prolongation of.

When the workers entered the struggle, were you there for their demos?

Yes, on May 13, I was there for a bit of it, and I followed the rest on the radio. I listened to the radio, Europe 1 mainly, which had a freedom of tone that was astounding: these journalists who became revolutionaries overnight.

And did you think that France was going down the road to socialism?

At that moment, insofar as I can remember, yes. But on the other hand, I quickly saw the cooling; I quickly saw there it wasn't going to continue, that something was broken.

There are so many memories that come flooding back as I talk …

Something that struck me far more than all the demos, that fascinated me and that has stayed with me, was the atmosphere of general discussion on the streets, where cars were no longer circulating, and I remember that near Condorcet there were groups of people—the neighborhood around Saint-Lazare was and still is a neighborhood full of offices, banks, insurance companies—and people went out into the streets to talk. It was the first time I'd ever seen it, people of all opinions talking together.

So going back to your earlier question about historical references, again, it's not the Commune, but it puts me in mind of '36, it was a return to something my parents both spoke about often, my mother because she was shocked that her Jewish family hadn't supported Léon Blum, and my father in particular, who spoke about the strikes of 1936. So this was very present to me. So when I saw the girls on strike at Galeries Lafayette it was as if I was seeing the photos in history books.[7] This was something really strong, a real bond with the workers.

I recall there was the famous Pentecost[8] when the big problem was whether there'd be enough gas to get away for the weekend, and I had the same reflex as I do today when the news talks about people going on their ski vacations. I say to myself, "This is absurd. Only 8 percent of the population goes on ski vacations." It was the same for Pentecost, and even today, when people tell me we can't have class on Saturday because people are going to their country houses for the weekend, I can't believe it. What country houses? This affects only an infinitesimal part of the population. But at Pentecost '68 there was a total shift: "We have to be able to go away, it's Pentecost weekend." There was a complete change in tone. I see this as a kind of turning point, when real, everyday life returned, winning out over left-wing dreams. At this point I said, this isn't a good sign. Just as when I saw my father—who was the soul of calm—who lived on rue Gay-Lussac, and who'd told me he'd helped people during the riots, who said this with a certain pride, after a time told me, "Enough's enough. This is beginning to be a bit much. What's the point? All they're doing is dreaming." So if he who had a natural sympathy for this movement and who raised me in the same spirit ... that this man was reticent led me to say, "Hmmm."

---

7   The fact that the workers at the department store went out on strike in 1936 is one of the outstanding memories of the general strike of 1936.

8   Pentecost fell on June 2 in 1968.

As a result, when de Gaulle made his speech it didn't surprise me that it succeeded so well.[9] It went as well with the fact that at the high school things were slowing down, that there were still the occupation and meetings and assemblies but there was a kind of void. I lived this again ten years ago at a demo I went to with my daughter and there was a confrontation with the cops that was really violent, with rioters on our side and the cops on the other fighting each other. And suddenly, the cops disappeared. Whoosh! And there was that same void, they had no idea what to do, and suddenly the rioters again became the delinquents they were without the police. It lasted for a few minutes, and it led me to think that if there's no outlet, if there's nothing that follows and rises, and if we're stuck in repetition there's confusion and helplessness and the machine goes into reverse. I felt this in '68 as well.

And at the high school, people spoke about what?

There were smaller and smaller crowds, things were starting to unravel.

And the leaders. What did you think of them? Was there one you liked?

Cohn-Bendit, and I'd later cross paths with him again by chance. After May '68 I was at a vacation colony. It was in Italy where there was an international anarchist conference. Dany Cohn-Bendit was working at the colony and I'd come there to launch a strike against it. He told me I was right, go to it. So there I was in contact with the great mythical leader! And the way he spoke then is how he continued, which is why he has maintained his popularity, since he avoids coded, hidebound language. He spoke just like us. I also remember his declaration to Aragon, calling him a Stalinist lowlife. He dared to say what had to be said. As for the others, Geismar, Sauvageot, they struck me as the usual.

---

9 Speech delivered on television in which de Gaulle dissolved the National Assembly, leading to the elections that would occur after the events had concluded.

Did you feel like there was Paris and there was France?

For me it was something like the famous cartoon in the *New Yorker* where there's a typical New Yorker's vision of America, where New York is gigantic and the rest of the country is a little spot. As a Parisian I had the same impression. Ahhh, things are going on elsewhere, that's nice. We were polite.

[He gets up and goes to his bookshelves.]

Here are some newspapers I saved from the era …

Looking at this, all of which dates from June, when things are already cooling off, there's all this talk about "*la lutte continue*," the continuing of demos … Was this all just for show?

Yes, but not with the pejorative sense. I always felt—and I still feel that way today in my activity in defense of the undocumented— that while I was in the events, I felt a certain detachment in order to be able to see what was what. I had a moment of exaltation when I joined the Jeunesse Communiste. Many people after a time abandon their activity and become good citizens and rally to all the filthiness of society. I never did, but I've always tried to take off the whipped cream, the vocabulary, the exaltation, which is not only disappointing but also counter-effective, and see reality for what it is.

How did it end at Condorcet?

The tradition is that high schools close early for the bac, from mid-June, and in early June there's already little going on. I passed my oral exam in '68 under incredible conditions, and this was also an impact of May '68. In history my topic was analysis and I began by saying, "The German bourgeoisie crushed the working-class …" and the teacher let me go on for a couple of sentences and then she said, "Very good …" It was crazy. The atmosphere was bizarre. And I saw this same phenomenon the next year at Louis le Grand, where we voted 30-1 for the end of bourgeois education, and many of the students went to work in factories, children of the big bourgeoisie who got up at 5:00 a.m. to work in the middle of nowhere in the north of France. All of this was a continuation of May.

I went into education myself, and now when people say that education is not the same, it no longer serves as a social ladder, I always contradict those who say it, since I took the ladder in the opposite direction, and willingly. And I'm happy about it. I'm happy not to have become a journalist or a college professor, and this is thanks to May. It rekindled a political engagement that was lying dormant in my family. May put me on the road to social engagement.

Do you think it brought about any changes in France that wouldn't have happened over the course of time?

I've often asked myself this question as a historian and a militant, but about '36 and not '68. In other countries, even the US, there were social advances without the strikes and occupations in France. More than the societal and cultural changes there were changes—though not enough—a change in the image of France held by the French. In the sense that for the French there's an image of France as "there's France, and then there's the rest of the world," which de Gaulle represented. He spoke as if he was at the head of half the planet, and spoke as an equal to the Americans. Many of my colleagues today still have this image, and I have to tell them we're less than 1 percent of the world's population. And so there's the image of omnipotent France—de Gaulle had allowed us to swallow our colonial defeats by masking them. But May was also a French epic. You said it yourself, that even in the depths of Brooklyn you watched what went on here with admiration, and in France this effaced what was going on elsewhere, like in Germany with Rudi Dutschke.

I agree though that cultural changes all entered under the guise of May '68, but, yes, they were long-term changes that were going to happen. I also say that there was a contraction that blocked the explosion, and like in '36, '68 was needed for that to happen. And so there's a connection that historians could make, that we passed to a more tolerant, softer society, where capitalism was able to pull through quite well. All this is true, but it hides the problem of how the social and cultural are connected. It was a cultural revolt that began in Nanterre, with the story about the dorms, and then it became political, which became social, which then transcended things so that people hid behind de Gaulle, who was a has-been. And yet a year later, my friends who went to class in ties no longer wore them.

$\wp \quad \wp$

PAULINE STEINER

Pauline Steiner was in the same neighborhood Action Committee as Suzanne Borde. From a family of Holocaust survivors, her account is an interesting portrait of what it is to feel alone in the midst of a great historical event in which you are participating. She had briefly been a member of the Trotskyist Voix Ouvrière (VO), but "left because I was disgusted by something I saw at a meeting. There was a group of people who weren't in agreement with a line of VO and there was a meeting supposedly to allow them to express their ideas. But the way they were mocked so disgusted me that I quit VO."

So you had a political consciousness even after you left VO?

Of course, and I have one still. I never retracted my ideas. I haven't repented. I can't even say I've changed. I don't think I ever thought it was possible to change society. But I always thought it was worth the trouble to stand up.

Where did you go to school?

I studied history at Censier.

Did you know anything about what was going on at Nanterre in March?

I didn't know a soul there, and I was isolated, tied to no group at all. But on the other hand, on May 3 it happened that I was at the Sorbonne, though I can't remember if it was by chance or purposely—I can't imagine it was by chance. But I was there on

May 3 at the Sorbonne when the police let the girls leave. That's how I was able to leave the courtyard of the Sorbonne. They didn't say anything that I remember, but as girls they let us leave. I remained in the Latin Quarter, we began to talk among ourselves, things began to heat up, and I saw and felt that this was something that was going to spread and have ramifications. Afterwards I did all the demos. But I wasn't organized.

There's an anecdote that might not mean much to you, but which really struck me, and that was that I had a paving stone to throw at the police, and I couldn't, because I was able to imagine the wounded head of the man. So I couldn't throw it. I saw that this was just not something for me: it wasn't fear—though I felt that too—but it was that I couldn't partake in violence that would harm someone else. This was on that very first day.

On May 10 there was another thing, and that's where I found myself alone—which was unusual, since I was usually with my friend Odette, who's now in a retirement home—and we did almost all the demos together. What happened was that I was alone and we were beginning to tear up the paving stones, forming a line to pass the stones to the barricade. You must have heard about this?

Tell me about it.

What we did was we began by tearing up the fences around the trees and then the stones, since at the time the streets in that part of Paris were paved with stones. We formed a chain and at a given moment during that evening I left. I felt alone. Perhaps I was afraid as well, but I was isolated. Despite the atmosphere, what I lived was a feeling of solitude. So I went home. So on May 10 I wasn't at the Night of the Barricades. I tore up stones, but I can't explain what it was, I just felt alone, too alone. I felt no desire to stick around.

Between May 3 and May 10 there were tons of demos.

And I did them all. I didn't spend much time at Censier, but most of it at the Sorbonne. I didn't do much there: I attended meetings.

It was crazy. People of all kinds spoke up, not just students. That was fabulous. People who felt like talking, who felt they had things to say, and that was more or less interesting. There was a freedom of speech that marked me.

When you entered the struggle, even if you felt alone there must have been a feeling of solidarity, a shared hope for something.

As for me, from the beginning, I had the feeling it would result in nothing. It's perhaps my personality, but I remember talking about it with my friend Odette, and I said this won't result in a change in society. Because it was students. I think that I was marked by my experience in VO, the idea that the workers must join the struggle for something to happen. I think this even now, that it's not the students, but the workers, the economic actors. And so on May 13 when there was a huge worker-student demo and then the general strike, perhaps things were then different. And at that point I felt it was part of a history that went back to the Commune.

But before that it was a student revolt, and that suited me fine, because I was a woman, a feminist, a rebel, also perhaps because I'm a Jew, and an only child. I always felt I was a Jew. For me being a Jew is tied to the Shoah. My parents weren't believers, they didn't transmit anything to me, nothing Jewish, except their story, which is that they were in Poland during the war, they passed over to the Soviet side of Poland, they refused Soviet nationality, were sent to Siberia and spent the war in Siberia. I was born in '46 after they returned to Poland. For me Jewish history begins there, with no grandparents, the extermination of the whole family. I think that without that I wouldn't feel like a Jew.

After that there was a moment of enthusiasm for me, and that was what was going on in the streets. There was the Comité d'Action that was formed in the neighborhood, I don't remember exactly when, and from the moment I joined the committee we went and spoke to people on the street, and that was something extraordinary. This was the most important thing I lived through.

Describe for me a little exactly what the Comité d'Action was.

In each arrondissement, I think it was Cohn-Bendit who had the idea, the slogan was launched, "Create Action Committees. High school committees, neighborhood committees ..." I lived in the third and I went to the neighborhood committee and that committee, what we did there, was to enter in relation with the Post Office on rue des Archives to distribute tracts, and then we went Sunday mornings to the market, and created what we called "dazibaos," putting up blank sheets so the people who passed could write on them what they thought

So the committee was the center of your activities, not the rest of the stuff?

No, I did both. I was still in the general movement. I think ours was the Action Committee that lasted the longest. It lasted almost four years, compared to the others that died during the election in summer '68.

Must have been tiring.

I was young and I was never tired. In '68 I was 22, so it wasn't a problem for me.

Did the media play any significant role?

There was the important role the radio journalists played in distributing information. At the demos we listened to the radio to know what was happening where. We had transistor radios at the demos to keep us informed where things were happening.

Why was May important to you as a woman?

After things changed and I frequented pro-abortion and contraception groups like MLAC and FAR, the feminist movement, but I was enraged by things, like when my father told me I couldn't smoke on the street. And when I asked him why, he said it was because only prostitutes smoke on the street. It was unbearable, this difference between men and women. This inequality existed in the political groups as well; I remember at VO I said I didn't know how to type and I said I'd never learn because it was always the women who typed up flyers. That always angered me, that women did that job, and not those that required thought. So I revolted as a feminist spontaneously, and that went way back in my story. My mother told me that she cried when I was born because I wasn't a boy. My mother depended on my father, who brought home the money. And when they fought I was the one who had to go to him to ask him for money to eat. It's normal that I became a feminist.

Did you hide what you were doing in May from your parents?

They were afraid, so no, I didn't fill them in. But they knew my ideas, since a few years before I was already active in a revolutionary group, which they did know about. It didn't please them.

Did you have political discussions with them?

Oh no. When I was active in VO there was one evening when I got home late and it was the only time my father hit me, because I'd been at a political meeting, I'd come home late, and my mother was worried. It was the only time. It ended with us crying in each other's arms. They were upset because I was seizing my freedom. They didn't agree with me but we never talked politics at home. For them it was all utopian and I was wasting my time and energy and putting myself in danger. But it could have been something else. Had I done hang gliding it would have been the same thing. But it was also because they had been in Siberia and were anti-Stalinist.

Did you continue to be active into June?

In the Action Committee.

So then you must have still had some hope.

I always thought it was better to die standing than to live on your knees. You have to defend your ideas, and even if I don't believe in the revolution I think you still have to say what you have to say and express ideas other than the conformist ideas all around us. I haven't changed my ideas; I still vote for the far left, when I vote. But back then I didn't vote: *élections piège à cons*. For years I remained faithful to that. And then a friend pointed out that in local elections, when there was a Socialist mayor there was more assistance for people in difficulty. I'm not in difficulty, but I still thought it right to vote for those who give more assistance. I never believed elections would change anything.

And how did you feel when the elections in June were so disastrous for the left?

I had a clear, lucid vision. In my opinion, from the moment you're beaten on the field the bourgeoisie regains control, and the vote that will be expressed will be one for the right.

How did the events change France?

The main impact on France was the liberation of speech, the liberty of women, of homosexuals. It liberated morality. Now these things would have come anyway, but more slowly. And these things were both immediate and lasting. The most important was the liberation of speech.

But did that last?

Unfortunately, no. But what lasted was that you could dress the way you wanted, could wear your hair the way you wanted. It seems like these things are nothing, but they're important to people. It allows them to find themselves. It opened and broadened people's horizons. And I think that has lasted until today. On the other hand, I think there has also been a depoliticization.

So then we can see people have retreated into themselves, that people no longer have a long-term political vision, and this has given rise to the racism that is so common in France: witness the rise of the National Front.

Did your life change after May, did it add something?

I think the fact there were more people that thought like me ... You know, before May '68 we were a tiny group, and for women, even then it was difficult. When I was in VO I was told that if you're going to go to a factory to distribute tracts you have to wear pants. There was a rigidity even in revolutionary groups, and with May '68 it's clear the group of people that I frequent, with whom I could feel at ease, expanded. It was easier to be feminist, which I already was. Helen Arnold then organized a women's group that I was part of. People reflected on difference.

And the Action Committee lasted until 1972, lasting so long because we got along really well. I'm a strong believer in the human factor and I think that if this group lasted so long—and none lasted longer—it was because we weren't affiliated with any political group, there was all kinds of people. It was a mix of people who didn't seek to do something specific, who weren't looking to join a political group. It all continued among us.

But the Action Committee died. It died around '72 and I have absolutely no recollection of how that happened.

Is there an image from '68 that stayed with you your whole life?

What has come back to me was this: sometimes on Sundays when we did our dazibaos we were arrested. And I remember that the cops were nice. This for me was May '68. In the neighborhood there was a kind of benevolence towards what we did. Even among the cops.

And then there's this: I was different from most in that I'd already lost my virginity at age 20. It allowed me to participate in group sex, but I didn't like it, so I never did it again. I had a lesbian relationship. I lived on a commune in Paris ... None of this would have happened without May.

ℰ꙰ ꙰Ɒ

PIERRE MERCIER

Pierre Mercier is a retired mathematician, living in his hometown of Saint-Nazaire. His family was politically active from the Popular

Front up to the war in Algeria, and family members taught at the Ecole Normale Supérieure (ENS). That family history set his career path: "It was unimaginable that I go work in the private sector and serve capital. It was impossible: it could only be public service. The teachers of Jules Ferry, you see." Though he had no politics when he arrived in Paris in 1965 to attend Lycée Louis-le-Grand to prepare for his entrance exams to the ENS (failing the oral exam), he was quickly inspired by the fight of the Vietnamese against the US: "That guerrillas could defeat the American army, the most powerful in the world, was enormously important. At the time there was a second thing. And that was the Sino-Soviet split. The fact that the Chinese were raising the torch of Marxism and the Communist movement was alight."

He was deeply influenced by Louis Althusser, saying, "Because I was a mathematician and physicist, at the Normale Sup there was Althusser. So for me Althusser was the return to the fundamentals, to the texts." In general, theory was far more important to Pierre than anyone else I interviewed. "We were very much interested in the Cultural Revolution and active in the CVB, but more than anything, we'd rediscovered Marxism. My God! We saw that it was a gold mine that couldn't be allowed to go unexploited and so we began [to study it in depth]."

For Pierre, May began just a couple of days before the events at the Sorbonne on May 3 ...

So it seems you were quite a workerist.

If that's how you'd like to phrase it, yes.

What did students reproach you for? What were you selling that they weren't buying?

If you will, we were considered theoreticians, which wasn't an incorrect characterization: the criticism was totally justified. We were thought to be more concerned with giving lessons than being involved in actions. But though not every student was concerned with seeing where the movement was headed, there were those who were interested in what we had to say, while the others were bored stupid by it.

And when you went to factories?

We were concerned strictly and solely with the factory strikes and occupations. We went and did our work in the southern suburbs of Paris, leaving early every morning to make a tour of the factories. For me this is one of the great memories of May '68, because as a rule we were greeted warmly, though not always by the CGT. But this depended on how we acted when we arrived.

What I recall is that the workers were on strike for bread-and-butter issues. The CGT was reformist and wasn't interested in any change in society. But we came and we were listened to by the rank and file and had to avoid clashes with the CGT delegates. If we arrived and spoke to them nicely and told them we'd come to discuss and distribute tracts and put up posters, and then, if all went well, we managed to form committees, and there was real curiosity about our ideas on the part of the guys.

So for you May '68 was a victory for capital.

Yes, it was recuperated by capital.

OK, so May led you to work in a factory. How was that? How long did you stay?

I was *établi*[10] until the army discovered I was no longer in my lab and ended my exemption. I had finished my doctorate of the third cycle and was working on my *doctorat d'état* when I left, so when I was 25 or 26 the army noticed I was no longer in my lab. So I was in a factory for two years.

And was it a positive experience?

Oh yes!

Did it confirm your theories, contradict them, add to them?

It showed me that when I said this was a long-term labor that it really was a long-term labor.

---

10   The French word—"implanted"—for those revolutionary students who gave up their studies to work in factories.

The people must have known you weren't one of them.

Look, I worked as a warehouse worker, then in a print shop, then as a metal worker, and it was only in the third job that after some time some of my co-workers felt that I was an intellectual. But only after some time. I wasn't like the people from the GP who, the day after they arrived would stand on a chair and tell them to fight the bosses. Since I saw this as a long-term project, I thought you have to understand people first, see what could be done.

Was it obvious to the others that you came from a political school or that you had ideas aimed at changing the social system?

Neither the one nor the other. I didn't place myself on the terrain of either reformism or changing daily life. As I said, I had no set theories. I did what I did when I later taught math: I was never the all-knowing professor who had all the answers. If someone said something, I'd say, "Yes, but …" or "Why not …" So if a worker said something, I never said he was wrong, I'd say, "If you do this, then that might happen," and he'd say, "Ahh, I see, that's not good."

What was the connection between May and being *établi*? Did the latter confirm what you felt about the former?

It was a continuation, a logical continuation. May '68 opened my eyes to many things, so when I started doing research in the lab I saw that there were things far more interesting to do. It will be a long task, but it will be worth it.

Nearly fifty years later, do you think it was worth it?

Oh yes! Things never progress as we would have predicted. Never. And again we're back to dialectical materialism, to contradictions … So if you will, the bourgeoisie tried to eradicate Marxism, but I can see today that more and more voices and people are saying that there are interesting things in it. That's one thing. Then there are the movements of the alienated: Occupy Wall Street, Syriza, the Indignados and Podemos in Spain … Obviously, one of the results of the eradication of Marxism is that today, in the former colonies, they turn to Islam and not Marxism. Now capitalism gives rise to no fewer revolts than in the past, and it's almost logical that it is now Islam that structures the revolt against global capitalism. So there's still a rejection of the system, but it's not a conscious one.

So I'm optimistic. There's room for us to work and we have to be up to it ideologically.

So you still have hope.

It can't be otherwise.

CHAPTER FOUR

May Outside Paris

... there was a kind of great, lyrical community.
—Jean-Michel Rabaté

JACQUES WAJNSZTEJN

Before entering university in 1967 in Lyon, his hometown, Jacques Wajnsztejn's sole political fight was over the length of his hair when he was in high school. "The principal of the largest high school in Lyon, Lycée du Parc, told me that either I get my hair cut or he'd throw me out the following Monday. And with my mother, who backed me, I led a mini-combat about my hair, and in the end I didn't have to cut it. After this mini-combat the school never bothered anyone about their hair."

At university he was close to the JCR, and was put in charge of work with high school students in Lyon. When the March 22 Movement was set up in Nanterre, his group in Lyon became part of that group, "distributing their texts, and having formal ties to the movement."

In May things began slightly later in Lyon than in Paris.

Right, it starts in Paris when all the *gauchistes*, the Maoists and the Trotskyists, are held inside at a huge meeting at the Sorbonne by the police, and the events begin outside with people who weren't organized cadres. We had news from Paris immediately—the radio was extraordinary at the time—and even within the demonstrations we were informed, mainly by Radio Luxembourg, about what was happening everywhere. These reports were live, and we also listened in on the police radio.

In Lyon the strike was voted that night. INSA was really important in the events in Lyon. INSA was an engineering school for the poor, and so there were many people from the south of France, among them many children of Spanish anarchists. So the politicized students immediately went to INSA to support them.

May 7 was the first big demo in Lyon.

Right. We stayed at the school for a few days. There were mainly young people, and things weren't organized yet. It was less organized than at Nanterre because it was newer: we stumbled around in the middle of the construction that was still going on of the new campus, and because this faculty was new, aside from INSA, the only students at the university were the first two years of the entering classes.[1] We also had the Cité Universitaire where we had the same stories as at Nanterre, about boys and girls having the right to sleep in each other's dorms. In the meanwhile, at the old location, in downtown Lyon, there was nothing going on. They came to see us, but nothing was happening there. We were far more numerous than they, since the first two years have more students than the last two years, which was all there was at the old campus. Just to give you an idea, I was in the school of law and economics, and of the 1,000 students in the first year in economy 300 zeros were given out, which meant 300 students were eliminated.

So the first demo was only young people, students?

Yes. But mixed in with the young were people who weren't students. My grandparents lived in the suburbs and I was often at their house, and I found young people from that suburb at the demo. But it was only the young. The GAs on the other hand were only students and only at La Doua. Later they would begin things downtown, but they couldn't throw the students out, while at La Doua there were no more classes. The discussions at the GAs began on the same basis as the discussions in the March 22 Movement: critical university, criticisms of the dominant ideology.

The UJCML put forth the need to address the issue of the workers, saying there was only one struggle and that we had to support the workers' struggle. But at the same time, from the beginning in Lyon, there were ties to workers, since there were large-scale strikes beginning in '67, like that at Rhodiacéta,[2] and so we quickly tried to re-establish ties with the workers who had gone out on strike for months before May. That's why on May 13,

---

1   The university in Lyon was undergoing physical renovation, with the campus called La Doua, northeast of the center of Lyon, under construction, while the old campus was in the center of Lyon.
2   Factory in Besançon where there was an important strike in February–March 1967.

after the call for the general strike, we went to a factory on strike in Veize that was about a half hour from the school.

But in Lyon we had great autonomy in relation to the workers, and there was total refusal to submit to the ideology that we had to serve the people. Even though there would be many activities directed at the striking factories, the struggle itself was autonomous. It was a fight of the young, of young students, but also of young people who came from the Maison de Jeunes founded by Malraux, where there were students, but also people from working-class quarters. We would go to them and discuss things with them, though they were often controlled by the Communist Youth. After a few arguments they would join us and drop the party. So it's not that we weren't concerned with the workers, but they came to us on our terms, not us on theirs. And in my opinion Cohn-Bendit, who I very much liked at the time, and Jean-Pierre Duteuil also felt that this was a struggle that wasn't only a proletarian struggle.

And on May 9 you did something I don't think was done elsewhere: there was a demo at the newspaper *Progrès de Lyon*.

What happened was that every day newspapers were posted, so in democratic fashion everyone could read them. And so we went to tear them all down, and we went particularly after *Le Progrès*, because that paper was widely read by the popular classes and, given the strength of the working-class and the unions in Lyon and its region, was always very respectful of the workers and covered their strikes, but because we were students, they didn't mention us. They'd put us on page 5 while the front page covered a flower show. Since we were unhappy with this, we intervened the first time at the newspaper offices and a second time at the printing plant. Later in the events, when we tried to have texts of ours printed in the paper and to connect with the printers, we failed, but the printers did go out on strike.

And all this just arose spontaneously? You were all so young!

Within these groups, or this group of 40–50 people, there were people who were slightly older and who were already of age, people born in the early '40s, so we weren't all young: I was among the youngest, but the others were a little older. Cohn-Bendit was three years older than me, but at that age three years doesn't matter. And we also had the ability to organize: you don't need a pre-existing organization to have the ability to organize, because acting as we did we didn't have the bureaucratism of organizations. You need an organization from the moment you say you need to organize, because after all, we were many but not that many, so there was no need to obsess over organization. That is, we were decentralized.

Were there dissidents? Those opposed to interrupting exams?

No, no. The first disagreements, apart from those with the Maoists and how to deal with them, were on May 23, and had to do with Cohn-Bendit, about his expulsion. There was disagreement among us because for most people, particularly the young, including me, this was an essential issue and we were fixated on it. We felt we had to demand he be allowed to return. There were others who were older who said we don't give a fuck about Cohn-Bendit, it's a waste of time to bother with him and that the movement had to carry on and move forward. That night we held a demo with about 500 people, and then we immediately organized the events of May 24, so the dissension lasted only about two hours. Later there'd be other issues especially about the equivalent of the *katangais*—we called them *trimards* in Lyon.

I know that you weren't against them.

No, there were even some who were among my stewards. Since I was at the school of economics the fascists wanted to kill me, and so I had the *trimards* to help me enter the campus. And I never backed down from supporting them. When the UNEF called on us to get rid of them I was against it. But it's true they scared a lot of people, though it was less than the *katangais* in Paris, who scared everyone.

You called them "my stewards"

No, not my stewards, my bodyguards.

So the situation was really tense.

Yes, because the first faculty we occupied downtown for whatever the reason was—I have no recollection of what it was—was occupied in one day, and we had to negotiate with the fascists because there were more of us than of them. They were real fascists ready to die, people from Occident. There were 200 of us and twenty of them. So we negotiated with them not to exterminate them, and they left. But when we went back the next day there had been damage done to one of the rooms, quite a lot.

And then later, because we prevented the exams from taking place, except for those in law and economics, for a year I couldn't walk around the campus without an escort. But it was no longer *trimards* but rather students armed with clubs made of newspapers dipped in water, which made them really hard. Even after '68, on one occasion the fascists were looking for me at a demo, and when they couldn't find me they beat up my wife—who was my girlfriend at the time—in my place.

So the least that can be said is that the atmosphere wasn't that of a carnival …

For sure. After the twenty-fourth the mood completely changed for the worse, first of all because we were more or less forced to hide for two or three days. Those who were the best known and were behind the attack on the prefecture couldn't go home.

Attacking it was quite a decision.

But at the time it seemed like something that was necessary because the prefecture was a local objective: it was decided, not by the GA but by the smaller group within the occupiers. For example, at the demo of May 24, the one that was violent, with the death of the cop, there were thirty people who'd taken the decision. But we'd infiltrated the official GA, which added perhaps ten more people, but that still meant that there were thirty people who'd decided on the attack on the prefecture of police. We were in the middle of a larger group, but even so, the decision was taken by at most fifty people. In 2008, for the 40th anniversary, I was interviewed by the regional press about the events and in particular the attack on the prefecture, and my account of the attack was contested by the leader of the UNEF. I was invited to speak about it at the library in Lyon and there was a woman in the audience who stood up and said it was shameful, we engaged in manipulation; that it wasn't democratic, democracy was at the GA. And this is all true, because the prefect wanted to maintain calm in the provinces in order to allow the police and the army to concentrate on Paris. We took this decision, in a not at all democratic way, so there'd be a confrontation in Lyon on May 24. So even though we were against vanguards, we acted this way.

While the GA decided the route of the demo more or less in agreement with the police, we were not at all in agreement with the police, because the game was rigged and they were seeking order in Lyon so everything could be concentrated against Paris. So we decided that we had to blow things up. Of course, we knew we weren't going to seize the prefecture but we thought we would disorganize the forces of order. So it was a strategy to unblock Paris. And in the back of our minds there was also the idea that power was in the factories and the streets.

But let's talk about what happened on the 24th ... You were going to attack the prefecture.

Let's say we were going to divert the demonstration. Instead of stopping it we had it continue towards the prefecture. So we crossed the bridge that leads to the prefecture and there, on the prefecture side, were two cars full of materiél: clubs, baseball bats, slingshots, etc. We were attacked by the police and there were many wounded. During this attack the demo split in two, and I found myself in the half that went back over the bridge and so blocked the peninsular side. Most of us were on that side, but the most important events of the demo took place on the other side, the side of the prefecture, where the lumpen and *trimards* were. That demo grew independently of us. The prefecture was on the city side, but it wasn't downtown, and we were on the more commercial side, so there were supermarkets that were ransacked.

And the death of Lacroix?

I didn't know about it right away. I'd only learn about it about 3:00 a.m. It didn't cause panic, but a kind of order arrived to go back to the university. Given the "military" impasse we found ourselves in, at a certain moment someone took the decision to have as many people as possible retreat to the university in order to avoid more serious incidents. I can't say for sure who it was, but it must have been the leaders of the UNEF, for we from March 22, at 3:00 a.m., were scattered on both sides of the bridge with no possibility of discussing alternatives. But we held the peninsular side. The battle continued even after the announcement of Lacroix's death on the prefecture side, and they were really violent.

Why were you poorly received by the *trimards*? Hadn't you fought the cops?

I think we were poorly received because they thought we were abandoning the field and they viewed this as an inglorious retreat. For the 40th anniversary there were stories in the papers about what had gone on in '68, and in one of the papers, *Lyon Capital*, they more or less hold me responsible for the death of the cop.

What did you know or hear at the time about Lacroix's death?

We were unaware of what happened for some time. For a long time we thought he was hit by the truck. The fact that he'd had a heart attack was completely camouflaged by the police and the authorities, so for a long time we thought he'd been killed by the truck. The truck was there as a kind of Trojan horse so we could hide behind it as it pushed into the crowd and toss things at the cops.

In your book you talk about how the days were dedicated to discussions and the nights to the making and stocking of Molotov cocktails. Is this true?

It's a good thing we did, so we were prepared when the fascists attacked. But it was also to learn how to make them. When the fascists attacked us, some time around June 6, we had a good supply of Molotov cocktails. But with all this the movement wasn't at all militarized. I think that in fighting the fascists or the police, except in rare cases, you can't win. So you have to propose something else, although you sometimes have to fight. I believe in causing a disturbance, but as a limited objective. There must be violence, because it unblocks things, but it has to be very limited.

There was another battle on the night of June 3–4.

Right, it was an attack by the law students and the right [*de droit et de droite*] on the Faculty of Letters. But this wasn't only students attacking, there were also people from the SAC [Service d'Action Civique], anti-communist henchmen organized by the Gaullists. So they sent men of 40 and 50 to attack us, and not just students. A short time before this we had prevented the exams from taking place in the law school, and there'd been brawls, but just with the law students, so they were fairly light. It was after the exams were blocked that they attacked the Faculty of Letters. The dean was so enraged by all this that the next year he suppressed my stipend.

You were there for this brawl?

Yeah.

Things went on for a few more weeks …

We held out for a few weeks, we held discussions, we wrote texts … Castoriadis had written a text called "La Brèche," which we read and analyzed, and in June we worked on other texts from SouB, during down time. And then there was more and more down time and fewer and fewer people who came to the school. Add to this the dissolution of the groups by the government, which forced us to become more discreet, and soon it was only the unorganized students who remained, because they had nothing to fear.

But after the 24th there was a feeling of depression and everything came raining down on us. The fascists regained their strength, there were the *trimards* who caused us problems and divided us, and now the older ones among us said they had to go, like in Paris. But while in Paris they were able to occupy the Odéon, here there was nothing like the Odéon, so many among the *trimards* went and started living under the bridges. The presence of the *trimards* came to an end not because they were thrown out, but because they no longer came to find out what the assignments were, because one day it just ended. They left of their own will, perhaps because the pessimistic attitude that began to make itself felt in early June didn't inspire them to stay, and the police investigation into Lacroix's death must also have worried them, since the police, the justice system, and the media sought to stick the rap for it on them. But it might also have been because the movement was re-centering itself around theoretical questions, things more properly student related or more traditionally political, like the matter of Charléty and the elections.

For the rest of us it was that we no longer planned anything, people no longer went to the university to learn what had to be done. A minority faction decided to go to the factories, not like the Maoists, but still, to go work in the factories. By mid-June I was broke, so I went to work at the government tobacco manufactory for two weeks. Since they had been on strike there was a lack of cigarettes, and so they started up another production line where they hired students. We were given the positions requiring the least qualifications—in fact none—those that were the most disgusting, that were usually held by women. And there we saw the harsh reality of the protected life of the state manufactories. They weren't civil servants, but were still very protected. For example, while at Renault they had no time to take a piss so they peed on the machines, where I worked were chaise longues in the rest rooms. On the other hand, we were frisked on the way out to make sure we didn't have cigarettes on us.

So it was only six weeks that it lasted for you …

Yup, from May 3 to June 15, six weeks when we occasionally went home, maybe to sleep, but six weeks when we were mobilized every day.

And it marked you for life …

It particularly marked those who didn't speak about it. Those who arrived right after—those who were four or five years younger are the worst enemies of '68.

In what way?

Because they didn't take part, and they're constantly confronted with those who did, who constantly refer to it because they were marked by it. They missed out on it. It was very different in Italy, because in Italy it lasted much longer and was not as strong, but was stretched over ten years. So the memory of the movement isn't the same, and having participated or not isn't the determining factor, rather it was the perception of the armed struggle. But in any case, it's not like in France, because in France, because of the brevity, there were those who were there and those who weren't, and those who were there either erased a part of their life for the reason that they didn't really participate—like the Maoists—people like Finkielkraut, Glucksmann, Castro … Castro for example participated in the demos the first two weeks clandestinely, since his group didn't take part.

Is there a before May and an after May as Zemmour said?[3]

But it's not only reactionaries like Zemmour who say this. Someone like Jean-Pierre Le Goff,[4] for them what dominated May was a guy like Cohn-Bendit, the libertarian liberal. Cohn-Bendit is the very image of what capitalism wants. He was intelligent, clever, open to ideas, he removed barriers and taboos, didn't want to have everything rest on the state. The movements of that time accelerated history. In this they were revolutionary, but it opened onto the revolution of capital, not the proletarian revolution.

There are few people who recount '68 from within. Many write about it who are younger and didn't live through it and no longer want to hear us; we aren't neutral and they don't want to have anything to do with us, and so our word is invalidated.

France was the only country to make a revolution to which the whole world refers, that of 1789. No one refers to the Chinese

---

3   In his right-wing recounting of French history in the twentieth century, *Le Suicide français*, the commentator Eric Zemmour wrote that "in the collective imaginary of our time there is a before and an after 1968."

4   Jean-Pierre Le Goff (1949–) is a French sociologist. Jacques Wajnsztejn is referring to his book *Mai 68. L'héritage impossible*.

Revolution, no one refers to the Russian Revolution, but all over the world France serves as a reference point. May '68 is the same thing. Whenever people refer to '68 they refer to France. If you go to Spain or Italy, even if something more important goes on there all eyes are still on France. As Marx said, France is the country of politics. So whether rightly or wrongly, events in France resonate throughout the world.

ℛ ℛ

JOSEPH POTIRON

Joseph Potiron, born in 1932, is a legendary figure on the left in Brittany. Living on the same tenant farm he grew up on in La Chapelle-sur-Erdre, outside Nantes, he has long been active in radical circles, and during the events in May played a central role in supporting the striking workers in the region.

When I think of peasants I think of individualists, yet you're a peasant syndicalist. How do you square this circle?

It's quite simple. I'm from a region of small farms, of people of modest means. The period around '68 that of the *trente glorieuses*, which everyone considers something really great. But the *trente glorieuses* were years that were paid for by someone, or by a multitude of people, notably by small farmers, who were in the process of disappearing at that time, or rather who were being made to disappear. But it takes time to kill a farmer: he never gives up hope. They were being led to believe it was all their fault, and they didn't understand why they were disappearing. And they still don't.

It was also being paid for by the OS [*ouvrier spécialisé*], the unskilled workers who were at the bottom of the social scale. And maybe it was because I was the fifth of seven kids, but I thought about solidarity, particularly between workers and peasants, because I considered all of them workers, and since I was an adolescent I'd seen that their exploiters were the same.

Because of this, I necessarily found myself part of combative movements. I fought because I was a peasant, because I heard myself called "hick," because people denigrated the world of the farmer. At the theater, in films, for people of "quality," it was acceptable to ridicule the work of the farmer. We were boors, we weren't civilized, we were less than dogs ...

In the region of Nantes there had been major strikes in '53, strikes in Saint-Nazaire and Nantes, and there were major movements in 1955 when I came back from my military service.

At the beginning it wasn't that I was there in support of all their activities, that of the workers. First there were peasant demonstrations, rough ones, starting in '66, and I increasingly came to think about solidarity with the world of the workers. But I thought that the students were people who were of no interest to us, since they were the sons of the bourgeoisie. And then on March 22 I heard Cohn-Bendit interviewed at Nanterre, saying we don't want to replace the capitalist system, we want to blow it up and start something new. I saw that this was what I'd been waiting for for years without knowing it. And that day said something to me. Of course, I didn't know all that was involved, but for me there was no other solution, there was no way to reform the system, and that we had to get rid of it.

And when things happened in Paris on May 3, did it take long to reach you here?

There was a demo of farmers on May 8 here in Nantes. Of course I took part in it, but I have no idea what the demands were. Demands were usually a rise in the price of milk, and I wasn't interested in that. For me it was the struggle of the farmers, because I knew they were being exploited. I didn't think that we'd succeed by raising prices; there were other solutions, and raising the prices of agriculture goods would set the workers—who purchased these products—against us. We had to find something else, so that each would think of the other and each would be able to find a way for all to live as if there were no exploiters.

It was strictly a farmer demo. Afterwards there were other demos that followed quite rapidly after this one, and the workers entered the fight, and between the demos the farmers started to support the workers.

When we got into the city we found workers and students, and we went with our tractors, with everyone following us, circling the statue that represents the tributaries of the Loire, and we hung up our sign. It was symbolic, and through it the farmers would understand, like me, that our enemy wasn't the workers. We were farmers but we were first and foremost workers, and the symbol was that we wanted nothing to do with the monarchy—because even though we were supposedly living under a republic we were living under a monarchy—since power was hereditary. Now we were entering democracy.

When we reached the main demo no one looked on us as hicks. It was a veritable festival. There was immediate, spontaneous solidarity between us. And of course the students and the leaders of the student movement as well as the leaders of the workers—I won't say of their unions—well, there was great sympathy among us and a great festive atmosphere. It was the worlds of labor meeting and recognizing each other, for we were all workers, even if we did different things. But there's no reason to be pie in the sky about this. We knew the barriers weren't going to collapse just like that.

In the meanwhile, many things had happened.

Around then we decided to show our solidarity with two factories to the east of Nantes, Chantiers Navales and Batignolles. We wrote a text and two or three of us went with some wine—because peasants are convivial—to show them we supported them. "We bring you a motion that we voted on," we told them. We weren't well received by the CGT union leader at Batignolles. The attitude was the peasants, the black market during the war, the usual stuff, and we felt we weren't welcome. So we left and went to the other factory and told them we supported them. The reception there was completely different from that at Batignolles. And they did indeed come out, they spoke among themselves and handed the mic over to us.

When we finished reading our text some young workers came over to us and asked, "What can we do together?" We told them there'd been enough blather, what can we do concretely, since they're on strike and have no money. What can we do to help them hold out? We thought about it and it was decided to hold meetings with the students, because it was the students who had put us in contact with the workers at a meeting held here in La Chapelle-sur-Erdre. We decided that the first thing we could do was supply milk. Now, we couldn't give the milk away, since giving it away meant more than giving away your salary. Within the price of milk are all the other expenses. So we told them we'll give you our milk, but at the cost the dairy processor pays us, half the price of what they paid at the store. But distributing milk isn't something simple, and we distributed 500 liters of it every day; 500 liters means you need containers. Then the next day I spoke with the head of an enterprise, a capitalist one, not a cooperative. He asked me "How many cans do you need?" I told him I needed two sets, one for us to send the milk out in, one to fill while the milk is out and which we would swap when the first set were returned empty. And that's just what happened. We met with the businessman in the morning, and in the afternoon a truck arrived with enough containers for 1,000 liters. The director told me you'll sign a receipt and take responsibility, and that was that.

Were you surprised it went so well with a capitalist?

It was a dairy industrialist who sent me the containers in support of a strike, which he normally would have opposed. I think he did it because the atmosphere was very open, something we saw in the streets, where people spoke with people they didn't even know. There was immediate sympathy. But this capitalist, I think he acted out of a feeling of solidarity. Without the help and solidarity of the businessman we never could have done what we did. We never would have had the means to transport the milk.

Anyway, he brought me the containers, so the next day the workers brought a van and they came to pick up 250 liters from us and 250 from some other farmers. So 500 liters went out every day under the control of the strike committee of Batignolles. It wasn't a union, it was everyone, unionized and not, and it was the women who organized the distribution.

None of this could happen if it wasn't organized on both sides. But it was set up quickly, perhaps two days. The strike committee already existed, but I'd bet they didn't expect to receive 500 liters of milk just like that. And they had to trust us, since 500 liters of milk represents quite a sum of money.

Who paid for it?

It was the strike committee, but I can't tell you how they did it, other than that the strikers paid the committee for whatever milk they got. And it's certain that solidarity played a real role.

I don't remember how I was paid either, but I do know I was paid.

By doing this we materially supported the workers' movement, and not only in words. What happened was that very quickly people—and it was usually students—came to see me and said we need other things, we need chickens for the workers. So we thought it over in our group meetings and worked out how to distribute chickens.

How many were there of you supplying the strikers?

There were two of us here, me and my brother, who provided half, and two others who supplied the other half.

So you weren't many?

No, and it would have been difficult to organize this among many. Not that people wouldn't have been in agreement, but it would have been vastly more complicated, while we had to get this done immediately.

As in Paris, there was a big pro-de Gaulle demo in Nantes. Did its size surprise you?

Absolutely. We'd had all this hope throughout May, a belief that things were going to change, that the people would organize, and then—boom! It was as if someone had poured a bucket of cold water over our heads. Though it didn't discourage me, it did bring me back to reality. It was too beautiful. The people couldn't follow the road to its end all at once, maybe a few leaders could, people who were already ready, like me. But it was clear that tough times were ahead.

But had things lasted we were organized so that we could head for something completely different. I'd imagined that with the workers in the slaughterhouses on strike we could organize our own distribution circuits of meat.

How long did all this go on for?

We supplied the strikers for about three weeks, and it lasted beyond June 3. I know this because the curate of Batignolles, of the factory quarter, who understood the workers' struggles, met the vicar of La Chapelle-sur-Erdre, who was on the same wavelength as me, in a square where we had discreetly put up a sign saying Strike Committee. The two met and greeted each other, and they were threatened by a bunch of idiots. After they were attacked they came to me and I took them in. A few days later there were graffiti on the walls of the presbytery saying it was the presbytery of the Maoists. There were thirty of them who insulted me and it's clear to me they were pushed to it by the local marquis. That evening thirty people came to support me. At the time there were 100 peasants here in La Chapelle-sur-Erdre, a third of whom supported me, a third opposed to me, and the other third stood on the sidelines. Those opposed to me didn't understand that I never acted against them; I tried to project myself into the future, and I never hid that I was always against land ownership and that I considered tenant farming theft, because the owners didn't create the land. If I make a spoon it was something I fabricated, while the land … Why don't they make us pay for the sun while they're at it.

And it all really ended after the Grenelle Accords and the return in June?

It ended when the union leaders pushed the workers to return to work. It was tough; we were in contact with the students and the young workers, and the atmosphere was really tough. But there was after all a 30 percent rise in the minimum wage, which is something. We farmers didn't gain much from it. I didn't give a damn, because what I was waiting for, hoping for was the revolution. That was when I realized that the revolution wouldn't come; that it was there, in our hands, and we had to know how to look into our hands.

Several times you've said "young workers."

Because we only dealt with young workers, workers younger than I. At the time there were a number of older people who participated, like a friend who was a leader at Sud-Aviation.

Were there extreme right-wing groups here at the time?

Had there been they would have had their heads handed to them. But remember that this is a region where, during the so-called Revolution, when the bourgeoisie took power, they used the people to achieve their ends and the peasants rose up in revolt against them, the Vendée. And the memory of this remains strong in people's minds. Remember that in 1792 and 1793 Paris sent Duroc to massacre everything that was living; there were the drownings, south of Nantes was the base, where men, women, children, and animals were killed.

If there was this strong memory on the right, was there also a strong memory on the left?

I don't know. I was raised with the memories of the Chouannerie and their songs; I learned them from my mother. I have ancestors killed at the head of the Chouans here in the commune who fired at the Blues and were captured and killed. Me at 14, I would have been a royalist. But at the same time, I wondered why we marched with the bourgeoisie who commanded us. People were misled then and are misled now. I think that at the time of the bicentennial in 1989 it was the moment to say the Republic made mistakes, it was two centuries ago, and we're not responsible for those errors, but in the name of the Republic we recognize these errors and in order to bring peace we're going to raise a monument in memory of those killed during that period. It's not possible to ignore history.

So what was May's lasting effect on you?

It made me take a giant step. I would have reached the same point, but it would have taken much longer. I was much influenced by my father, who wanted to limit land ownership to no more than 50 hectares. I realized there was no need for landowners, not me any more than anyone else. I didn't have to own land, since I contest land ownership. What I need really is security, which led me to wonder about security in housing, health, in education. We don't need to own the teacher, we don't need to own the doctor, so we don't need to own the house. We need to be housed, and we farmers need security in land. I never owned a centimeter of land, and though I accept paying tenant fees, it should not be to a landowner but to a collective. It's intolerable that someone should hold land as a form of speculation. The Quechua, who I visited, say that the land is their mother, and you don't sell your mother. Nature is my guide.

How did it change France?

What leads me to say something changed is the ferociousness with which the bourgeoisie insists on saying that May '68 was a mere comma in the history of the world. May '68 was something really important.

There was something I saw on the walls in May that I thought was essential: "Dare to Say No. Dare to Struggle." When I was in the army we'd say, "Seeking to understand is the first step in disobeying." I love expressions like that. It's extremely important to disobey, and in order to do so you have to understand. If you don't understand you follow the herd.

℘ ℞

GUY, BERNARD, DOMINIQUE

Guy Texier was a veteran CGT leader in Saint-Nazaire, and Bernard Vauselle was a young man working at Sud-Aviation in Saint-Nazaire; Dominique Barbe was a Young Communist in high school in Nantes. All of them were Communists in 1968, all of them remain proud of the party, and its positions.

Guy: I was a militant at the shipyards in Saint-Nazaire, and in May '68 I was in charge of the CGT laborers union. At the same time I was secretary of all the metal workers in Saint-Nazaire. At the shipyard we had a pretty strong union: there must have been 1,000 full-time workers who were members out of around 8,000 employees. We had 47 percent of those included in the professional vote and were number one, both among the workers and the supervisors. I was also in the PCF, after having been a member before there was a Jeunesse Communiste, joining the Union de la Jeunesse Républicaine de France (UJRF)—as it was called until 1952—right after the war. Afterwards I wasn't a member of any party until I joined the PCF in 1960. I was never someone who was fixated on this or that personality, like Stalin. I always developed my own ideas and analyses. What led me to join in 1960 was the war in Algeria, the situation in Berlin, but above all the war in Algeria, since I'd served there.

Bernard: I'd been back from doing my military service for three years and had been at Sud-Aviation ever since then, from 1965. I did my apprenticeship there and soon afterwards we went out on strike. Then, in '67, we went out for two months, so '68 wasn't something spontaneous, it grew out of years of struggle. I joined the party after '68.

137

Dominique: In '68 I was 17 and I was in high school, and had joined the Jeunesse Communiste (JC) in 1967, so I was a member when the events began. What led me to join was my family. My father wasn't a Communist, but I read *L'Humanité* which we had at home every day, and I can't imagine any better training for joining the JC. I was never tempted by groups further left. Being attracted to what I was reading in *L'Huma*, I was totally imbued with the Communist culture. I'd read Marx and Lenin, and after all, they're the basis for Marxist-Leninist theory, and I think we could read and learn from them today. I didn't go out on weekends selling *L'Huma Dimanche*: as young people we had activities aimed at the young.

Let's jump to May. How did you get involved?

Guy: Right after the repression in Paris on May 10, where I'd been that first week, the CGT proposed a national twenty-four-hour action for May 13. So we spent the weekend in Saint-Nazaire preparing for the demo, which was huge, with a meeting at place de l'Hôtel de Ville. So this was the beginning. Later that week—it was about the 14th or 15th—we began to talk about occupations.

You in the CGT spoke about it? It wasn't spontaneous?

Guy: Perhaps it was different at Sud-Aviation, and Bernard can speak about that, but at the shipyards we called an assembly where we usually held meetings, and we had a meeting on Friday at noon calling for the occupation of the place. It wasn't at all spontaneous. There was a vote at the beginning of the week to see if we'd occupy or not. The vote, out of the 8,000 employees, was a minority— no point in telling stories—but there was a large percentage for the occupation.

And why was that decided on?

Guy: Listen, much is said about May '68 as a political movement. But '68, as we lived it here, was not a political movement. It was a bread-and-butter movement that was the continuation, as Bernard mentioned, of the strike in 1967 of all levels of metal workers in Saint-Nazaire, workers, supervisors, everyone, that lasted two months. The workers were locked out for participating in this movement. The results of '67 were quite important, regarding salaries, with all levels of workers reclassified and made full-time, that is, paid by the month. So for us the movement of '68 was a continuation of this, of this bread-and-butter movement. That's essentially what it was. We were concerned mainly with wages, but also with working conditions. Elsewhere it had political repercussions, but that can't be said about here.

Bernard: While I was still in training in 1966 we were already engaging in work stoppages; we'd go out every day for months to have our demands met. So I was already deeply involved. And then in '67, as Guy mentioned, I began to take things in hand—and turn them over in my head—and I began to be a militant. Small things, I was still young, and later I'd become a delegate.

Now as Guy said, on May 13, 1968, there was the big demonstration in town and then the 14th—I think that was the date—at Sud-Aviation Coblay we voted to occupy. There are famous photos of the event, of people sleeping on cardboard boxes, but we occupied the factory, and all of this gave rise to lively conversation throughout Saint-Nazaire. Now it wasn't spontaneous in the sense that there'd been preceding battles. The first thing we did was solder shut the gates. But actually the real first thing was to protect our work tools against outside—and sometimes even inside—attacks. There were workshops where the risk of fire was worse than others, so those were the first ones we made sure were sealed.

Not to be provocative, but why was your primary concern protecting your tools and machines? Why not sabotage them, since they belong to the bosses?

Bernard: That wasn't our reflex, and before going out we cleaned the machines so that they'd be ready to function again, knowing we'd be gone for some time … We did it out of pride.

Guy: It's a rule of ours—of the CGT—to refuse outside intrusions. Protecting the work tools was one thing, but it was also a matter of the security of the workplace. I'm thinking of the Naval Shipyards, where the ships are built in slipways and in the slipways there's no protection. So you have to protect them and the people who work there. The occupation of a factory requires a great deal of organization. It's not something you do just like that. And this is the role of the union, ensuring protection.

Now Dominique, you're young, you're a Communist, and you hear of the events in Paris. Did this inspire you as a student to do something?

Dominique: Well, I joined the JC in 1967 and in '68 I was a high school student. The question that was posed to us Young Communists was how to participate in this movement when the students are in the struggle. This was the question we posed, and we answered, we too have our demands in our high school and we're going to organize and put them forth. So we set up a Comité d'Action Lycéen (CAL), and in fact there was even a UCAL, a Union of CALs—and set out to participate in this great movement that was on the rise. The majority of students joined the movement, so classes were stopped, but it can't be said we occupied the high school, since we went home at night, though we were there every day. Though we were on strike there were other schools that weren't, and our objective was to have as many high schools as possible involved in the movement. We went to the schools that weren't on strike to get them to join in and issue their demands. Sometimes we succeeded, and sometimes we didn't.

What about the *gauchistes*? Were you well received when you spoke as a Communist?

Dominique: I didn't speak as a Communist. This was my first union post—so to speak—and my place was putting forth the demands of the students and not that of a political movement. That I was a Communist had no bearing at the high school. In fact, there were no political labels attached to those who called for the students to fight.

Once the occupations occurred everywhere, who was it that decided who would do what? Who organized things?

Guy: We at the shipyards wanted to put a strike committee in place, because we'd already had experience with them going back to 1955. At the initiative of the union there were people who were put in charge of security and of provisioning, since the strikers had to eat and sleep ... The organization of the workshops in the shipyard was different from that at Sud-Aviation. The workshops in the shipyard were, forgive the expression, disgusting, there was sheet metal all over the place, and we couldn't sleep on the ships. So it was the offices, including the design offices and those of the managers, that we occupied and slept in. So here again, we live there and don't want to damage the place. And then there were the union offices and the worker-management committees, and all of this has to be organized.

At the beginning the people came with their food, and then we organized that. There were people who took charge of food, of drinks ... There were also factories that had contacts with fishermen and farmers, who brought fish and farm products, and since people drank a fair amount, there were also barrels of cider that were brought to the workers. So you can see there was quite an organization. We used the funds of the labor-management committees, illegally, incidentally, since we really didn't have the right ... But in a situation like this we settled up with the boss afterwards, and in fact, at the end, the bosses are always so happy that it was over that they don't ask too many questions. But in any case, the provisions weren't free. That is, you had to pay for a glass of wine or beer. But not to make a profit. It was at cost.

And at your level, Guy, was there coordination with the CFDT and FO (Force Ouvrière)? How were relations between you?

Guy: We had good relations, we had tense relations, but relations are always difficult; you have to achieve a result ... There are those who along the way are fine but who up the stakes at the end: this is a classic maneuver. This isn't how we act. And especially as the largest union ... At the end of May, beginning of June, there were demands that were less bread-and-butter and were more political. We were always the ones with the most political awareness and experience. I always said we weren't there to accompany a political movement. The demands of the workers were the most important thing, since we understood the experience of 1936 ... People say it was the Blum government that gave paid vacations, but that's totally false. It was thanks to the union movement that began in 1935 and 1936, and that exploded in May '36, so at Matignon[5] we had our demands met, like paid vacations, and the government translated this victory into law. But we had a left-wing government then. In May '68 we didn't have that. It's better to have a government of the left that's really on the left, but this wasn't the case in '68.

Bernard, during the picketing and the occupation of Sud-Aviation, were they supervised by the unions, was everyone who was there involved, or was it just the leaders?

Bernard: Everyone was there; it was the militants who ran things. There had to be stewards and all the rest, and again it was the militants who ran things. But listening to Guy I was thinking, where were the others? The other unions. I didn't see them active during the occupation. While at the end, they were there saying we had to carry on until political victory. Then we clashed.

But during the occupation, how was the atmosphere. Was it like 1936, that great, festive spirit?

Bernard: There was no tension, but, of course, we needed to set up security, and this was mainly handled by guys from the CGT, plus we had to set up nighttime teams, and there was also security outside the factory. We sent people to the train station at La Baule

---

5   The accords signed between the Popular Front government, the bosses, and the unions granting workers raises, paid vacations, and union rights.

to picket, since there were no railroad workers to assume the task. Even so, we opened the factory to people from outside; for example, there were folklore groups that performed for us. During the three weeks we were there it wasn't party-time every day, but we had events with personnel from the factory who had cultural interests who put on shows.

Dominique, during all this, at the CAL, were the demands mainly student ones?

Dominique: The central axis of our demands was dignity. Being recognized as young adults and not as children in short pants. That was the focus of the high school fight. Because, in fact, there were people among us who were 20 years old, those finishing their studies. I remember an important demand was the right to smoke, that we not be forced to hide in the toilets to smoke a cigarette. We wanted to be recognized and have the right to smoke like the others. And we won. And it was a victory that was symbolic of the fact we were young adults and not kids.

Were there GAs?

Dominique: Yes, and we spoke of our situation as high school students, but also of the political situation. As Young Communists we spoke out so as not to validate the ideas of the anarchists. The question was to see what politics the conflict would result in beyond the immediate situation. For me the ideas of the anarchists were short-sighted. It wasn't enough to mount the barricades. I witnessed the barricades in Nantes at the prefecture, a barricade on rue Paul-Bellamy; there were young anarchists who were throwing Molotov cocktails at the building and the cops threw three or four grenades and everyone scurried behind the barricade. Even with that, the way I saw things, it was the forces of order who organized the disorder.

But at the GAs, we didn't speak much about uniting with the workers; we spoke about our situation as high school students.

On the other hand, Guy and Bernard, you had visits from students.

Guy: Very little, in truth. There was one attempt, notably with Gabriel Cohn-Bendit,[6] at the shipyards. His brother Dany came once for half a day for an assembly on the beach in Saint-Nazaire, but Gaby lived here. So Gaby wanted to speak, and there was a discussion at the shipyards as a result of which we accepted that he come. He wanted to sit at the tribune, but we told him we're the ones organizing and your place is in the hall. We made things clear. Our opinion was that this was a strike for specific demands, and that it was interesting to hear what the teachers wanted, since they too had their demands, but for them the goal was revolution. Everyone has the right to want to make revolution, but to make the revolution you need revolutionaries.

But weren't you Communists revolutionaries?

Guy: Yes. But even though as a political party we understood what was going on at the national level, we didn't accept that the movement in support of the workers' demands should follow after the political movement. There was no prospect on the left at the time for a left-wing policy. This has to be remembered. So for us, there were the demands. Our experience—and it's possible we were wrong—was that the social movement, with its demands issuing from the factories, was the most solid one. It could result in a political movement, but our analysis was that we weren't in that situation.

Let's get back to Gaby Cohn. He certainly wasn't there to talk about your bread-and-butter demands.

Guy: It's what Bernard just said. No, we had to get rid of the government, he called for workers' self-management. That was something fashionable at the time, even if it is something that is worthy of being reflected on. But it's not something that happens spontaneously; it comes after reflection. Our analysis was that

6   Gabriel Cohn-Bendit (1936–) was a teacher in Saint-Nazaire. He was at the heart of much far-left political activity in the region. See interview with Myriam Chédotal below.

we're living under a capitalist regime and we weren't living through the ten days that shook the world of 1917.

OK, but let me ask you this: if these days in May weren't the ten days that shook the world, when would they ever be? And if it wasn't then, is it something even doable? You never felt like you were putting the brakes on something that would go further?

Guy: Yes, that was part of the political objectives that the CGT supported. But the political conditions of the period were the de Gaulle government, the prime minister was Pompidou, and our analysis was that the union movement wasn't the bearer of this demand in the first instance. People weren't on strike to change the government.

But is that true? Dominique, you were on strike, and maybe it didn't go further for you than the cigarettes, but elsewhere in France there were people who wanted more. Slogans like "It is forbidden to forbid," "Power to the imagination"—how did you view that, Bernard? Things like the nights of the barricades?

Bernard: That's a good question, but in '67 and '68 it was really the bread-and-butter demands we were interested in, not the political demands. The workers weren't on strike to go to the barricades. And in the elections that followed you can see we were right.

Right, there was all this enthusiasm, and then in Paris there was the pro-de Gaulle demo on May 30, though in Nantes it was June 1, and then the elections and the left takes a beating. But what I'd like to know is could things have been different if you'd acted differently? You surely know that you are held responsible for the fact that it all failed. That if the party had been ready to go further, perhaps things could have gone further. But let's finish with Gaby.

Guy: For us he was insignificant in '68. We had the experience … The world of labor wanted a political change. Yes. But were the conditions in place for this change? This is an important question. We had the experience of the presidential elections of 1965, when

Mitterrand was candidate for the first time, and Duclos pointed out that Mitterrand and Mendès-France had 5 percent of the vote, the two of them together. There was disunion between the Communist and Socialist parties and the PSU, and there was the famous meeting at Charléty, with Rocard, which we CGT militants took part in, and we saw that the political prospects weren't propitious. It's true that a movement of such power could have resulted in something, but only if the conditions were right. This was the first time we spoke of a common program of the left.

Bernard, during the occupation, did you talk about remaking the world?

Bernard: No, we only spoke about the demands, the need for uniform demands, for raises. That's what we discussed. Never about the revolution.

Dominique: As a young person it was easy to recognize yourself in slogans like "It is forbidden to forbid," because within demands like these we can find things like feminist demands. So as young people we recognized ourselves in these types of demands, in these cultural demands, and we joined in on the basis of these ideas.

But as a Communist, there aren't only these slogans, there are also the actions that go with them. Occupation, barricades …

Dominique: True, but on the other hand, I didn't subscribe to those other ideas, things like the barricades, which I saw as a kind of theatrical mise-en-scène on the part of the authorities to lead the movement astray. We talk a lot about May as a student movement, but for me it was a working-class movement. What was our experience at the time? It was that there was no more gas. There are things that weren't available because the workers were on strike; not because the students were on strike, but because the workers were. And for me, as a Young Communist, it as a workers' movement first and foremost.

In accounts about this region you read about the blocking of the roads.

Guy: There were none. Movement was handicapped because there was no gas.

Bernard: No.

Dominique: No.

And what about barricades?

Dominique: As far as I remember there were none. The only one I remember was the one on rue Paul-Bellamy.

Guy: There was one barricade in Saint-Nazaire, in front of the Nouvelles Galeries on place des Droits de l'Homme. One barricade. And you know what it was made of? Vegetable crates! There was one comrade I knew who was on the barricades in Nantes, he was a sailor who was in the PSU who thought, "We're going to make the revolution, so let's put up a barricade." Perhaps there were some obstructions on the highways. Maybe that's the blocking of the highways.

OK, but what about the rationing of gas?

Guy: That, yes.

Bernard: That was part of my assignment. To run the teams at the gas stations. I distributed coupons and people went to the gas stations with them, and it was my men from the union who controlled the pumps so there would be no damage.

"My men?" So it wasn't the station attendants.

Bernard: No. It was us.

So you had seized power!

Guy: A small amount of power. But we paid for the gas. And those who went to the gas station to fill up paid for their gas. There was also the responsibility for the provisioning of the city, because people had to eat. There were people who were responsible for ensuring that merchants didn't engage in a kind of black market. People had to be able to buy food, and the merchants weren't our class enemies, you see. We needed them and they needed us. So there were contacts with the merchants, because not every store was open: You could wait to buy clothes, but food, you needed meat, bread ... they had to be supplied, including gas so they could continue their work. So all this was our responsibility.

So you controlled gas. Anything else?

Bernard: We had to control it so there'd be no incidents; there was nothing police-like about it. It wasn't authoritarian, it was simply organization.

Dominique, the students were never called upon to handle this?

Dominique: No. But as Young Communists we were opposed to anarchist ideas. At the time I was imbued with the Leninist culture of *Left-Wing Communism: An Infantile Disorder*.

And now back to Gaby ... He wanted to speak and he wasn't well received.

Guy: No, because he wasn't in sync with what the workers at the shipyard had in mind. I think that as much as the political situation interested the workers at the shipyards—and elsewhere—just as much was it not the discourse they wanted to hear. Because they had demands. We were in a situation where, even after the strikes of '67, the salaries were low, the work was difficult, there were all kinds of things. So this was the main thing in '68. And also Saint-Nazaire wasn't Nantes; there was no university. Our situation was different, and it was a working-class city, more than it is today. Metallurgy was essential to Saint-Nazaire at the time. We weren't in the situation of Nantes, Paris, or Nanterre ... So when Cohn-Bendit came ...

Gaby or Dany?

Guy: Gaby. Dany came for a half day for a talk on the beach. A few thousand people came but not me. It didn't interest me. I knew what he'd say. He went to a factory and told them the director had to be changed so there'd be a kind of rotating management, it was a bit far-fetched: today you run the factory, tomorrow it'll be another, etc. It's not very convincing.

But Bernard, if someone had told you, "Bernard, you've been working here long enough, you can run the place," what would you have said?

Bernard: There were joint labor-management meetings where we'd tell the bosses what we thought had to be done.

So Cohn-Bendit wasn't that far off base.

Dominique: The question of self-management was at the heart of our demands in '68 and in the '70s. You asked about the tools before. Well, you can look at them as the tools of our exploitation, but as workers you could view them as our property.

Yours? What about the other tradition, that of sabotage, that the tools are theirs not ours?

Dominique: That wasn't my idea nor was it that of the working-class. It goes back to the Canuts:[7] they protected their tools. The idea of sabotage wasn't that of the majority of the workers.

But it's an idea that's an integral part of the history of the French working-class movement. Emile Pouget[8] wrote about it, it even figures in the founding charter of the CGT.

Guy: The workers' movement, notably the CGT, comes out of the anarchist movement. And we come from a region where the debates over this were important, with people like Pelloutier[9] and Briand.[10] But the Charte d'Amiens settled all this, giving a sense of class struggle to our activities. That was the basis of the charter, the recognition of classes—there's a working-class and the bourgeoisie, and there's the struggle. It was the anarchist movement at the end of the nineteenth century that said that when there's a strike the machines have to be destroyed.

---

7 Silk workers in Lyon, famous for their nineteenth-century revolts.

8 Emile Pouget (1860–1931), anarchist writer, theoretician of sabotage.

9 Fernand Pelloutier (1860–1901), anarchist and leading figure of revolutionary syndicalism in the nineteenth century.

10 Aristide Briand (1862–1932), native of Nantes and Saint-Nazaire, began as a revolutionary syndicalist and later became a powerful politician, occupying the highest government posts.

The question was never one of destroying machinery. The question was, were we capable of taking power in the factory? We think—in the CGT and the PCF—that workers should be given more power within the labor-management committees. This is our goal, so the workers can decide on investments, etc. In '68 the question was under debate. As it was before and as it was after. And what is the goal of labor? The question was posed in '68, and we posed it differently. We felt the benefits of labor should go towards education and health care, while the right wants to just increase profits. The rich are richer and the wage earners' power grows weaker. In '68 this question was posed. And we had no political response.

But you were looked on poorly by the others and you looked at them in the same way. Bernard, when Trotskyists or Maoists came to see you ...

Bernard: It wasn't so obvious to us that they were. We met some in our organizations and they came to our meetings, and what they said had an impact.

There were never students who came to your factories and had their tracts torn up?

Guy: Oh yes, we kicked them in the ass. Because they came to undo what we'd built. At a given moment it's a question of relations of force.

What about democracy?

Dominique: Their presence among us could be viewed as non-democratic vis-à-vis the workers who were organized and had made their decisions.

But what gives you the right to tear up their leaflets?

Guy: You're right to ask the question.

Dominique: But was it democratic on my part as a member of the CAL to go to other high schools to convince them to go out on strike?

Absolutely! You gave them the choice, while tearing up leaflets ...

Guy: Yeah, but we kicked them in the ass. On principle, and also because the work of union militants is complicated, it's not something where you come and everything is immediately decided. There are discussions … We built and then the others came and instead of attacking the bosses they attacked the union. That's another thing entirely. And the Trotskyists you talk about, and in Saint-Nazaire it's principally Lutte Ouvrière (LO)[11] which was the most influential of them, they never stopped criticizing the decisions of the CGT, decisions they'd contributed to making. So they attacked the union militants and the bosses just feasted on this. This isn't acceptable and can't be done in the name of democracy.

Bernard: And the split we were talking about before, between protecting tools and smashing them no longer exists, even among the Trotskyists.

Dominique: There's no denying this old tradition was a strong one, and even in the strikes after '68 there were those who wanted to go into the offices and smash them. And we never had a problem with sequestrating the bosses. For legal reasons we didn't call it sequestration, it was holding them for negotiations. It would happen that we'd hold a boss. I remember holding them overnight and it never posed an ethical problem.

So for machines it's one thing, and for bosses another … I'd think sequestration was much more radical than smashing.

Guy: Recently there have been actions where there was real violence. Including some that led to the destruction of tools and even threats to destroy factories. But this is a reaction based on despair. It's not a revolutionary reaction. That is, we have our backs to the wall, we've tried everything, like the guys in the north who drove their tractor into the river. It's that the people's political consciousness, the consciousness of the workers, is so weak: it was that

---

11   Heir to Voix Ouvrière, it was firmly implanted in the region, and the first strike and occupation, at Sud-Aviation in Nantes, was led by a Trotskyist member of LO. See interviews with Eliane Paul-Di Vicenzo and Michel Andrieu below.

way in '68, and even more so now. But there were never violent reactions at any point in '68, because we arrived at something, at a compromise. The union movement always reaches a compromise. I have some experience in this, having been a union leader for 56 years: we have our demands and in the end the results are a compromise compared to what we wanted. This is the difference between us and the others.

We've reached the Grenelle Accords.

Bernard: People were tired of the strike and it was then that things got more complicated, since there were people who wanted things to go further but who'd never made these demands before. And what was a really important outcome was the official recognition of the unions; before this we had to distribute our tracts outside the factory. And from one day to the next we entered the factory and had our own office.

Dominique: That's something that's often forgotten about '68, and that's the recognition of the union in the factories. Before, when there was an election for delegates from the personnel people presented themselves as members of the CGT, but there was no legal recognition of this membership. It's only in '68 this was recognized, and this is essential to the workers' struggles.

Bernard: And I remember the meetings of the metal workers in late '68 when people were in tears because we'd obtained an office with a table and two chairs. It was a great victory. So the agreements were dynamic.

How did the vote go on the agreement to go back to work?

Guy: People have focused on Grenelle, but it wasn't an accord, it was the record of a decision that affected several things, like salaries and union recognition. But every factory had its own demands. So unlike '36 the focus wasn't really on things on a national level. Back then the strikes continued after the Matignon agreement. In '68 I was kept informed of the national discussions, but in every factory there was something particular. But people talk so much about Grenelle, about how when Georges Séguy[12] went to Renault he was booed—I don't doubt there were some who booed, that's always the case—but in the end it was the workers at Renault who voted and settled the strike. We didn't vote on Grenelle, but on the demands of our enterprise.

We've forgotten the students. How did things go there, Dominique?

Dominique: As I said earlier, this was my first mandate as a union delegate, my first involvement in a strike. I gave the demands to the principal, demands having to do with our being treated with respect, with the conduct of the authorities towards us. There were more demands that were cultural in the spirit of "It is forbidden to forbid" than specific items. The idea was that of recognizing we were adults. Concretely I can't remember anything aside from the cigarettes. But I do know there were changes in the authorities' conduct towards us. It was more in the general climate of '68 than anything else. And May '68 was more than anything about freedom of expression. For example, TV was muzzled by the Gaullist state. And there was the feminist movement that had its place in '68, which we don't talk about enough.

And were your "members" happy with the way things were done?

Dominique: Yes, I think they were happy with the way we carried their voice; that's all we were.

After the pro-de Gaulle demos and then the elections, did you as Communists see this as proving you were right?

Dominique: This validated our position that there was no political alternative at that moment. As I've said, in May there was no political perspective for something else.

Bernard: I had the conviction that we were on the right road, and the results didn't upset me.

---

12   Georges Séguy (1927–2016), leader of the CGT, was famously booed and driven out of the Renault factory in Billancourt when he called for accepting the Grenelle Accords.

Guy: I was 30 in '68 and our analysis was that we weren't in a revolutionary moment that would bring a majority. The movement was essentially for daily demands, and that because of divisions on the left, the possibility of political change wasn't posed. So we weren't surprised by the elections.

Dominique: This reminds me that one of our demands was the vote at 18. Which came in 1974.

Did May '68 forever change something in France?

Bernard: Yes, it is a reference for the union movement, just as '36 had been thanks to all its successes. And now the revanchists attack it—capital, who want to roll everything back.

Dominique: What changed was cultural, it was victory for individual freedom.

Guy: It was globally positive. But whenever we obtain something the bosses want to take it back. They want to put everything into question, everything from '36 to '68 and after. In '68 we were in a period of conquest and said we no longer want to discuss the bosses' demands, we want to discuss ours.

What did May change in you?

Bernard: The fact of becoming a militant came from '68. That was something concrete that came from it. The responsibilities and the disappointments, all of this came from '68 for me.

Dominique: It was my first engagement and it was my birth as an organizer.

Guy: As for me, I continued. It reinforced my conviction that when the world of labor is united and fights, it's capable of winning. That's what's important.

MYRIAM CHÉDOTAL
AND ELIANE PAUL-DI VICENZO

Eliane Paul-Di Vicenzo was a university student in Nantes in May 1968; Myriam Chédotal one of the few girls at the technical high school in Saint-Nazaire. Both would be extremely active in their schools and cities, and remain politically active today. I had been told by several people how repressive France was from the sexual point of view, something that hardly resonated with what we in the US had always assumed. I began by asking them about this.

Eliane: It wasn't something at the level of the right to speak: the right to speak is something you naturally take. It was rather on the level of daily life. I was a student at the Ecole Normale de Nantes, and we didn't have the right to wear pants, tights, short skirts … There were tons of regulations that meant that we didn't have the right to our own appearance, our own bodies. There was that. Plus, I had a mother who was Sicilian and Catholic, so I had no right to go out alone: if I went out I had to be accompanied by my little brother or sister. I lived in a poor neighborhood of Nantes, the north, where there were a number of associations, among them a group there from the Young Communists that had a club, and my mother trusted me to go there, but that was it.

Myriam: It was a little different for me: I'm three years younger than Eliane, so in this area the differences were tremendous. I was far from being of age in '68 and there was the great fear of pregnancy: obviously there was no birth control. As for speaking, perhaps in some families girls were less listened to than boys, but in high school I had no fear of speaking out, nor did I feel girls were less capable of doing so than boys. On the other hand, being in a family where I had a brother who bore the halo of someone about to do his military service, you didn't feel you had as much value when your future was getting married rather than doing your military service. Though I had no hesitation about speaking up, later on, when I was in high school during May, when I was in the Comité d'Action Révolutionnaire Lycéen (CARL), it was mainly boys who did, as was the case in the CAL. The leaders—though everyone would have been ashamed to be called a leader—were boys.

Did you rebel against this?

Eliane: The student movement in Nantes was tiny. In '67 we went to occupy the girls' Cité Universitaire so the boys and girls could visit each other's dorms. And in March '68 I was the first to have the right to live in the boys' dorm. This was the first strong, collective movement.

Is there one example of backwardness that really stands out?

Eliane: I was at the Ecole Normale of Nantes and we were all given numbers based on our rank in the entrance exam. According to the number we were assigned a pedagogical mother, a pedagogical grandmother, and a pedagogical husband. Every year there was a ball organized by the director and directress of the school so we could meet our future spouse, and normally this was our pedagogical husband. For the ball there was a mass of rules about how we should dress, the distance to be kept between us when we danced, what to say.

Myriam, did you know this was what awaited you when you went out?

Myriam: No, because I was already unhappy with the path laid out for me and I lived in the hope of an explosion. Had it not happened I'd have provoked it on the individual level. I couldn't imagine myself going to the Ecole Normale—though parenthetically it must be said that I became a teacher—and for someone like me, not exactly from the popular classes, but molded by rural life, living in a tiny town of 3,000, 50 kilometers from Saint-Nazaire, I was constantly forced to lie, to get around the surrounding hypocrisy, which meant either pretending to conform, and sometimes by insolence or rebellion or lying. Because everyone knew that we were going out with boys, that boys and girls of my age were sleeping together. So I quickly found myself confronted with lies and the need to lie.

Did the two of you feel that all you were doing to free yourselves had a political dimension?

Eliane: It was only when I was in high school in Nantes that I gained this awareness. That I was political. I was at a girls' school with reactionary teachers, but it was when a teacher spoke in praise of Lenin that I first gained a political consciousness. Before it was all on a personal level.

Myriam: For me it was different. It's always a matter of a confluence of experiences and encounters. I had a mad desire to liberate myself from my family milieu, not so much on a personal level, since they were nice people with a certain narrow-mindedness, with moral ideas that didn't agree with me. But in '66, '67 I was led to anarchist groups in Saint-Nazaire that were already following in the wake of Gaby Cohn, who taught classes at the Université Populaire, so my aspiration to emancipate myself, to go a little mad, to accept my insolence and do things that were a bit extravagant, found their legitimacy in the fact that there were groups with a theoretical reflection concerning things I was doing completely spontaneously. With them I found political legitimacy for my desires.

And you, Eliane, you felt the same thing?

Eliane: Exactly. Though I'd read *Capital* it wasn't my cup of tea, and my first action was against Juquin when he came to Nantes to give a talk at the Centre d'Etudes Marxistes in 1965. I asked a question and he answered me with utter scorn, saying I hadn't understood Marx and he treated me like I was wet behind the ears. He raised his voice to me to make fun of me and all. And since then I've never accepted a man raising his voice to me. And I decided I'd never become a Communist.

When did you hear about the occupation of Nanterre on March 22?

Eliane: I went to Paris on March 22 because there was already a group in Nantes that had connections with the Parisian students. So there were three of us who met with students from Nanterre.

What did you learn?

Eliane: Many things, about the GAs, on how to conduct them, how to see to it that the movement takes hold everywhere. And it was Nanterre that gave us the idea to live in the dorms of the other sex: I was in the boys' dorm in March '67.

Myriam: The news from Paris inspired me. I was already frequenting a group of anarchists around Gaby Cohn, not that we were his students at high school, where he taught German, but we knew him from the Université Populaire, where he gave classes on the Russian Revolution and Bakunin ... But already there were documents that reached us from Nanterre, so we knew what was going on. Plus, high school students had already joined the workers at one of their demos in Saint-Nazaire, the first time this had ever happened here. So I was ripe for the events. And I was ripe for another reason, and that's because like Eliane I had had problems with the PCF. I had many Communist professors at the Lycée Technique my parents had had me attend. And they were like Juquin: since I was insolent and rebellious in class they categorized me among those who put their authority into question. Who destabilized them. So through this teacher-student conflict I began to detest the Communists. Though I'd later join the party. So when the moment began in my high school, and since there were many students who were Communists who were behind the organization of the CAL, I immediately joined with the three or four Enragés to form a CARL, the Revolutionary High School Action Committee, which was opposed to the CAL. We spent more time combatting each other than we did the authorities. That is, the CAL for us were reformists, *collabos*, because they negotiated with the leadership of the high school for better rules inside the school, while for us in the CARL, we didn't give a damn about changing rules, we wanted a revolution.

Eliane, you hear what's going on in Paris, you go, and when events explode on May 3 you're ready in Nantes.

Eliane: Oh yes, from May 4. Nantes followed Paris immediately. We occupied the University of Nantes and I took over the switchboard, sending messages all over the world. To Berkeley, for example.

Switchboard operator ... So they gave you a traditionally woman's job. Did that bother you?

Eliane: Not at the time, because we laughed a lot. We did it gleefully. We met so many people. In fact, I didn't even realize it was a woman's job. Nor did I realize at the time that it was mainly men who spoke at the GAs. It took me two years to realize all this, but at the time it was so euphoric, so enjoyable, so different from what we'd lived until then that it never even occurred to me I was doing woman's work.

How did the occupation function, was it round the clock?

Myriam: The school was occupied all the time, and the CARL occupied the school overnight. The people on the CAL, if you were to ask them, probably wouldn't know we were there all night. I remember bringing in a duvet and sleeping in a classroom, so we definitely occupied the school at night. We didn't occupy on the weekends, but during the week at night, yes.

Eliane: For us at the university, there were professors who supported us and there were even security guards who were on the strike committee, so we could come and go as we pleased.

Did the women speak at the GAs at the high school?

Myriam: Yes, not many, but then there weren't many at the technical high school. And even when we had the big spontaneous demo on May 7, my friends and I went around the school telling people to join the demo with the people from the Aristide Briand, a more literary school. When we spoke to the classes, one of the two Communist teachers was dumbfounded by what we were doing, and in the end there were 400 of us who marched, mainly from Briand, but some from the technical high school as well. This was the first time they'd gone out other than on orders from the organized. We already had news from Paris and we had our slogans from them. We spent a lot of time imagining slogans.

Had you read the Situationist pamphlet *De la Misère dans le milieu étudiant*?

Myriam: In fact, it was the subject of much discussion when the CAL was talking about grades. We read excerpts and commented on them.

Eliane: And we received Situationist texts from a small publisher called Editions Barbare, and we reproduced them on a mimeo machine, including comics *detourné* [diverted] by Raoul Vaneigem.[13]

Was it common to talk about the Situationists?

Eliane: All of my friends and all the student leaders at the university were Situationists or pro-Situationist. There were some in ICO, some Maoists, some in the JCR, but they were a minority. The hard core were Situationists.

Myriam: In high school there was a cleavage. The CARL was nourished on the Situationists, while the CAL was completely foreign to all that, more sensitive to Communist and union arguments and slogans. But honestly, maybe because we were all young, aside from one or two who were very theoretical and read reviews, none of us called ourselves Situationists. We were anarchists. Which marked us off from the others. We were anars, period.

Eliane: There were some among us who went to Amsterdam to visit the Provos and brought back their reviews. We kept up with everything going on everywhere.

So for both of you the references were more cultural than political. Or a mix of the two with the cultural predominating.

Eliane: Oh yes.

Myriam: Cultural, but within an international environment, with myths which we constructed around events going on in the world. Let me give you an example. The school had a photo lab,

---

13   Raoul Vaneigem (1934–), a central figure in the Situationist movement.

and the idea was to reproduce the image of Che, who'd been killed shortly before. We felt the need for an iconography, for a myth.

Eliane: We for our part were against any kind of chief. When Raoul Vaneigem came to Nantes he was going to speak to the UNEF downtown and not at the school. So the rank-and-file militants went to tell him we had no need of leaders and we didn't need him to speak. We were angry because he'd been brought clandestinely without our being told, and because he was going to speak in Nantes, where we had refused leaders.

Is it safe to say, Eliane, that the leaders of the period didn't interest you?

Eliane: I'm a literature professor now and I have much admiration for Vaneigem's writings, but it's not because I like his writings that he could be our spokesman. But at the time we were organized, we had our inter-professional/inter-union committees, which were expanded to include the non-unionized strike committee that functioned collectively. We had no need for a leader and we were outraged that Vaneigem could even think he could come to Nantes to speak. So we didn't boo him or anything, we simply had a discussion with him.

Myriam: Listening to Eliane there's something that comes back to me. It's that there was a kind of fundamentalism, with everyone battling everyone else, and so the least initiative was contested. During May the claws came out very quickly and ad hominem attacks were a regular feature. Looking back on it, bringing a speaker was something interesting, but just because he was being brought to Nantes that meant he was being idealized, and as soon as someone distinguished himself a bit he was immediately suspect.

There were strikers everywhere. Did you seek connections with them?

Eliane: Oh yes, absolutely. In Nantes on May 9 we went to Sud-Aviation, and after that we went out every evening, sending delegates to factories around the region that were on strike.

And what did you do?

Eliane: We'd spend the evening occupying along with them. Most of the time it was something truly festive. And we discussed issues like self-defense, how we were going to defend the places we occupied. And we were always well accepted by the workers. I never went out alone, there were usually three or four of us, among whom I was usually the only woman, but we were well received, though I have to say that at Sud-Aviation Bouguenais the leader Yves Rocton[14] scorned us: I was young, I didn't have his experience, he was a member of the OCI, a convinced Lambertist and member of FO, plus for him women counted for less than nothing. He held recruitment drives all over the Nantes region, and at the events they'd have games of *belote*, and we'd play it just so we could play against him. He ridiculed us, so we ridiculed him in front of the people who he recruited.

Myriam: I didn't go to the workers very much at all. I was a boarder, so aside from the demos I didn't get to do too many things. There was a worker who was close to the anarchists who wanted to make connections with the students who came to the high school. We had no means of transport, while he came with his pals and told us what was going on.

What did the workers go to the high school for?

Myriam: There weren't necessarily GAs, but the weather was beautiful and we had meetings outside almost all the time. There was even a daily program, with discussions about sexual emancipation, political emancipation, talks about authors, historical events. All of this happened outside. The workers came to inform us and they stayed to participate in our meetings.

In the discussions, what did you want to achieve? Myriam, you said earlier that you wanted not to reform the school but to destroy it.

---

14 Yves Rocton (1938–2008), member of Lambertist Organisation Communiste Internationaliste (OCI) and Force Ouvrière, he led the strikers at Sud-Aviation during the May events.

Myriam: Absolutely. It was utopian. The less experience you had and the younger you were, the more you wanted revolutionary change. I would later join the Ecole Emancipée,[15] but after a time I left that and joined the PCF after meeting some members during activities I was involved in. But that didn't last, and in general whenever I was part of something I would quickly find myself in opposition and would feel it no longer made any sense.

Eliane: I didn't have that experience. My father was in the CGT and the PCF; I read much about the Commune and the Spanish Civil War, so I came to realize that sooner or later the parties betray the working-class, so it was out of the question that I join a party, even an anarchist one. They're antonymic. So I was never tempted by a party.

Did you feel that what was happening was going to overturn France?

Eliane: That was our objective. I wanted to be done with the old world. At the time I was utopian as well. I thought the formation of workers' councils—and we had them in Nantes—would spread and change everything. We quickly realized that the army was lying in wait and it didn't last very long. Afterwards I still had the rebellious streak which I carried wherever I went to live.

In the region there were attempts at self-distribution.

Myriam: I was one of those who went to buy products from Joseph Potiron. A few of us would go to his farm to purchase goods. Back at the school people would come get the things we'd brought back, milk, vegetables, and paid us cost. It was the strike committee that paid the farmers. We only provided for the north of Nantes.

Eliane had gone to Paris at the very beginning. Myriam, did you ever make it there?

Myriam: I had a monitor at school who I liked who had a 2CV, and we took off for Paris where, as in so many cases during the time, I lied to my parents. They thought I was preparing my

---

15   Radical current within French teachers' unions.

school leaving exam, and I left with the monitor in his car, and we went to Nanterre and the Sorbonne. I remember it was the day of the Gaullist demonstration. So for three days we went to the GAs and debates, but not the demos. Seeing all of this amazed me, but didn't make me enthusiastic, because I was horrified by the dissension. Where I was coming from, in Saint-Nazaire, we'd had the split right from the beginning of the movement, the reformists on one side and the revolutionaries on the other. While there what we saw were revolutionaries tearing each other apart.

Eliane: It's always like that in Paris, with their intellectual debates ...

Myriam: So I didn't return home fired up and full of ideas I'd want to apply. I came home happy to be home in Saint-Nazaire with my comrades and subjects of discussion in accord with my concerns.

When there were disputes in the GAs, was it over day-to-day questions or the larger ones, or arguments over what happened in the Soviet Union in 1927?

Myriam: All of the above. It was often on questions of immediate strategy, and indeed, on historic analyses that we did to avoid reproducing errors, so you had to analyze this or that event.

Eliane: And at the university we did it with much humor, asking the Trotskyists, when we discussed Kronstadt, exactly what Trotsky wrote about Kronstadt.

With all this it's clear that neither of you was all that much interested in immediate reformist demands.

Eliane: I remember that at the end we put up a poster for the 30-hour week and increases in our grants, so we did have demands that were acceptable, and not just those that were unacceptable. And let's not forget our demands for the mixing of the sexes.

Myriam: No. Certainly not. What we reproached the CAL for was for negotiating things we considered mere details. We were more utopian, seeking transformation of society. Perhaps had we been at the university it would have been different, but immediate demands seemed to us to be the prerogative of the workers.

Eliane: The things we wanted were concrete: abortion, the right to own our own bodies.

Dominique Barbe, who I spoke to yesterday and was at the technical high school in Nantes, spoke about how the basis for their demands were that they no longer wanted to be treated like children ...

Myriam: That was common to everyone. But the things they wanted, like the right to smoke, were all symbols of what interested the people in the CAL, who would discuss these things for hours, and we thought that these issues were fine, but for things like cigarettes and attire, well, instead of waiting for the authorization to wear pants we just put on pants.

Eliane: Exactly.

Did you pick up boys?

Myriam: Yes, yes.

Eliane: A lot. One of the first slogans that we took from the Situationist International was "*Les réserves imposées aux plaisirs incitent aux plaisirs sans réserve*" (The hindrances placed on pleasures incite unhindered pleasures). This was one of the first things we put up everywhere. It was the sexual revolution. There were even chicks who came to the school to pick up guys and nothing else. And we threw them out. Guys I knew complained that I had a nasty attitude in May '68, because I'd thrown out these girls who didn't come for the occupation but strictly to pick up guys.

It was a carnival ...

Eliane: Oh yes, every minute.

Myriam: Absolutely, that's just how I remember it.

Eliane: Songs ...

Myriam: Eating whatever we wanted whenever we wanted, listening to music. This was all important and we haven't spoken about it, but we wrote songs, we sang them together, there were revolutionary songs we adapted to the situation.

Myriam, were you still a boarder?

Myriam: Well, no. I'd been thrown out at the beginning when I called for everyone to leave school and join the demonstration; I was thrown out by the correspondent—the person who was responsible for me. So I squatted and I spent a lot of time with the Cohns,[16] and my boyfriend who was a monitor had a room at the boys' school. My parents didn't know because I simply told them that Cohn was my new correspondent. They thought it was great, since he was a teacher and it was he and his wife who were taking me under their protection. They didn't ask questions.

It was all so hypocritical. I lied all the time.

If there is one image of May that remains with you, what is it?

Myriam: It would be the day when everything crystallized for me, everything changed for me the day when my friends from the lycée classique—who tended to look down on us at the technical school—encouraged me and I dared open the first door and I said to a stunned class and teacher, "Comrades"—because they were already my comrades, you see— "here's what's going on, here's the news, I propose we all go to town to demonstrate for the abolition of wage labor." [Laughter] Sometimes I'm not proud to repeat the things we said, though now I see it was funny. That was the first time I spoke in public, before students who didn't really care, before teachers. The first class I said that, the second I said a little more, the third I expressed myself even better, and my life shifted: I realized I had a gift for speaking, for finding the right words. It was that day I gained confidence in myself. It was brilliant.

Eliane: I have two. The first was when I settled in the boys' dorms, and all of them came to greet me. Plus I was on the fourth floor so the school authorities would have had to climb the three

---

16 Myriam and the other people from Saint-Nazaire usually refer to Gaby as "Cohn." Not "Cohn-Bendit."

others before I could be dislodged. That was a great moment. And then there was the first visit to Sud-Aviation, where we spent the night around a campfire with the workers, drinking, singing, fraternizing in a way I'd never done with workers, even though my father was a worker. And workers who sang revolutionary songs like us, French songs whose lyrics they'd changed. And there were accordions.

Myriam: We only had guitars.

There's the difference between the workers and the students.

Myriam: There's something that you said, Eliane, that I want to talk about. You said how you felt close to the workers in a way you never had even though your father was one. It makes me think how in families there was always a barrier between parents and children, but now we were dealing with adults as equals. The first step was dealing with teachers and monitors, and the next was with the new school year and the workers, where no one considered us adults, but now there was no difference.

Eliane: And at the university it was the same thing: we grew close to the professors and assistants who supported us. And to go back to the workers, even though I hadn't had good relations with the CGT before, we were greeted with open arms, no one was hitting on me … It was real fraternity in struggle.

ഔ   രു

JEAN-MICHEL RABATÉ

Born in Bordeaux in 1949, in spring 1968 Jean-Michel was preparing for the entrance exams for the Ecole Normale Supérieure, which he would attend the following school year. Thanks to a professor who "was really extraordinary, because he had managed to make his face look exactly like that of Lenin: he was absolutely identical to Lenin," he worked with immigrants in Bordeaux as well, helping them to learn French. Active in the anti-Vietnam War movement, before the events, he proudly describes himself as being one of the "unorganized" during the events. He now lives in Philadelphia, where he is a professor at the University of Pennsylvania.

What was May in Bordeaux?

There was a great commotion, even in an average provincial city like Bordeaux.

And even in Bordeaux, which wasn't a very politicized city, there were many demonstrations, occupations at the university, to a certain extent following Paris's calendar. I remember an immense demo in Bordeaux, and the slogan was "Fight the Repressive University." As far as I remember, there were no real confrontations with the cops. There were huge demos and the school was occupied: at the time there was a campus in the middle of Bordeaux that was occupied, but they just let it go on. People came and went, they distributed flyers. I have to say that I didn't know the "Occupation of Paris" side of things, the nineteenth-century aspect that occurred in Paris.

I had friends in Paris and they were really excited, but what I lived, what I see now when I look back, was all the groups, all these different groups, the same ones you could find in Paris. Let me list them: there were the Maoists, the Trotskyists, and there were the anarchists. The Trotskyists were all followers of Krivine, but the people I knew were all shared out among the different groups. Many of them were Communists, and they were very well organized. As far as I know they were very critical of what was happening, but gradually they saw there was a popular movement that came out of the factories, so they joined in. But the Communists were very, very critical. That's why they called us *gauchistes*, which for them was an insult: it meant petit bourgeois, anarchist, etc.

You weren't a Trotskyist, you weren't a Maoist, you were accused of being an anarchist, so what were you?

I had, let us say, anarchist tendencies. Well before this, when I was very young, I would attend meetings in Bordeaux of the Spanish anarchist groups, the CNT-FAI. These were really interesting meetings, held in the old city of Bordeaux, which is now a tourist trap but at the time was a rundown spot. They held huge meetings and this led me to read Bakunin and Stirner. So my points of reference were the anarchists. As for the Trotskyists, I had many friends among them. Now the Maoists, I found them Stalinists, and in fact they were hyper-Stalinist. There was a curious paradox: they were Stalinists against the Communist Party, who they accused of not being sufficiently Stalinist. Later on, when I went to rue d'Ulm I would meet up with them again.

Once the events began in May there were no classes in the high schools and the university. People were out on the streets handing out leaflets, arguing ... But that would soon end for me, in July or August, because I passed the entrance exams to the Ecole Normale. When I got to Paris in September I saw there was a kind of return to the events, so I participated in several small demos with the Trotskyists, which was pretty interesting.

We don't hear much about Trotskyists on rue d'Ulm.

No, no, no ... They were there. Anyway, I went to their meetings, but it was kind of the tail of the comet. Many of the militants, like one of my Maoist friends, had been arrested, had police records. So they had suffered, and would suffer again: when they did their mandatory military service they were treated poorly, that's clear.

Did you have the feeling in Bordeaux that you were mimicking Paris, or did it seem you were doing something original and particular to the city?

I feel like we were living both sides of your question. First because things came from Paris, and it's clear that in Bordeaux we were psychologically far from Paris: it took seven hours to get there by train. But many of my friends were involved with the Situationists, who were based in Nanterre and Strasbourg, and we all read issues of *Internationale Situationniste*. So we were aware of what was going on and many of us made the round trip to and from Paris. But I have to say that the events were really in Paris and not in Bordeaux. So it's true, we mimicked them. On the other hand, it was something like a game of make-believe. We spent an entire night arguing Marxism, arguing Marxists against anarchists, Trotskyists against Stalinists, so we discussed politics, and since my friends were either historians or philosophers they knew history well. I remember long, long, long discussions about the Russian Revolution, things like was Trotsky right in crushing Kronstadt? So we discussed many things. Cuba, we argued over Cuba. In Bordeaux ...

If you went to the ENS you must have been familiar with Althusser.

Among all these groups, all these tendencies, I wasn't an Althusserian. I'd read Althusser in 1966—*Pour Marx*—but I wasn't Althusserian because I thought he was wrong to exclude the young Marx, who I like. For me there wasn't a young, idealistic Marx and an older, scientific one. And I was attacked for this, people telling me I was naive, I was an anarchist, we who have read Althusser know what should be thought. The Maoists believed this. As for me, at the time it just made me laugh.

But back in Bordeaux?

Well, since there was little that happened there, what I remember is that the university and a few factories were occupied and that it didn't last very long. We started late and it went on for about two weeks.

The university was in the heart of the city, the building we occupied was on place de la Victoire, a lovely nineteenth-century building, easy to occupy. What did that mean? There were no classes, people were there day and night, there were studios for producing leaflets and posters. There were General Assemblies every day, and I attended them, though not every day. I don't remember what was said, but you know, it was a lot of verbiage. The police kept an eye on things but they were forbidden to enter ... Except when they entered the Sorbonne. Afterwards the authorities understood that it was a mistake to have universities in the heart of the city and they started building them 10 kilometers outside the towns.

I have to say that I saw and participated in huge marches but I never saw police repression. Perhaps here and there were cases at occupied factories, but I didn't see any police violence. The French cops had orders not to kill, so this wasn't Tiananmen. Why? Because they knew the people who'd be killed were children of ministers and judges.

For you was this a matter of fighting for something or against something?

For me what it was, was that Gaullism was dead, and we were rebelling against it. But I think that the current of thought that gave me the most was *Charlie Hebdo*—which at the time was *Hara-Kiri*;[17] it was the spirit of *Hara-Kiri* that mattered to me. I would read it in secret, since my parents would destroy it when they found it. But I loved its spirit, its anarchist, irreverent spirit.

But what we rejected most of all was de Gaulle, de Gaulle with his wartime halo. France before May '68 resembled Franco's Spain more than it did England. Ideologically France was very backward. It was interesting to see this in a provincial city like Bordeaux, with its old bourgeoisie and all the petty scandals. It was *this* France that was being rejected, more ideologically than in the modes of production.

You shouldn't forget just how reactionary and repressive France was. The March 22 Movement—perhaps I'm wrong, but what set it off was when the students at Nanterre wanted to sleep with their girlfriends in the same room. These days this seems normal, but at the time it was strictly forbidden. So there was this absurd sexual repression, but sexuality was only one element, though the most obvious one, and the Situationists understood and played on this, because this was a visible element of bourgeois repression, of a bourgeoisie that was still in the nineteenth century. For me, May '68 is when France entered the twentieth century.

---

17   Satirical magazine, founded in 1960, predecessor of *Charlie*.

What was interesting for us—and what was thrilling for me—was discovering the social reality of immigrants, those who were totally excluded. Something I truly appreciated in the discourse of the Situationists and the anarchists was that we had to stand by the excluded.

Do you see May as signifying a break in French history?

Yes. May changed something. That doesn't mean that what was changed was the structure of production: French capitalism still functions and continued along its rails. What changed was the popular consensus, the relations between people. That's clear. And there was a kind of liberation of the word that was quite remarkable. As for the rebellion against parents, that was less clear. For example, my father taught literature and was in agreement with May '68. But it was difficult for people like him, formed under the old, authoritarian system, to adapt. That said, someone like my father thought it was something positive, and I was a little surprised by this. There were six of us, six sons, and we argued all the time; in fact, everyone argued all the time. This was the hysterical side of things. We spent whole days arguing, not sleeping, smoking, drinking coffee, etc., there was a great ferment.

Can you think of one striking event of the time? Something the image of which has remained with you since?

If there was one really striking event of the time it was the huge pro-de Gaulle demo. This I didn't understand at all. It was then that I said to myself: here we are in our little group and we don't really understand what's going on. It was then that I said, "Aha! After all, this is just like the revolutions of the nineteenth century: a small group of people in a big city"—essentially Paris and Lyon, the main cities where things happened—"and in the other cities they were in the process of settling accounts with the old order." It was really like the French Revolution. There you had the moderate Girondins against the Mountain, and so what characterized Bordeaux was the mix of epicureanism and irony. People liked to enjoy themselves, and even in May we went for swims and then said, "Let's go back and occupy something." This wasn't the case for the Parisians: you don't go swimming when you occupy the Sorbonne.

How would you define May: a revolt, a revolution, an event?

I call it an event: I think that's a good term: "something happened" in the philosophical sense that Badiou speaks of as an *événement*. It was foreseeable and not foreseeable; it was shocking; it was unexpected; it took on an absolutely particular dynamic.

There are people who do so, but I never denied May '68. There are many in France, bad philosophers, who say that everything that is evil in France comes from May. They understand nothing. May '68 was complicated: there were many actors with different ideas and there was a kind of great, lyrical community in their expression. This is what was remarkable about the slogans of May '68: they were so amusing, so Lacanian, so disenchanted: "It is forbidden to forbid," etc. There was great novelty: something was finally happening. Afterwards the French state changed somewhat in its policies. What's interesting is that in Italy and Germany they didn't succeed in having that same spontaneous poetry, and so the fight there was much harsher, with their groups on the extreme right and the extreme left, with kidnapping and assassinations … Which didn't happen in France.

I find this very interesting. This didn't happen with us because for us this was much more an affair of language; it was a change in discourse. There were acts, like throwing stones and smashing cars, but these weren't acts as radical as assassinations or killing clergy. Think about it: had the *gauchistes* of May '68 been very, very radical they would have gone into churches and carried out massacres. Why not? Nothing wrong with that. But they didn't do that kind of thing. Of course, had they done so the air force would have been unleashed on them. It's clear there was no delirium to carry out irreversible acts. So for me, and for the others who lived it, it was an enormous liberation of discourse that forced people like my parents and others to listen to what was going on.

May is famous for its slogans, and language is your subject matter. Did you come up with any?

I had a magic marker and I wrote slogans on banners. I wrote a lot of them, but I can't remember any specific ones, they were usually something about the stupidity of the bourgeoisie. Because everyone insulted everyone else; insults were bourgeois, but in this way we were all bourgeois.

How did it change your life?

It's not May '68 that changed my life, no. That happened when I came to Paris the following September, and especially in '69 there were still all these debates, since Althusser was there at the ENS, as was Lacan, and Derrida. I worked with Lacan, I attended his seminars: he was tremendously important because many *gauchistes*, who had really hoped the revolution would come, became depressed and found themselves in psychoanalysis. It was the moment of the psychanalysts of the left, the Maoists and all that, people like Jacques-Alain Miller. I worked with Derrida and someone like Derrida, who at the time was in the PCF, wasn't all that interested in May '68. There were those who thought it was a good thing, but that the work had to be done differently.

Did I ever tell you this story? A few years later, in 1973 I was in charge of the ciné-club at the ENS, and with a few of my friends we assembled all the documentaries on May '68, just five years after. We had a festival, "May '68 and Film," and it was extraordinary: we made posters like those of May and the people who came to see the films were absolutely astounded by what had happened. In five years we'd changed so much: in five years we'd become more hippie, there was no more short hair. We were astounded to see everyone—except Cohn-Bendit—in white shirts, ties, short hair, a discourse a bit stiff. And it was in seeing this that we realized just how much in society had changed. It wasn't only because of May, but even so it allowed France to reach a level of what was happening in, say, England or the US and other advanced industrial nations. It was a little as if the same thing had happened in Salazar's Portugal. It was as if something happened to Salazar, Portugal's repressive dictator, and poof! it turns into Carnaby St. And this is what happened in France. The France of de Gaulle, with all his bizarre apparatus, its outdated chivalry, and suddenly there's a modernization.

And the day after, the *lendemains qui chantent*?

I imagined a more or less just society, a society that was less closed. France, you see, wasn't a country with a great vision. De Gaulle lied; he lied to everyone. He made people believe that France had never collapsed before Germany. There were so many lies, so many lies about our heroic past. France needed more truth, and *that* was the effect of May '68: May '68 allowed for greater truth. I didn't like the idea of a heroic France and all that, since we saw all the lies: like what about colonial France? OK, he got us out of that, but if you looked at our history there were all these lies and the remains of repressive Catholicism. May allowed for the destruction of all of this, and for me that was very, very good.

May was: we're going to be more true, and that was the case. We came closer to the truth.

℘   ℭ

JOSÉ AND HÉLÈNE CHATROUSSAT

The Chatroussats, José and Hélène, have been together for over fifty years, a life of political activity, travel, and shared readings.

Hélène dreamed as an adolescent of humanitarian work, of providing medical care to the poor of the world; José, raised in a family atmosphere of anti-militarism and anti-colonialism, fought against the war in Algeria, but knew that "even if the war in Algeria ended we had to continue the struggle against that state and the social order in all areas." The question was, how? Feeling certain anarchist tendencies, "I was never very sure of myself, in fact I never was, and that's why I didn't want to immediately say, 'That's the truth.' I was always in a state of doubt, of hesitation, but also one of permanent seeking." And, as Hélène said, "Our navigation through all these organizations—as well as our travels—we did all of it together."

José worked in Algeria in 1963 as part of a youth group, but despite the Algerian Revolution not turning out as the left had hoped, wasn't disappointed by what he saw there, "Because I went there with no illusions. The benefit of my anarchist vision is that I didn't expect anything."

After a flirtation with Pouvoir Ouvrier,[18] they discovered the Trotskyist Voix Ouvrière, Hélène explaining that they joined it because "When we were 16–17 we were thirsty for life. We read a lot, discussed a lot, but above all we wanted to act."

Famously dogmatic, in both its VO form and its later Lutte Ouvrière form (and maintaining so strict a control over its members' lives that Hélène would be told to end a later pregnancy), they nonetheless found the group exciting. "The discussions were lively. And there was also a nucleus with a great sense of humor, who joked around," José told me.

As 1968 approached Hélène and José were in Voix Ouvrière ...

Did you have pseudonyms?

Hélène: I was Ida, from a tale I loved by Andersen, "The Flowers of Little Ida."

José: I was Samuel.

José: That was the thing with VO; there were all the rules, the bureaucratism that took on painful, unacceptable proportions. But at the start there was also the young, dynamic group side, with its original analyses. For example, no state was acceptable, we had no illusions about Cuba, China, the USSR. It was a Trotskyist analysis, but far more critical. The idea was that the best way to defend the USSR was to defeat their bureaucracy. There was nothing reformist about it. And the radicalism of VO was stronger vis-à-vis the PCF and the CGT. That's why VO made the greatest efforts and had the greatest success in winning over industrial workers, and not just college kids, say, who worked at the post

---

18 Workers Power, a council-communist group, outgrowth of Socialisme ou Barbarie, founded in 1963 by Jean-François Lyotard, Pierre Souyri, and Alberto Vega.

office. Winning a student over is one thing, but a worker is quite another. The other groups didn't do this or succeed in this.

So we found ourselves in brutal confrontation with the PCF. The result of all this was pride in being in a group that wasn't fooling around, pride in being confronted by people who absolutely did not want revolutionary ideas to penetrate the working-class. And so we had a real optimism.

May arrives, and you'd been optimistic something is going to come ...

Hélène: Absolutely.

It's May 3, you're in Rouen and you're very workerist. How did you see the events in Paris, which were all student-led?

José: In the first place, we were students.

Hélène: And I worked as a substitute teacher ...

José: I think there are several things that have to be pointed out. There's not a single young revolutionary of the period, including those in VO, who wasn't won over by what was done by the Zengakuren in Japan, by what the SDS did in Germany. We never said, "Oh, they're nothing but petit bourgeois, we don't give a damn." Never! Even in VO the analyses were very favorable to student agitation. There were articles to explain to the workers that the students want a better life, that they were bearers of freedom, but they can't succeed on their own. They're not a force that can change society on their own, but they're right and we should do the same as them.

When did things start in Rouen?

José: I don't remember exactly, but we reacted quickly. The campus in Rouen was outside the city center, on the heights, which might seem an irrelevant detail but it played a role in the events. There was already a group, JCR in particular, extremely solid, and dynamic, of about a dozen. That had already organized demos in the past that would bring together hundreds of people, and there was the UEC as well, but they were increasingly marginalized, so you see there was already agitation in Rouen well before the events, in March and April. The fascists of Occident attacked us as well, so there was a great deal of activity.

So where did things start in Rouen?

Hélène: At the university, but it was Le Cirque, where there were normally performances, that was the place of the revolution.

José: We did stay at the university, and we also went out to the factories. As for the Cirque, it was perhaps less spectacular than Paris, but the offices were occupied, people listened to music, there were talks, but to be honest, we didn't go to the university very often.

Hélène: We pretty much did what we wanted.

José: I can't even tell you what the other members of VO did, who they were with.

I assume there were GAs. What was discussed at them?

José: What struck me when workers went to the university was how they discussed how we were going to construct a new society, what it was going to be. What would self-management mean, how would it be done. We discussed the war in Vietnam, and the black protest movement in the US excited an enormous number of people. All these themes were discussed. There was a dream-like side to it, a resemblance to the Paris Commune in the sense that nothing was settled, and even though de Gaulle was not gone we had already moved on to the future society.

Did people discuss what was to be done right now?

Hélène: No, never.

José: No. Perhaps this was done less in a provincial city like Rouen than in Paris, where the shock of events was far more immediate and stronger. In Rouen things were far more attenuated. There were no barricades in Rouen, no confrontations with the police. But there were enormous demos that were very peaceful. Plus, the weather was beautiful, so there was a vacation-like atmosphere. It was all something never before seen. Though things would eventually go bad, for most of the time it was as if we were floating on a cloud, it was all so relaxed …

In Rouen too was speech set free?

José: Yes, but things would regress qualitatively. There were people who spoke—there were no spokesmen—but it never led to anything. It was clear it was a movement with no direction. The problem was that certain groups spontaneously pushed themselves to the front, some of them more often than others, like the JCR, which had some excellent speakers, while we for our part didn't push our way to the front. We never made grand speeches, but rather discussed and discussed and discussed in small groups. But even the good speakers, if someone asked for the floor they gave it. I remember a guy who worked at Social Security, a boss in a tie and well dressed, and he got up and said, "Above all, you can't turn back, everything must be changed from top to bottom." It was amazing! His attire was so opposed to his speech …

Did you go to the factories?

José: Hélène was still working, since the strike hadn't yet started and the university was already in an uproar. Sud-Aviation was already on strike. So I took my car to head to some factories around Elbeuf, because I heard things had begun at Renault-Cléon. There was a small factory I saw along the way, where I saw two or three guys, so I asked them, "Are you going to go on strike?" And they answered, "We're waiting to hear what our delegates tell us to do," which showed me there were lots of areas where they were waiting for orders, where the workers didn't just immediately go out on their own. I went to the Cipel, a factory that manufactured batteries, and though the CGT was there it wasn't all that strong, so there were no problems when students went to talk with the workers. It was even a joyful experience.

At Cléon they'd held prisoner the factory's director and the head of personnel, and there was no question of setting them free before every single demand was met. And in fact it was really festive there for three or four days, with a great crowd there at the factory. But the union bosses said to release the people they were holding, and when I returned a few days later the atmosphere had completely changed and there was no point in my hanging around. What happened was that the factories, which had been occupied more or less spontaneously, well, after a few days it was only the union leaders and those close to them who occupied them, who blocked the gates, not the workers. The workers for the most part just went home. It was easy to know if you were talking to a worker, who was interested in hearing what the students had to say, or a union …

Hélène: … bureaucrat.

José: They'd tell me to show them my hands, they'd look at them and say I had the hands of a loafer.

Hélène: And they'd tell the women they should go home and wash the dishes and clean the house.

José: One day, before '68, as we were in front of Rhône-Poulenc, a chemical factory, there was a young CGT member who said he'd like to see my newspaper, and then he grabbed it and tore it into shreds, and they called us every name in the book. As a result, it really wasn't worth the trouble to go to the factories.

Were there joint demos?

José: Oh sure.

Hélène: With young workers.

José: The demos were peaceful and there wasn't much tension. The tension would mount after May, when we had our *gauchiste* march with the JCR, VO, and the anarchists, and the unions would place the longshoremen at the tail of their section of the march. When we would hear a voice in the megaphone saying, "Longshoremen to the rear," we knew we were in for it. Now during the events they didn't dare do this; they waited till after. And the people from the UEC, we'd make fun of them for being part of the PCF. These people dragged us through the mud during the events; there were flyers they put out attacking the students at the beginning, but after a few days they no longer dared to do so. Even so, the PCF was strong in Rouen and controlled all the municipalities ringing Rouen, we had a red belt like Paris, the department of Seine-Maritime being a Communist stronghold. They only have two left now.

What did you expect of the general strike when it came? It was so enormous, all over France, was it the beginning of something that would shake up society and the state? Or was it at the best a dress rehearsal?

Hélène: I wanted to go into it head first, but I had no idea where it was headed.

José: It was clear that May 13 wasn't a day of action like the others. This wasn't like those days in previous years when you marched and then you went home, since nothing else was going on. But on May 13 … And it was the next day, or a couple of days later that Renault-Cléon went out. This was clearly something enormous, but where it was going was impossible to say. It was what we were waiting for, and then what we were waiting for surprised us. There was a fissure in the working-class. There were those who no longer followed the union leaders, something that had already occurred in places like Renault in Le Mans and Saviem, and Rhodiacéta, in '67, where it was workers, not students, who fought the CRS. So those who argue over who started things, was it the workers or the students, it's really not a serious discussion: it was everyone. There was constant student agitation and constant worker agitation. It was kind of a chicken-and-egg situation.

When you were in it, was it from day to day, or was there an overall plan?

José: We had no vision.

But you did, given your political past. And now there you are, the whole world has risen up.

José: And we were happy. And we would do everything we could so that it went as far as possible. But there was one thing, something I reflected on, that was surprising: there was so little violence. We thought things would develop, that there'd be a trial of strength, and in the end there were things everywhere in the world: there were riots in the US, contestation in Eastern Europe, in Spain, revolts in the Third World ... But though there was a lot of violence, especially with the Vietnam War, we were confident in the future. Even our leader, Hardy,[19] was optimistic. He had said, during an internal seminar, that we can hope to build an international party in about ten years, then, after some years of revolution, counter-revolution and a transitional period, maybe, if we were not killed in the meantime, our generation would be the one to know the beginning of a socialist society.

Did you have the feeling that you were part of a historic movement that went back to 1830, to 1848, to the Commune, to 1936 ...

José: There's absolutely no question about it: we were inscribed in a history, we had a strategic aim in VO, and the most we could hope for was that there emerged from all this a working-class revolutionary party. For some people the aim was to overthrow de Gaulle—not that we were against it—and it was a Mendès-France government that would follow, no point in dreaming: it was something short-ranged and short-sighted as that, though the notion of creating a revolutionary working-class party [laughter] ... well, that's another debate and we've evolved greatly on this question. Today we don't think at all that the building of a party is the answer to overthrowing capitalism. Inside a would-be revolutionary organization, some people like too much to have power or a kind of power. It's pathetic. And many militants lose their intellectual curiosity and become conformist in the long run, as we have seen during our long militant life. But at the time we thought that it was necessary that all of this energy succeed in bringing forth a revolutionary party, including all tendencies, all of the *gauchistes*, and afterwards we'd perform the triage of the problems. This was the main thing we had in mind. The aim of VO's strategy was that all these events create an experiment, a bit the idea that May was a kind of 1905. That was the idea, in a way. In fact, 1917 would not

19 Pseudonym of party leader Robert Barcia (1928–2009).

have happened had there been no 1905. It was necessary to take as much as possible from that first event and then ...

Everything seems to be going well on May 13, but for how long was that the case?

Hélène: It was my first post as a teacher in a school just on the other side of the street where there was a big factory, the zipper factory, Fermeture Eclair.

During the strike I had the responsibility to pick up our newspapers, leaflets, and posters at the Sorbonne, where every group had their table, even the UEC. The atmosphere was very fraternal. I was enthusiastic. There were singers, poets ...

I had the opportunity to take part in two important demos. One of them was at the ORTF[20] with thousands of students, young workers, and older people. It was to protest against the lies and slanders of the government. The other one was the enormous demo at Renault-Billancourt. The workers were there on the roof, fists in the air singing the "Internationale," and the CGT was there at the gates, blocking the entrance to the factory so no one could break the work tools. I said to myself, they are many, they're with us, they're on the roof with their raised fists, so why didn't they tell the Stalinists to get lost so we could come in and they could join us. That really did something to me ...

José: I was in a state of denial that things were going bad. I thought things were going well until the time of the dissolution of the groups. There were alarms, like the big demo of the right on the Champs-Elysées, but that seemed to us to be nothing but human dust.

Hélène: They were coming out of their holes, that's all for me. '68 lasted until the funeral of Pierre Overney.[21] It was then that it became crystal clear that the *gauchiste* movement wasn't going to

20　Office de Radiodiffusion Télévision Française; national agency in charge of public radio and TV.
21　Pierre Overney (1948–1972), Maoist militant, member of the Gauche Prolétarienne, killed by a guard at the Renault factory in Billancourt. His killer was later assassinated by an armed group.

create a revolutionary movement. It was too late. Then, starting in '73 the crisis began and a veil of sadness—a light one—descended on the working-class. On the political plane Overney's funeral was a caesura. The working-class had not reacted to a security guard gunning down this young man in front of the factory. We understood then that the union leadership, the CGT, had taken things back in hand, that they controlled the situation and they were preventing anything happening like what we'd lived in '68: the contestation, the going beyond the leadership.

How and when did things end in Rouen?

José: It happened slowly ... It's only an anecdote but it's important ... From the moment we were banned, if you were to ask comrades in Rouen, if they were sincere they'd all admit they were afraid. There were some who went into hiding in the forests and didn't return home, for fear of being arrested. There were those who buried any compromising documents, and they weren't people who were fraidy-cats: even the leaders of the organizations were arrested. The publications director of VO was arrested, but since he had a feeling it was coming he had his bags ready and packed when they came to take him away. All of this cast a pall over the students. The moment when we understood the movement ended—and I do know how this happened—was when the evacuation of the Cirque was decided on.

Hélène: The JCR were not prepared for this kind of situation, unlike VO. We were more prepared because we did not trust in bourgeois legality and had some good habits. It's the reason why we were the first organization able to republish a newspaper, *Lutte Ouvrière*.

And those elections were a real pounding for the left. Did it surprise you?

José: Not all that much. My non-spontaneous side, my experience told me that ... Well, the heavy side of French society, I know it well. That is, even the fight against the war in Algeria was that of a tiny minority. The overwhelming majority of the big bourgeoisie, of the petit bourgeois, of the middle bourgeoisie, and even the working-class never moved on that subject. They did nothing. I know just how ponderous France is. I don't focus on everything that's in movement: I know that France is an imperialist country, with conservative social strata, with small landowners who might have good ideas but who run back into the ranks as soon as there's any danger. So the tidal wave in support of de Gaulle didn't upset or even surprise me. I knew that we had to have confidence in certain people, in certain movements, but France was a country where things just aren't all that easy.

Anyway, I never expect any real change from the electoral process, because that's when the conservative side, the reactionary side of France really rears its head.

Capitalism was shaken by May but it recovered; it was shaken by Mitterrand's victory, but it recovered. Will it someday be shaken for good? And would the changes that followed May, like the advent of feminism, have happened without May?

José: Perhaps, but it would have been more laborious.

Hélène: Conformism lies heavy on France.

José: There was the new phenomenon of young workers who detested working, who wanted to love, who wanted to educate themselves ... It was a real joy to work with them, and this is why we remained in VO: otherwise there was no reason to do so. And we also stayed there because we had warm, human, joyous relations with our comrades.

And May's cultural impact should not be downplayed.

And in the movement of today, like at Notre-Dame-des-Landes, Education sans Frontières, you'll always find '68ers in them: and they're easy to recognize, they all have a look—one I don't have. There was no break, rather there is a connection and passing of the baton.

In France can it be said there was a before May and an after May?

José: There's definitely a break.

Was it a bigger break than Algeria, when France lost a part of the country?

José: They're difficult to separate. It was precisely because of that defeat of French imperialism that there was an opening, that there was in '68 a settling of accounts with all we detested. And bear in mind it was an extremely hierarchical society. At Hélène's high school boys and girls were separated.

There was an unquestionable rigidity in all domains that May blew up; the usual efforts didn't suffice. So the two sequences are connected, the defeat of imperialism in '62 led to an intense politicization of a large sector of students and intellectuals, people seeking across the board.

Hélène: What's certain is that all the old racism has remained in the heads of many of the French that re-emerges on the first occasion. I'm very chatty and talk with everyone, and sometimes there are things that come out of peoples' mouth that send chills down my spine. May '68 is certainly far behind us, because when there was Bataclan and all the other terrorist attacks, it was the occasion for old things, old racism to come out.

José: What's saddening compared to '68 is the deficit in ideas. Ideas of emancipation. They'll perhaps blossom, but it has to be said that the historical background is very weak today. Which wasn't the case for our generation. We'd involve ourselves in strikes everywhere, go to Belgium even, and we'd have long discussions about the Commune. For the young of today it's a tabula rasa, even for those politically involved. Now they're young, active, dynamic, but they're lacking in a historical grounding. There's much going on, and I think the next couple of years could be very rock 'n' roll in France.

CHAPTER FIVE

May and Film

We didn't think about posterity,
but we knew we were filming history.
—Michel Andrieu

MICHEL ANDRIEU

Filmmaker Michel Andrieu, like Pascal Aubier, whose interview follows, went to high school with Paul Thorez, son of the leader of the PCF, and tells of a philosophy teacher there who would tell young Thorez: "Be quiet! You have no right to talk to me like that, I a former Resistance fighter who quit the PCF in 1956 because of Hungary. You've heard of Hungary?" He told me of being invited to the Thorez home, decorated with Picasso paintings, where he would play cowboys and Indians when they were younger.

Andrieu was staunchly "anti-Stalinist with an anarchist tinge," being a member as a teenager of Socialisme ou Barbarie (his cousin was married to Cornelius Castoriadis), as well as having met Guy Debord,

Though he was originally a law student, due to poor grades, "caused by the fact that I was firmly anchored on the left," he entered the prestigious film school IDHEC in 1962.

Attracted to both the New Wave and outsider Hollywood directors like Orson Welles, Michel immediately turned to the political cinema, but he also went to Algeria for six months to help the newly independent nation set its film industry on its feet. Though "we were well received everywhere we went," he quickly saw that "I had nothing to do there."

He returned to France.

Did you think of making political films before May '68?

Yes, in the group I was part of, there was Jacques Kébadian, who was before me in IDHEC. We made a film about the big miners' strike of 1963, a film that escaped us. We shot it using material from the school, and after we made it we gave it to the CGT and that was that. We were wrong not to keep the material.

It was important that we go all the way down the road, not only make a film and edit it, it was important that this group, and some others we met, form a cinema group open to society, open to letting the people have their say. And then in '67 we met some former students from IDHEC who were connected to Debord and Guattari. At that moment there was a possibility for a fusion, or at least for interactions, for a political movement of the left outside the control of the PCF or any similar movement; one that was interested in psychoanalysis as it was practiced by people like Félix Guattari. So we found ourselves connected, but not too closely, to a sphere that had great importance at the time, a movement blending psychoanalysis and politics. *Psych et po.*

We didn't pose the question of form very much, we discovered forms while filming: we were in a movement of body, of spirit, of camera more than a formal one. But we had a cinematic culture: we were at the Cinématheque all the time.

Were you already a director?

Before '68 I worked as an editor, I worked on TV magazines writing shitty little things, I worked as a scenarist a little, I wasn't yet shooting my own films: I was learning. My filmmaking friends and I were part of the current of films like *Loin de Vietnam*, Chris Marker and all that, and we wanted to be there, to film what was going on, film the social movement. We filmed demonstrations between May and December 1967 that were all lost. Things like that happen …

So you worked as a group?

Yes, and we gave ourselves a slightly absurd name: ARC.

What's that? Association Révolutionnaire …

No, we chose one that was very neutral: Association de Recherche Cinématographique. But afterwards we were just ARC, and no one any longer knows what that means. There were seven of us in the group. We had a stolen camera, an Eclair Coutant, that someone had stolen and passed on to us. I have no idea where it was stolen from, but we were always careful it not be seized, because it could have been traced through its serial number; it was, after all, a professional camera. We also had some smaller cameras that we'd bought or found but that didn't shoot direct sound. The big recording device of the time was a Swiss thing, the Nagra, but that wasn't what we had. So we used Heuer which didn't synchronize all that well, but that's what we used throughout May '68.

So when things begin …

We were ready. This is very important, because we understood we were part of the movement that had just arrived, and that we're militant cineastes, or rather that we're with the people, are part of them, and at the same time we were filming.

For us, we can say it began with a film we made in Berlin in late January '68 called *Berlin 68*. We were approached by people who would later be in March 22, like Dany Cohn-Bendit and from the JCR, which Jacques Kébadian was a member of, who were going to Berlin as part of a large movement—well, large as far as we were concerned—for a conference against the war in Vietnam. There were huge demos. So we made a film about the German movement, and we spoke with Dany and all those people and we're in the heart of the movement and advance along with it. So this was late January, and we showed it around in the months preceding May. We also made a film about the critical university, an idea very important to the people at Nanterre. We went to Nanterre on May 2 to show a Cuban film. Dany was there and he said we're going to go into that room there. It was locked, and the people started screaming and carrying on, and it turned into a real mess. And there we were, right in the heart of it! There'd been many things before, but this crystalized things, and at this point Grappin[1] closed Nanterre. Because of us? No. But we were there, they refused us a room, and this was the event that was the straw that broke the camel's back. We were the butterfly that causes a hurricane in Beijing.

So we begin filming everything the next day at the Sorbonne, and we were off …

Later on there was another guy who went on to be an important cinematographer, who shot with Truffaut, Pierre-William Glenn, and the three of us set off for Sud-Aviation in Nantes, where the strike had begun just a few days before, saying we had to go to the factories. We saw this was a great movement, and from the earliest days the slogan was "Worker-Student Unity," which was

---

1   Pierre Grappin (1915–1997), dean of the Faculty of Letters at Nanterre.

something we understood. So Sud-Aviation was the first factory occupied and we had to go there. But we had no gas. So what did we do? We siphoned gas from the tanks of parked cars and set off in our 2CV for Nantes.

How were you greeted?

We were very well received.

Even by the CGT?

It was mainly the Trotskyists who held the factory, Rocton, the Lambertist in FO, I think, was the boss.

What was funny was the way we worked. The first occupied factory, we have the camera and sound, and we have to film all that was happening. Glenn wanted absolutely to film Rocton and that Rocton recite Trotsky's Transitional Program. I was the one doing the sound and I said, "It's simple: we're making this film together, so if you want to film Rocton, I'm going off and I'm going to record, and you can film Rocton, but there won't be any sound." At least this is what I remember; it's possible he'll remember things differently. So we ended up filming the workshops, the picket lines ...

You let the workers speak for themselves?

In fact, I can't remember, but what I do remember was that I was up to here with Rocton and his Transitional Program. In the end the film kind of escaped my control and Glenn edited it for himself. It's called *Nantes Sud-Aviation.*

How was it edited? Where?

Glenn edited it himself. Our collective had expanded in late '67, early '68, and he was living with a famous actress, Juliette Berto, who had played in Godard's *La Chinoise.* There was a meeting and I recall Berto being there with Glenn, stretched out on the bed, sucking on a candy ...

The film labs were functioning?

For a time they did and we worked with them. And when we no longer could, we worked with a lab in Belgium. This is part of the mysteries of the period. We would cross the border to Belgium clandestinely, fearing repression, that they'd take our reels from us. We'd cut through the woods and be met on the other side and be taken to a lab in Brussels.

And to get back?

The same thing.

Did you make several prints?

A few, and as soon as we had them we'd send them out. Especially the first film I made practically on my own, along with Françoise Renberg, who would later marry André Glucksmann, who'd gone to IDHEC with me, so we edited the film, which I did the commentary and voice-over for, and which was the first film we made about May '68, called *Ce n'est qu'un début*. We made it at the very beginning and it circulated throughout the events, and was sent to the US to Newsreel, which we had connections with. It was sent to the provinces, to Italy, to Germany everywhere.

How long did this whole process take? Your idea, after all, was that the films be seen as quickly as possible.

As quickly as possible yes, and it's true that the editing was a tad rough, because we had to work fast. But we never went back and fixed them up. One of my good friends, a Maoist who wasn't in the group but who we helped out with film stock by giving him what we had left over, would later re-do his films. For example, in one of them there was Stalin and Mao and he removed Stalin.

So what was the timetable? Let's say you shoot on Monday ...

We met almost every day, so we met, say Sunday, and discussed what was to be done, we had to coordinate things and decide who was going to go where. Now we'd made some money by selling things we'd shot to TV stations, like excerpts of our footage at Berlin earlier in the year. We invested our money in film and lab fees. So we met often to decide who would film where and we'd meet after the shoots.

But if you had to go to Belgium to have the film developed, that must have taken some time.

That was a few weeks in; I think the labs in France shut down like May 18 or May 20.

Were the films able to be seen within days?

No, after all they had to be developed, edited, so they weren't really available until June or July or August.

So they weren't seen during the events.

No, the only film that circulated during was *Ce n'est qu'un début*, a film that was about ten minutes long and the one on Berlin, and there were ones at the Sorbonne and the barricades, since that was at the very beginning … But in any case, nothing was shown in Paris. People were so active there was no time to watch films, so it was rather they were sent to the provinces and overseas. And there were some truly evil people—journalists—who took the films to Canada, to Los Angeles, and San Francisco, and I don't know what became of them after.

Were your names in the credits?

No, and that was an understandable and normal error: there are no names and no credits. For us these were the films of the people, these films of '68, so there was no name to put on them.

Did you change roles or was there specialization within the group?

There were director-cameramen, there were cameramen who became directors. But everyone was more or less cameraman and director.

What did you normally do?

I shot and edited. But there were also all those meetings, where we discussed the revolution. And we discussed practice, or rather practical questions, like who would take the small camera and who the big one, do we have enough film, which film … We always shot in black and white, since color was too expensive, and never had lighting. We used Kodak 4X.

Did you shoot interiors?

We did, for example at Sud-Aviation and the Sorbonne: 4X is a very sensitive film ... We never used lighting.

Did your group ever discuss the big questions of cinema? What is cinema and all that?

Absolutely not! We had no time. We were in the middle of militant action and we were filming; we slept little, hardly ate. I had a two-room apartment in Montparnasse where I slept, but often late and then got up early. And I have no memory, but none at all of what I ate or when. Odd ...

Were you there filming on May 10 at the barricades?

Oh yes.

Filming or throwing stones?

Filming.

When you did that, did you ever think maybe I should put the camera down?

No, never. It was important to film: there were few people doing that and we thought it important to be there and film the events. And it was a risky thing to do. We'd be chased by the CRS and we'd hide in cellars, in buildings until it was daylight and we could discreetly come out.

Must have been hard to change reels while you were shooting.

We had small reels, 15, 30 meters and a little Bolex. It was perfect on the barricades. I have no idea where that camera came from: we had three non-sync cameras and one big synchronous.

How did you choose what to film?

For example, on the barricades I was alone, and I was up close to what was going on. We didn't have much film, so we were careful of what we shot so as not to waste the film. This served me in good stead later when I'd shoot regular documentaries: for a film of an hour and a half I never shot more than twenty hours.

When you shot, did you think of current use or of posterity?

We didn't think about posterity, but we knew we were filming history. From the beginning of our group, from Berlin, we strongly felt that history was on the march and we were in it, both as individuals and as filmmakers. And from January '68 we felt we were headed to a revolution. There was much confirmation of this movement, March 22 was a confirmation of a movement that was growing, in which we were actors and witnesses.

This was your chance to film the storming of the Winter Palace.

Voilà! That's it. We had the impression we were actors who were filming. It's an extraordinary impression, and there's nothing since that so clearly demonstrated what I've just said.

So at the time you thought this was leading to the revolution.

At the time. We saw that authority was crumbling, and we also understood that when there was the great demo of May 30 we saw it was over, that the old France had returned, the strikes little by little ended, and we saw it was the collapse. We had the impression that power was falling; what was going to happen was obscure though. And for a time I'd thought France was with us. Everywhere I traveled I felt that, and that everywhere everyone was speaking out. Everyone had something to say about everything. Priests, workers ... Not only students. Far from that. There was great effervescence that was visible everywhere. And this continued afterwards.

Did it shock you, the demo?

Yeah, it was what we didn't see. We were too much in the heat of the action and not enough in political discussion. When you're in a movement you see the movement more than what's stable. And that's going to recover.

Did you ever go to a demo without your camera?

No, because in fact either we were in the thing and filming, or outside and doing the things that were indispensable, like transporting the film, editing ...

How did the people feel about being filmed? Were they happy about it?

There were a few incidents, I think it was May 13, when the strong-arm men of the CGT threw us out of demos, they didn't want to be filmed and tried to grab our cameras from us. In the middle of everything. In Paris.

There was something else that happened on May 13 that struck me. It was a huge demo, it might have been May 13, but I wouldn't swear to it, but I saw a guy who was wearing a beige raincoat who resembled Pierre Goldman. At a given moment he took out a gun and put it in his pocket. He was right next to me, and I said, hey, that's Goldman, but was it for sure? I have the impression it was.

Were there confrontations between you and the Communists, or did you see any between the Communists and the students?

In the film we made, *Le Droit à la parole*, there was a large cortege of the *gauchistes*, of the JCR and we—Jacques Kébadian and I— each had a camera at the back of a truck, or I was filming and he was doing the sound, and we made the circle around Île Seguin, the Renault factory, the fortress of the working-class. So there's the immense cortege and the workers and the picketers are on top of the walls, these immense walls, but there was no contact. There's banners saying, "Workers and Students Unite!" but there was no contact. Elsewhere in the film there are scenes in small factories, and those places there are discussions: it's extraordinary, because we see people talking, and there are workers there from other places who call out to the workers behind the walls, with their flags and their things from the CGT, and they're shouting to them, "We have to do something, comrades." It's extraordinary, it's moving, it's poignant. There were the people, staying behind the fences … So we knew that this barrier, that was put up by the CGT, was unbridgeable. And it never was. Except in Flins.

What most people didn't see was that the students were the spark that set off the prairie fire, as Mao said. I accept that there had been strikes over the past two or three years, so the fire was there in the factories, but nothing had taken except in Saint-Nazaire. But the student movement made everything suddenly come together. And it never would have happened without them.

Did you see the barriers at the time?

No, for example, there were optimistic moments. At the enormous GAs at the Sorbonne there were a lot of workers who were there and spoke, and they'd say, "I, a worker, my union tells me this or that blah-blah-blah, but I think that, etc., and we have to unite with the students …" There are scenes of this in the film. So there were many workers who came to the Sorbonne, to hear what the students had to say, to see how we could work together. But this didn't happen in the factories. Outside their walls the workers were able to speak more freely.

Was it usually young workers?

Yes. Sometimes some older ones. I remember in the film there was a train conductor, who must have been between 45 and 50, who came to the Sorbonne to talk to people and we filmed him.

When did you stop filming?

Must have been early June, after Flins. There was nothing afterwards.

Did you film the return to work? Were you at all involved in anything like the *Reprise du travail aux usines Wonder*?

That's an extraordinary story. The two people who made that film still fight over who made the film. They were students at IDHEC, and the two of them set out, one with the camera, the other with the sound, and they both claim credit for the film, for an event they just stumbled on. And in our film there's a similar scene, where there's a woman at a factory gate shouting at the picket line, "Wait, wait, we can't do this." It's exactly the same thing, except we edited it and it's just part of the film, while they just shot this sequence. And this sequence took on a historic and symbolic value.

While ours was just part of a film. So everyone lived that, everyone who was in front of the factories.

So now you've finished shooting and it's time to edit. With what goal in mind?

We started to edit the film, an important one that would be *Le Droit à la parole*, with Jacques and Françoise who wrote the commentary for the film. From a cinematic point of view I think this was the most successful of our films, because for certain scenes we adopted an extremely rapid rhythm, following the rhythm of what was happening, everything that was so lively, the demos … It was an editing process that was in keeping with the intimate life of what the camera filmed.

When you showed the films, was it in order to give rise to discussion?

For that and to publicize what had happened. In the provinces there wasn't that much TV so they didn't really realize all that had gone on. And now everything is filmed, so nothing is filmed.

Did you have an audience in mind?

Not at all. And we ended up being *the* film group of May '68—which Godard understood very well … Godard came to see us and he said, "You people who filmed all of May, I'd like to do a film about May"—I'm trying to imitate his accent—"I don't want to choose, so you're going to go to your laboratory and you're going to take one minute from every ten minutes of negative and you're going to give it to me." He had a kind of butler with him and he said to him, "Give them some money,'" and this money allowed us to purchase film: it was quite a sum of money. So I went to the lab, and I couldn't just cut things in the middle of shots, but I more or less did what he asked and he made a film that's not very well known, interviewing workers in Flins at Renault, which was very important in June '68, when there was a powerful revolt, and so he edited this with excerpts from our footage of May.

Did you have any contact with Chris Marker during all this?

Yes, and I recently wrote about this. When I spoke about the truck before, well, we arrived at the big plaza in front of Renault and

Chris was there with his Leica and he saw Jacques and me on the truck with our camera, and he said to us, "Now it's up to you to do what I've done." That it was up to us to carry on. This was extraordinarily moving, a passing of one generation to the next.

Speaking of Chris Marker, like in *La Jetée*, is there an image from May '68 that marked you forever?

It's something I filmed, in fact, and which is an incredible image. It was on the Champ-de-Mars, it was nearly empty, and there was a crowd that ran towards the camera at a mad speed. There was a flood of people, and it was the very image of May '68: they ran and ran and ran.

How did May change the French cinema?

I think that for a long time it changed it little. There was criticism that no one filmed May '68. And this is false, because there wasn't only us, there were many people who filmed things in many places. Perhaps it didn't result in important films, but the events were filmed.

And how did it change you as a man and a filmmaker?

As a person I think, well, I lived it and prolonged it for a few more years, and in 1975—and for me this was really the end—I made a film with someone who was one of the members of our group. We made a film together about the end of colonialism in a French department—the island of Réunion, it was called *C'est la France*, a film that had no career because no one wanted it. That was the last militant film I made, and it was seen by almost no one. It was something really extraordinary: we showed it in postal sorting centers where postal workers worked by hand—there weren't yet the machines to do the work—many of who came from Réunion. So we showed the film in an enormous sorting station on rue Brune, and three quarters of the people left. Even though most of them were from the Caribbean. They said Réunion? We don't give a damn about Réunion! And there we were, the working-class, the Caribbean, they were all together … We showed it a few more times, and it made it to a couple of festivals, including Cannes in a short-lived section called Cannes Politique or something like that … So for me militant practice lasted until this film, about '75, '76.

As for putting in question cinema practice, for me there were two types of cinema I was torn between: the classical cinema, with Bresson on one side, and the cinema of intervention, with Jean Rouch on the other. I remained with this, with these different things. So there was a classical film that I made that was a big success, that won prizes in the US, *Bastien, Bastienne*, while I continued to make documentaries, since I always like doing that. At bottom May '68, at the cinematographic level, was very rich for me.

As a man, May '68 remains for me an absolute reference.

℘   ☙

PASCAL AUBIER AND
BERNARD EISENSCHITZ

Pascal Aubier is the son of the publisher Jean Aubier, a man who greatly influenced his son's political life. Not himself a Communist, Aubier père instilled in his son an admiration for the deeds of the Red Army during World War II. Pascal quoted his father: "He always said that it's the Soviets who won the war against the Nazis and allowed us to win it. And if they tell you it was the Americans who liberated us you can tell them it's false." This attachment would ultimately lead him to join the PCF, independently of the fact that he had attended high school with Paul Thorez, son of Maurice, secretary of the PCF. But his membership was not only sentimental: prior to joining he had accompanied his friend Michel Andrieu to a meeting of an heir of Socialisme ou Barbarie, Pouvoir Ouvrier. "There were about thirty people there. And there was one worker. That struck me. I said to myself, we can't do without the working-class in making the revolution. So as simplistic as it might sound, the PCF represents the working-class, and so I joined it."

Aubier had studied ethnology, but while still young was active in film, shooting a film of a miners' strike in Valenciennes in 1963, which was confiscated by the police at its sole showing for failing to have proper authorization. Perhaps more significantly, Aubier worked as assistant on five of the six shorts in the New Wave omnibus film Paris vu Par, *working with Jean-Daniel Pollet, Eric Rohmer, Claude Chabrol, Jean Rouch, and Jean-Luc Godard. He would continue to work with Godard as assistant on* Pierrot le Fou *and* Masculin Féminin. *He would go on to make a number of films, including* Valparaiso, Valparaiso, Le Chant du Départ, *and* Le fils de Gascogne.

Bernard Eisenschitz describes himself as "something of a child of the Resistance." His father was a German émigré who fought in the Resistance and was deported during the war. But he continues, "I was above all a cinéphile," and it was at the Cinématheque that Bernard and Pascal met in the 1960s. He worked primarily as a critic, writing for the Cahiers du Cinéma *and writing important books on Humphrey Bogart and Nicholas Ray.*

He dates his politicization to two events: the fight against the war in Algeria ("I took the time to be clubbed a few times") and the Langlois Affair, when the minister of culture, André Malraux, fired the director and founder of the Cinématheque, Henri Langlois, "which was very important because we had the feeling of an unjust authority, and the power of the old." Both were outside Paris when the events began in May.

Bernard: I was invited by Bertolucci and his musician Gato Barbieri, who were finishing a short film with the Living Theater. I returned to Paris and the films had started up again at the Cinématheque on rue d'Ulm—films were showing at that location and not Chaillot. I took a night train from Rome and arrived in Paris on the morning of May 10 and went to see a film by Dovzhenko—I think it was *Arsenal*—and when I came out it was the demo of May 10 that became the Night of the Barricades.

Like a character from Stendhal I strolled around behind them, observing the events.

And you, Pascal, were you already in Paris when things began?

Pascal: I was at the Festival of Young Cinema in Hyères with my short feature, *Monsieur Jean-Claude Vaucherin* when everything began, and on May 10 I had just returned, exhausted. I had gone to sleep with my girlfriend when in the middle of the night I got a phone call, and it was Valérie Lagrange, who was at the home of Jean-Jacques Scholl in the Latin Quarter and they were stuck at his house because of the tear gas. She asked if I had eye drops. I was stunned and I said, "Yeah, I think I have some," and she told me we're stuck on rue Royer-Collard and it would be good if I could bring it to them. So I asked her, what's going on and she said, "What do you mean, what's going on? It's war. The cops are all over the place, there are barricades." I was already living in this building, here on rue Fleurus, and I heard the echo of the noises across the Luxembourg Gardens in the background of the call. I grabbed the drops and I didn't take boulevard Saint-Michel: I went around the other side of the garden and reached Gay-Lussac by rue de L'Abbé de l'Epée. I wasn't able to get to my friends to give them the drops, finding myself in the middle of the mess. I was quite alarmed, because it was really astounding: I'd never seen anything like it, cars were burning, barricades and all, and there I was, right in the heart of it.

So like Bernard, at the beginning I was a flaneur, alarmed in the middle of the battle.

So you didn't join in and toss stones?

Pascal: No, not that evening. That evening I was discovering the thing: it had happened so quickly. And the next day there was no choice but to be part of this movement. This was obvious. Many of my Communist friends from the Latin Quarter found themselves in the thing. There was no order from the party to join, nor was there a prohibition.

That's interesting, because I interviewed someone in the Communist Youth and he said he was expelled for participating in the events. You didn't have this problem?

Pascal: No, not at all.

Bernard: Things were much less rigid. If you do the lived history you'll see that it was much less rigid and everyone lived it in a different way. And that even a party that tried to be Soviet and monolithic differed from place to place, from cell to cell.

Were you assiduous in your attendance at cell meetings?

Pascal: I went to them, but remember, it was a cinema cell.

Bernard: And each lived its own way of dealing with the events. I joined a year later and the expulsions I knew about could be counted on the fingers of one hand. That kind of thing was pretty much over. There was still a great rigidity and sectarianism, which we'll talk about later, but these kinds of things, in May '68 and before that in '67, with the Central Committee of Argenteuil, things were no longer exactly the same. The Communist Youth, being made up of the young, was more rigid, so it's certain there were expulsions, but at the same time things weren't entirely rational or ruled by one sole logic.

Did you continue to go to the cinema?

Bernard: No, there really wasn't the time, but I think I saw Bergman's *Hour of the Wolf*, which came out around then, but that must have been towards the end.

And you participated in the demos?

Bernard: Of course.

Pascal: Of course. How should I phrase it? We didn't feel any prohibition at all. On the other hand, the UEC had already been infiltrated by the Trotskyists and the Maoists, who had entered it. It was then that things blew up and the *gauchistes* began to really exist and things became more radicalized.

In the meanwhile, there was the story of the article Georges Marchais had written in *L'Huma* where he'd said what he said about Cohn-Bendit. Obviously he meant the state allowed a German anarchist to stir up such a mess in France, that it was in the state's interest that he do this.

So with Jacqueline and Masson and a couple of other guys we went to see Marchais at the offices of *L'Huma*. At the time, he was in charge of the metal worker section ... There had been the demo where everyone chanted, twisting what he said into "We Are All German Jews"—what he'd said was not "German Jew" but "a German anarchist." Anyway, he explained his point of view, about the working-class, all the struggles that were ongoing since 1966, struggles taking on ever greater importance, and suddenly there's this mess, and he said it was going to end badly and will above all serve the ends of the state. And he was perfectly right. So that was the direct contact we had with party leadership.

So tell me about the Etats Généraux du Cinéma. How was it decided on?

Bernard: How was it decided to occupy? Well ... It can be said it was spontaneous.

Pascal: First there was the occupation on rue Vaugirard.

Bernard: And in the middle of the general hubbub someone spoke of the Etats Généraux du Cinéma and it worked. Everything like that worked.

Pascal: When we began the Etats Généraux du Cinéma we began by occupying the Ecole de Vaugirard, the technical school of photography. The funny thing for me was, that it was my elementary school where I'd learned to read. We expanded the occupation and took over the school itself, and I found myself in my old classroom, at my old table—which was a little bit too small for me. It was there that everyone spoke about everything, about what had to be done, and we decided to establish commissions that would concern themselves with this or that sector or this or that thing. Along with a friend of mine, who was an editor and was in my cell, we decided to be part of a commission that saw to the respecting of the strike, that is, the prohibition against shooting commercial films during the movement, and at the same time to allow those who wanted to make films on what was happening to be able to do so. Very bizarrely, we occupied a place called Antegor, which was a production company, and there, along with my friend Jacqueline, we ended up being the ones giving the authorizations to film, using Antegor letterhead that we stamped. I never heard about many things being stopped, but in any case, commercial filmmaking was stopped. After three days or so of stamping and signing in a dark room in Antegor, I said to myself, I have no reason to be here and I said to Jacqueline—who was more serious than I—that I wanted to see what was going on outside.

During the meetings of the Etats Généraux, did those who were better known dominate?

Bernard: No. Those who knew how to speak spoke. For example, there were assistants like Bernard Stora who were very good, who represented the point of view of the party, though he was very rigid, but he was able to turn a room, so it had much to do with rhetoric. It's like everywhere: those who know how to speak make people do anything at all. So when someone said we have to abolish the Centre National du Cinéma, if he said it well, people believed it.

Pascal: And we continued the struggle. The Etats Généraux du Cinéma settled in Suresnes, and there it was a kind of extraordinary happening. There were commissions presenting proposals for the functioning of the cinema to be presented to the government that would follow '68.

And what kind of government would that be?

Pascal: A government of the revolutionary left.

Bernard: It wasn't as simple as that. It's absolutely true that the PCF showed no interest in the students and concentrated on the strike movement, viewing the students with distrust and even hostility, because of the leaders, because of the workerism of the party, because of a certain ignorance of the questions concerning the young. Yet the renewal was real, but it was one pushed by Aragon, who wasn't young but who did a magnificent job, and who came to the Latin Quarter and was booed, so there was that.

So if you read *L'Humanité*, what people said in it, it was quite unpleasant and as a result it was natural that "German anarchist" became "German Jew." There were rumors about rumors that functioned very strongly. So the party was pitiful in dealing with the youth issue.

But there was also this: for the party, power wasn't there to be taken. The state wasn't going to collapse simply because you demonstrate and put up barricades. There was the demo of the entire left, except the Communist Party, at Charléty, where Michel Rocard presented himself as the savior of France who was ready to take the leadership of a government that obviously wouldn't have been revolutionary, Rocard being who he was.

De Gaulle had left, he'd disappeared—he'd gone to Germany to talk to Massu to make sure he could count on the army, it was quite a simple affair—and he didn't know how to react. The moment he reacted, I was at a demonstration at the Gare de Lyon—we shouted, "He's bullshitting us," but he'd simply said enough fooling around; it's time to stop. And in fact, things came to a halt, the demonstration on the Champs-Elysées brought together what was a huge number of people for a right-wing demo. The elections in June were elections completely of the right, and on all this the PCF was right. Though everything that wasn't workerist in their rhetoric was pitiful.

And now for the Etats Généraux: I find assemblies where everyone speaks horrible; I detest that. Now I'd followed what had gone on at the school on Vaugirard, and I went to the meetings in Suresnes which were appalling. That said, there was much work done. There were nearly twenty motions, people having devised quite serious projects—to my surprise—almost always with the fall of Gaullist power in view, and a new departure of a new government.

On rue Vaugirard we'd voted the abolition of the CNC.

Pascal: Which had been created under Pétain.

Bernard: Which had been an excellent thing, though that wasn't its name at the time, and Barbet Schroeder went around painting graffiti on the walls about the Centre National du Cinéma that said "CNC = SS," his revision of "CRS = SS."

Wasn't he on the right?

Bernard: He was an aesthete.

Pascal: When we shot *Paris vu Par* he said to me—I wasn't yet in the party but I defended its positions and was seen as someone committed to the left—"You're no good, you're a zero. All the guys from the *Cahiers* and the New Wave are all people on the right."

And he was serious?

Bernard: And there were proposals, like those of Louis Malle for the internal reform of cinema, that weren't revolutionary, far from it, but which were interesting. These were reforms people expected at the time but that weren't coming because with de Gaulle and an aging Malraux things weren't moving very much. Malle wanted a cinema that wasn't a cinema of the monopolies. He wanted an independent cinema, which was what he continued to do.

Pascal: We were participating in something important, and the Etats Généraux gave birth to the Société des Réalisateurs de Films (SRF), whose administrative council I immediately was part of. The SRF created the Quinzaine des Réalisateurs at Cannes. There were many things it did that changed the cinema: filmmakers were present at the Cannes festival right after '68 in a way completely unknown until then. It was really exciting. So indeed it was a mess, but it was exciting to live through, and it gave birth to things that weren't at all bad.

Bernard: But to go back a little bit, I remember two events ... I was at the *Cahiers du Cinéma* and a friend there decided he had to quit when he heard a certain C. say that cameras should be given to all the peasants, and the other thing was something the same C. said, "Those who want to take part in the clandestine committees are requested to write their names on the blackboard." So this was the kind of thing we were in the midst of. And I'm not exaggerating: this is something I can personally certify. And this wasn't the most idiotic thing I heard. We were in the middle of a kind of madness which by the end totally disgusted me, and I left for Italy with films we had wanted to edit but were unable to because of people from the Communist Party. I came back, I was active, and a year later, brought into it by friends and conversations, and not by grand ideas, I joined the party.

During the events you weren't tempted to shoot militant films?

Pascal: For me it was a period where I shot militant films that weren't militant, and my first feature film that I shot in 1970 was one I'd begun to write in '67 and which evolved. The point of view I adopted was critical and self-critical about commitment to the revolutionary struggle by intellectuals who thought it was a form of absolute romanticism. I made this film, which was called *Valparaiso, Valparaiso*, after I made other films that ... Well, I wanted to tell my stories, but I remember there was a period when I began to think I'm not a Communist filmmaker but a filmmaker who's a Communist. And one day one of my comrades from the party, a terrific guy named Jacques Brière, who was in charge of intellectuals for the Central Committee, he came to see me and he said, "You know, Pascal, being a filmmaker who's a Communist is fine, but what the Communist Party needs is artists, is poets, that's what you should do and not think you have to make agit-prop like in the '20s. It's not the moment for that." So there were people in the party who weren't idiots, and my idea of being a filmmaker who was a Communist was already a leftist idea. When I made *Valparaiso* there was a whole bunch of my friends, among them Michel Andrieu, who decided my film was unbearable because it attacked the revolution and I felt quite good being ostracized. And all these people, who were good friends, I didn't see them for five years. When they passed me on the street they pretended that they didn't recognize me. Fortunately, at the time I was living a full life, I had my children, who were little at the time, I traveled, made films. But it pained me, and one day the ostracism was lifted when I made my second feature-length film *Le Chant du Départ*, which they all thought was terrific. I still throw this story in their faces, but they were people committed to their thing and they didn't want to laugh. I was more on the side of those who laughed.

Bernard, you joined the party after '68. The way the party was looked on after the events didn't cause you any hesitation?

Bernard: Rather the contrary. For me the horror was the totally abstract violence that Pascal suffered in a soft form that was completely cut off from everything, the *gauchiste* groups that couldn't stand each other and that threw each other out the window, who brawled with each other because this one was a Trotskyist and that one a Maoist. Their discourse was that of parrots, repeating and repeating the same slogans. It was absurd and also very dictatorial. So I arrived at the Communist Party quite naturally, since on the one hand I was an intellectual and was in the cinema, and through *La Nouvelle critique* I discovered things outside the cinema, and was speaking to others; while on the other hand the PCF was also sectarian, of an abominable sectarianism towards all that was not only *gauchiste*, but everything that seemed to be opposed, and this was a Communist tradition since the '30s. If we read today Gide's *Retour de l'URSS* it's a book that was more or less favorable to the Soviet Union but there were three sentences that led to him being viewed as a traitor. So there was this thing of who is not with us is against us, which was very tiresome.

Pascal, you never had any hesitation about the party line?

Pascal: One always has hesitations. Of course; it's normal. But at the same time, I didn't take myself for a theoretician. I joined the party for fundamental reasons, and of course I was attracted by things, but fortunately I quickly understood about *gauchisme*. I saw the Trotskyists who practiced entry-ism, entering the Socialist Party, and people like Weber and Jospin became apparatchiks of the PS and all of that seemed terrible to me. Already being a *gauchiste* struck me as stupid, and entering the PS ...

Bernard: Being a PCF apparatchik was no better.

Pascal: Right, but among party apparatchiks I saw people doing important things, people who were exciting, people who were brilliant.

For how long a period did May change the cinema? Or did it change it at all? Let's take the demands of the Etats Généraux: did you get what you were demanding?

Bernard: On the idea that directors be recognized as an autonomous force in the cinema, the Société des Réalisateurs was a success.

Pascal: It gave directors recognition and we were able to defend their rights; I was later involved in organizations that were terrific, that defended writers, this is important and significant. It allowed people to make films. On the contrary, it didn't allow *me* to make many; I was seen as an eccentric, a joker, a partygoer, a party member: I wasn't taken seriously and it wasn't my intention that I be taken seriously. I didn't want to be Lenin. I wanted to make films and believe in the revolution. And all these things. I grew tired over time with what the party became.

It was in '78 there was a manifesto signed by 300 Communist intellectuals that said the party needed more democracy at the base of the party, in the cells, because we were increasingly used to receiving a motion from the Central Committee and voting for it rather than really discussing it. After the manifesto was written the guy who wrote it took it to *L'Humanité* and Leroy refused to run it. But 300 people, it's quite a crowd, so the thing appeared in *Le Monde*.

Now this caused some noise, and I was in Cannes during the festival and was invited to lunch with some party leaders. They asked, "What's going on? Your name is on that manifesto. Did you see who you're next to?" I didn't understand what they were getting at. "You're alongside people like Frank Cassenti;[2] they're one thing, but you, Pascal ... If you have a problem you can call [party headquarters on] place du Colonel Fabien, you can call Marchais. We can talk it over." The others, they viewed them as asses, while I would have privileges. I said to them, "If one day we reach power it's you who'll exercise it, and it'll be without me. It's

2   Frank Cassenti (1945–), jazz fan and filmmaker who was briefly a member of the PCF, during which time he made his most important film, *L'Affiche rouge*.

not possible that it should be people like you," and I put my card on the table at the Blue Bar and said it's over.

Bernard: I must have slid out at the same time. At the time the media were interested in people who noisily left the party, but I was among those in the period from '76 to '78 who left without hostility, without a scandal, without causing a scandal, without denunciations, who'd simply had enough.

But I wanted to say another thing on the cinema. Something that wasn't political but in a way was. It's that '68 corresponded to the period after the New Wave when new, lighter equipment and new ways of filming made their appearance, thanks to a technology that was advancing and people who wanted to do things on their own without passing through film school. These people existed before '68, obviously. But May '68 crystallized something, simply because there were militant filmmakers who set off in teams of two to make real films and not to make TV reports, or finished films that were recognized as such. All this gave rise to a desire— one that had existed before—to make films alone or with a crew of two, people like Philippe Garrel.[3] There were thus many ways of making films, that were shown in theaters, and that didn't respond to the professional criteria of the profession and the CNC. The result was that for the next ten years there were many films shot in 16mm that were showed in theaters, conceived in terms of 16mm, totally independent films, with small crews that had their dignity as films. In the '80s there was quite a harsh reflux. But May '68 crystallized something that had existed before. But it was good.

A last question Pascal: is it true you had a Rolls with a red flag?

Pascal: There you go …

Bernard: Print the legend …

Pascal: Listen … In 1967 I was at the Edinburgh Festival and I met a guy who was a journalist at the *Scotsman*, who invited me to his father's house, who was a Scottish lord. A really funny guy

---

3 Philippe Garrel (1948–), filmmaker, author of numerous extremely personal films, including *Les Amants réguliers*, set during May '68.

who'd been the governor of Gibraltar during and after the war. He had castle that had a shed and in the shed, under a tarp, was a car. I asked what it was and he told me it was an old thing, an old government car. I asked if I could see it, and it was an absolutely sublime Rolls. He said he wanted to get rid of it, so I asked if I could buy it. He began by saying that was ridiculous, that I should buy a new one. Make a long story short, he sold it to me for peanuts, 300 pounds sterling. It cost me twice that to modify it to meet French norms, but I had a brilliant car, insane, sublime, that I'd paid little for. Well, I still had it in May '68, and of course I had a red flag on it. It seemed very anachronistic, and bizarre: there's Aubier with his Rolls, and when I went to pick up some miners in it people were really angry with me. The symbol was stronger than me, a guy who liked to fool around, women, who went out, who loved to eat and drink, and who drove a dream car … It caused me some important enmity, particularly among the professionals of the profession, even more because I'm a loudmouth and all, so producers didn't approve, and they'd say it was because of my extravagance and because I was imposing, so the Rolls was part of a whole series of things that cost me on the professional level way more than what I'd paid for the car. I don't regret it, in fact, I enjoyed it, but it's true that I hadn't considered the impact of the symbol. People just couldn't accept it.

CHAPTER SIX

Some Anarchists

I'm here. I exist!
—Daniel Pinos

DANIEL PINOS

The youngest of the participants interviewed, Daniel Pinos, who now lives in Paris, lived in Villefranche-sur-Saône, a suburb of Lyon, in 1968. Like Wally Rossel (see below) he was the child of a veteran of the Spanish Revolution.

I was 15 and a student at a technical high school in Villefranche-sur-Saône, in my second year, studying tinsmithing, boiler making, auto body work, I guess you'd say. I was born into a family of Spanish anarchists, my father being a member of the CNT, and in my house we always cast a critical gaze on events. I would sit in on meetings between my father and his friends, all of whom were anarchist militants and Spanish refugees. My aunts, uncles, my grandmother, all of them were Spanish refugees in France who'd fought in Spain and then in the French Resistance, so throughout my childhood I bathed in an atmosphere of combat, of activism. I had lived in this atmosphere of revolt, in the desire to change things all my life. Even though the Spanish Civil War was lost and we were forced into exile, and though their youth—and some of their illusions—were denied by the defeat, they'd managed to maintain their spirit of revolt and combat. And I, very quickly—at around 13 or 14—was imbued with this. I was also imbued with the French environment, even if there was a kind of lead weight that crushed everything, with the presence of de Gaulle and a right-wing government that denied much of the libertarian spirit.

But even so, here and there, there were certain strikes, like in 1967, when there was an important strike in the Lyon region at Rhodiacéta, one that prefigured May '68. The workers occupied their factory seeking improvement in working conditions and wages, and though it was a strike over bread-and-butter demands, it was still an offensive strike and prefigured the later ones in Nantes. And my father who was a militant in Villefranche was the CGT delegate at his textile factory.

CGT? A Spanish anarchist with the Communists?

Yes. In France if you wanted to be active you had the choice between FO and the CFDT. But as an anarchist, if he wanted to have a presence in his workplace, he had no choice but to join the CGT. And it must be said that those old anarchist militants gave great importance to being a union member, to being connected to a union organization. Even though many anarchists joined the FO, that union didn't exist where my father worked, so he was in the CGT. And he had good relations with the people in the CGT, who were in the PCF. He considered them workers and that he had more in common with them than with the factory's leadership.

When May '68 arrived I frequented people who were 15 to 16 years old, and among them was a group of people who were close to the PCFML. They put out the paper *Front rouge*. Now the Maoists in France were very divided, and there were three groups of them that claimed to be the real Marxist-Leninists. So during the year leading up to the events I spent time with these people, who were a little older than me, and we would discuss the issues of the day. The result was that when the first student movements broke out we were already sensitive to and interested in the spirit that was incarnated in this movement, which was largely made up of students. We were already interested in the counter-culture, in the anti-war movement: I listened to Dylan, to Joan Baez, to Pete Seeger, so I was imbued with all this. I wore my hair long, which caused me problems, because it was rare among working-class people at the time.

Anyway, when things first exploded and there were the first strikes, we had discussions with a teacher who was unionized and a member of the PCF, and we said, "We have to do something. Everyone's going out on strike, and we, the future workers have to do something." So we were very much concerned, precisely because we were the future workers of France. We spoke about this at home. The catalyst was that my father's factory went out on strike and was being occupied, and this completely turned things upside down in the town, in the neighborhood ... So we said we have to be part of this. On the Monday morning after it all started in Paris, with this teacher who I was very close to (he taught French—which doesn't have much importance in technical high schools—and I was really good in that subject), anyway that morning I decided it was time to say something. Most of my fellow students were completely apolitical; May '68 meant nothing to them, though I knew that some of the older students were going to hold a GA, so I told the French teacher, "Everyone's going out on strike, there are beginning to be echoes of it here, we have to talk about it." The teacher said to me, "If you want to talk about all this, no problem. I'm all for it." I spoke of the strike and how we had to be involved in it as future workers ....

So it was strictly the worker aspect. You weren't calling for a strike as a high school student.

Not at all, since I was a student at a technical high school and because at my house we were workers. My brother was on strike and occupying the factory he worked in. And at the high school we spent half our time in coveralls working at machines, plus we worked at the school, which was a subcontractor for companies in the city. Now, in the politicized group I was part of we were aware that we were workers and would soon become producers. We were workers and sons of workers. That said, at the time I had many aspirations. I was reading novels—Zola, Hugo, Ferenc Molnár—that I discovered in my father's library, since like many anarchists he read a great deal. Spanish anarchists gave culture a great deal of importance. But it was only with May '68 that I began to read political books. I was aware that it wasn't on our own that we were going to change things, it was only through social struggles that things would change, that we would change our condition.

At the time, there was an attachment to the fact that you were a worker, that you wore coveralls. For my father it wasn't a uniform, but an attachment to values, values he'd tried to maintain all his life, fighting in Spain, participating in collectivization, fighting fascism, fighting in the French Resistance. For him there was a pride in being a worker. And that we were going to be the motor of history, thanks to the general strike ...

So to return to the classroom, since it was difficult in the class to come up with demands, I said, "Let's go to the GA and let's say, 'Let's go on strike in solidarity with the workers and students.'" Everyone applauded and the teacher said that was great. The GA was organized by the students in their final year and word of it passed along in the corridors: we weren't yet militants, so we didn't know about tracts or posters, though the oldest students at the school had experience in the PCFML and were more knowledgeable about the ins and outs of activism. For my part I was just discovering all this. I'd seen my father and his friends in action, but this was *my* first time. So we go to the GA and during the assembly, obviously it was the oldest who spoke, as well as the teachers, the most politicized among them. And right away the people were excited, even those who had no politics. It was something that had never happened in a technical high school, where we're much less free to express ourselves, where the weight of the hierarchy is very strong. It was like an explosion, and we voted a strike with occupation. I remember exactly how I felt, it was "Shit, we exist!"

The next day we went out onto the streets, there was a demo of all the factories in Villefranche, the two high schools, and us, the technical school.

We'd voted the strike, we'd set up a committee, but it was all a little off: it was always the same people on the picket line. Every day we attempted to provide updates from the newspapers we received. At a certain moment we tried to get the cleaning staff and the cafeteria workers to go out on strike. We told them, "You're workers too. What's going on in the country involves you as well." But we had a hard time with them, since they were separate from the rest of the personnel. It wasn't easy, and we didn't succeed.

But we managed to hold out, thanks to that spontaneity we demonstrated. In most high schools this was easier, because there were people who were already older, more politicized; those in their final year were very political. But it was a real feat at our high school to get the students to go out on strike.

How many people attended the GAs? Were they full?

At the beginning yes, almost every student attended, between 1,800 and 2,000. All of them boys, since our apprenticeship center had only boys: the segregation was total.

The next day something fascinating happened. There was a demo and we found ourselves shoulder to shoulder with the workers from every factory that was on strike. And it was almost every factory: even small ones, that had never been on strike before had gone out. It was incredible. At my father's factory, a big textile factory, they were used to strikes, strikes that lasted a day, that's all, never prolonged ones: occupations like these had never been seen before. So there we were, shoulder to shoulder with all these workers on strike, and it was the first big demo of my life. I was only a kid, there with my father and my brother, and I was totally swept away. But I also discovered something there: the Spanish anarchist press, printed in France and then smuggled into Spain. It was a terrific press, produced with the collaboration of well-known people, like Albert Camus. Papers like *L'Espoir*, *Combat*, *Tierra y Libertad* ... These were newspapers that interested me because on the front pages they talked about the general strike, about the movement. And seeing things through the eyes of these anarchists I felt close to them and what they wrote. They talked about the general strike and how there had to be social combat that would lead to social change and the end of capitalism.

In the end, what were the demands at the school?

In the first place, we saw that we were part of a large movement that wanted to change things in France, which began in the universities and spread to the factories, and then the demands were simple little things, like ending the iron discipline imposed in the workshops by the teachers; then there were the working conditions, since we felt we were being exploited, given that we didn't receive a salary. There was also the access to jobs, because when we left school we were pretty much assured a job—it was a period of full employment—but when we left with the diploma in our pockets we were hired at extremely low salaries. I remember we included the demand to be treated better when we began our work lives. We touched on what concerned the quotidian: like the cafeteria, but in the end we never demanded the firing of the supervising monitor, since we realized if they got rid of him they'd replace him with someone who might be even worse.

And your more political friends, the Maoists, they didn't try to push things further?

Of course, it was very much a question of a political change, of a social change, but it was tough to get this accepted, because not many people were politically prepared for this. So things remained on the level of simple demands. This was the case too in factories. The CGT, which was in the majority—and this was something that saddened my father—often stuck by the slogans put forth by the PCF. We don't want social change, just a change in government with a new majority. It was revolution versus reform. Fortunately, within the factories there were more radical elements that issued deeper demands that attacked the roots of power, of capitalism. I remember my father tried to put forth an anti-capitalist discourse but he had problems with it. I remember he'd say, "We're not in Spain here."

And at your father's GA, at his factory, was it different?

I remember that in what people said there was a real hope that things would change. Spontaneously, it brought out all the hopes and aspirations that were imaginable. But we were quickly brought down to earth: the CGT and the CFDT negotiated with the bosses, and in the end a few demands were met, but they weren't going to profoundly change things.

But I found the assemblies fascinating, because there was a real fraternity, and then there'd be people who'd come to our house to continue the discussions. On the picket lines my mother, who was also a Spanish Red, would regularly bring food to the strikers so people could remain at the factory and resist. In the neighborhood where we lived, a working-class one, where most of the people worked in factories, the events also subverted relations.

Did you learn things when you went to the GAs at your father's factory?

I discovered the world of the working-class. The difference in sensibility and consciousness that was possible. What I also discovered, and this was a pity, because I'm an anarchist, is that in a certain way you need leadership, you need leaders to carry the struggle forward: without it, it quickly becomes any old thing. I spoke about this with my father, and he'd known the same thing in Spain during the revolution, and he always said that the French were more bourgeoisfied than the Spanish during the revolution, that they were more integrated into their society. While in Spain— he came from a peasant world, the world of the landless—they had nothing, a mule and a plot of land, and so the people had nothing to lose. It was frontal combat against fascism: they took up their weapons because they had nothing to lose. But in France it was different. There was a form of integration that limited their actions.

How was the atmosphere in the factories? Was it like '36 or was it under the discipline of the CGT?

It wasn't at all comparable to 1936. The movement in May didn't bring about things that were nearly as important. And the CGT had ferocious control over things, and most of the CGT leaders were also in the PCF, whose aim wasn't a break with the existing society. There was no question of overthrowing de Gaulle's Fifth Republic, and the PCF was aligned with the position of the Soviet Union that it was only at the ballot boxes that changes could be made after we obtain a majority. There was no question of social revolution.

But the 15-year-old Daniel Pinos, did he see further than that?

Of course! There were so many things we thought were possible, and there were so many things that came to us from outside.

There wasn't much you could get in my working-class town, but in Lyon it was different. Che Guevara, I discovered him in *Tierra y Libertad*, the Spanish anarchist paper printed in Mexico. And it's true I had a great deal of sympathy for him. Later I discovered he had his dark side, but it's true that at the time he was a symbol. I had his portrait hanging in my bedroom and even carried his picture in my wallet. My friends didn't even know who he was!

You wanted a revolution, you thought that you'd achieve one.

Yes, I had immense hope, even at the end of the events, even if I had to return to school, and the factory. There had been this major event that meant you couldn't look at reality in the same way. And it was afterwards that I began to be a militant, though when I entered factory life I didn't go to the CGT, like my father, but to the CFDT. I was very active, and the CFDT represented a form of unionism that was a break with the CGT. Just the fact that in their program they spoke of self-management, of the workers taking control of their struggles was important to me. The CFDT was the first union in France to take an interest in the lot of immigrants, to support strikes of foreign workers, support that I shared in strikes in Lyon and the region. I found in this union—which grew out of a Catholic union—people of great honesty, people unlike those in the CGT, who were manipulated by the bigwigs. The CFDT was more open, even to us young people. As soon as I joined the CFDT the CGT people in Villefranche no longer greeted me, they turned their backs on me. I was a traitor! At a young age I was in the leadership group of the CFDT in Villefranche. I spent all my time being an activist, giving out tracts. At the same time I joined the Organisation Révolutionnaire Anarchiste, a group mainly of young people in rupture with the traditional anarchist groups. We had a newspaper called *Front libertaire de lutte des classes* and we put an accent on the class struggle as the only way to bring about change. Some of us were in the CGT, some in the CFDT, but we were all anarchists, communist anarchists. This gave rise to some truly important things at the time, since all my comrades started factory newspapers where they worked. We involved ourselves in life in the neighborhoods, we tried to give anarchism back its social meaning, which it had somewhat lost in France. May '68 brought all this about; without it none of this would have been possible.

Were things falling apart at your school during the final period?

Yes, by the end there were fewer and fewer of us, though I remained faithful to the bitter end.

You and the Maoists?

Yeah, it's funny because they were people I wasn't in the least in agreement with, but they were friends, and afterwards we did things together. But yes, the end of the strike was difficult. There were the leaders who wanted it to end and we could feel that at the level of the country it was fading away. My father told me about a GA at his factory and his colleagues in the CGT voted for the return to work, and my father said there were two who voted against, him and a Spanish comrade. They were the only ones. There were more combative places where things lasted longer, big factories, but no, with us it ended quickly, within a few days. And things were complicated ... or maybe not. The workers weren't going to be paid at the end of the month and it would have been difficult for them. At the end the discussions revolved around how are we going to eat? How are the kids going to eat? Villefranche was a town that was held by the Socialist Party and it issued coupons for food, and with them they were given food in grocery stores. It was a dramatic situation. People had to live on their savings, and there wasn't much of that at my family's house. Despite that fact, my father wanted to stay out, but then, he was a revolutionary.

Your father, who'd lived through the defeat in Spain, did he think he'd finally see victory there in France?

No. He was extremely enthusiastic at the beginning. And I think that the fact that my brother and I were involved in the strike was something very important to him. But I don't think he had many illusions about the end of the movement and about changing things. Afterwards he continued to be active, continuing to fight for Spain until his death. Unfortunately, he wasn't able to return to Spain, which he had a hypertrophied image of, and when we finally went to visit we saw that the image he had was a totally idealized one.

With this idealization, were there moments you thought you were in Barcelona in 1936?

Never! No-no-no. You have to see things as they are. We were enthusiastic, my brother and I, but my father's point of view towards the events was always critical, and with reason because of the role of the PCF, which limited the movement, outside a few factories. So he was conscious that it was an important event that would allow for the radicalization of part of the youth, and which indeed occurred, with people joining the fight five or six years later, but in the long term he didn't have any illusions. Sometimes I found him nihilistic, but he was old, while I, as a young man … Sometimes I was shocked by what he said. He wrote articles for Spanish papers, and his final texts were full of bitterness.

And how did you maintain your optimism after the defeat that was May? How is it that you began to be active afterwards?

I think that what allowed me to go on, to resist, was that I met tons of people who participated in May, people who were my age and some older. In a working-class city like Villefranche, when you wear your hair long, when you think differently, in a town where people don't have great aspirations, where young workers go out Saturday night and go to dances, where they spend their time at the cafes, I was with those who were different, who looked at the world with greed. We wanted to travel, we read Kerouac, we read the Beats … America was very important to me, the counter-culture. And I was also anti-militarist and refused to go to the army. And that too was because of America, because of the war in Vietnam. I was one of the young of the time who couldn't bear imperialism and wars of aggression.

What happened to you immediately after May?

In the immediate period after May, things went badly for me. I was considered a revolutionary, a troublemaker, and I didn't finish school the next year. I was completely different from what I'd been the year before and was a serious activist. For the school authorities I was a rotten kid, a pain in the ass, and I continued to be what I was, but more radical. There was a teacher who hated me, partially because I was one of the leaders of the strike, and partially because I was Spanish: he hated the Spanish. So one day I was in class just before Easter vacation, and he was demonstrating a machine and as always happened, he asked a student to do the same thing to see if we understood. He called on me, but my thoughts had been elsewhere, and I hadn't listened to a thing. He shouted, "Pinos, get up here and show how we set up the machine." I was paralyzed because I had no idea, so he grew furious, and he screamed, "Pinos, you troublemaker, you're finished here. You don't pay attention to anything," and he started punching me, which was a common thing, something that had gone on for generation after generation. He backed me up against a machine as he was punching me, and I slipped away, ran to the locker-room, took off my coveralls, put on my street clothes, and said to myself, "That's it. I'm never going back." This caused trouble at home, since my father didn't see what I could do without a diploma, but it didn't matter: I couldn't accept such an attitude on the part of a teacher.

I paid for my attitude in May, and I wasn't the only one.

You were called to do your military service at 18 …

No, at 20, and I didn't go. I didn't go because I was working with anti-militarist groups, and we carried out many actions in barracks, even occupying some. You really had to be athletic to do that: we were dealing with the military police, and they're no joke. But after May '68 there was a whole generation of draft dodgers, very politicized, many anarchists, along with many non-violent anarchists. I participated in support actions, and even helped Spaniards who refused military service there, and in Spain they were sent to penal colonies in the Sahara, eight years of military prison, while in France it's only two years. That's what I was sentenced to, though I never served it.

Particularly since the war in Algeria there'd been a strong anti-militarist current in France, and I found myself among people who'd refused to serve in Algeria, who went to prison for it, who'd continued the political fight. And so, naturally, I reached 20 and received my call-up notice. I wrote a very political letter to the Minister of National Defense, calling him "Minister of War" so it would have more impact, and explained why, as a worker and an anarchist communist I refused to serve in an imperialist army, in an army in service to a government that helped break strikes. You can see this was part of my global combat and when they came to look for me I was gone, to Amsterdam. While there I met American anti-militarists and draft dodgers, and I went to live in Spain, closing the circle, living in Barcelona. I even came back to France. In all I was underground for eight years.

How did you cross the borders?

I had the luck to be part of a very well-organized group that made false papers for us, and we had doctors who took care of us. All this was the inheritance of the war in Algeria and the resistance to it. If you were stopped on the highway and you had your real papers you were dead, but we had fake ones, so I traveled to Holland, to France. And I never would have done this without May '68. I would have been another man, had there not been May '68.

How did your exile end?

When Mitterrand was elected president, part of his program was amnesty for political prisoners, for those who had refused military service, and those who had deserted. The problem was that we all received letters telling us to report to our barracks. Everything was turned back to zero, but I was still being told that I had to perform my military service. We didn't take this well. We formed a committee of draft resisters and we did all we could so that we would not be made to serve and that we would not be arrested, because the law hadn't changed: if we again refused to serve we'd be arrested. So we formed a committee and decided we were going to go and make trouble. Charles Hernu was Mitterrand's minister of national defense, a firm militarist, and we said we're going to bust his balls as much as we can and make him retreat. And at the first congress of the PS after their victory in May 1980 we marched in—and all the minsters were there—while Jospin was speaking and we entered in force with an impressive group of stewards. When that wasn't enough, we carried out an action at the office of the general-in-chief of the army, we decided we would stop him on the street and pour a bucket of paint over his head, a symbolic action to remind him we were here and we hadn't forgotten. We were arrested, because his security force was enormous, but a few days later we received letters informing us we didn't have to serve, and were out of danger.

You've already told us how it changed you, but is there one moment you lived through that really stands out for you?

I think it was the moment at the GA when I first spoke. But it was all so impressive, everything seemed possible, you felt free, you felt things so intensely when you're young, so it's the first time I spoke. I was a timid young boy and there I found the words. I spoke for the first time, and it was "I'm here, I exist!"

ஐ ௸

WALLY ROSELL

Wally Rosell was a student at a technical high school in Paris, on a track aimed at construction and public works. Sports were his main interest (he played field hockey with Thierry Porré, the next interview subject, in the '60s) but he had noble anarchist political bloodlines. His father, a Spanish anarchist, crossed the Pyrenees into France in 1939. "He escaped the French concentration camps for foreign political refugees and lived underground, and through a French network he reached Angers and then Saint-Malo, where with a number of friends from his region, some Catalans and his brother, he reconstituted a solidarity group." The woman in Saint-Malo who provided his group with support had a daughter, who Wally's father fell in love with and married. His entire family was involved in the Resistance, organizing escape networks for imprisoned members of the International Brigades, and ultimately participating in the armed liberation of Saint-Malo. The family moved to Paris, where his widowed grandmother would meet and marry the anarchist leader Maurice Joyeux.

Despite his background, Wally admits that he was not active politically in the period prior to the events, but he did have some political notions, due to his family's activities and their association with the anarchist journal Le Monde libertaire. *"Every year, sometimes two and three times a year, my grandmother organized a gala in support of* Le Monde libertaire *and the Spanish exiles. This was always a family outing, since it was held on Friday nights and there were no classes on Saturday. So there, I saw Leo Ferré, Georges Brassens, Serge Reggiani, Barbara, Hugues Aufray ... there were speeches and things like that, there was the selling of newspapers, and I'd attend to have a laugh, to give a hand, to work as a steward, control the entrances, and all that. And so I wasn't politically ignorant: I had a clear political consciousness." When I asked him what he did in school his answer was simple and blunt: "Jack all. I was a real troublemaker, always pulling stunts at school, locking teachers in closets, bedlam in the cafeteria." And there were two topics in his home, sports and politics: "First politics and then football, cycling, the Tour de France ... and the sports discussion was every bit as animated as the political one."*

And yet, there was a general political air that surrounded Wally and his friends that would lead to his participation ...

But let me give you an idea of the atmosphere. How should I put it? All the boys and girls of my generation, if they were the children of Spaniards—in which case it was worse—or if they were French, their parents had done what? They'd been in the Resistance, they'd been involved in the Spanish Revolution and the Popular Front in high schools like ours, that is, where there were working-class kids, so we were immersed in all this: both my parents had been in the Resistance, participated in the strikes of '36, the Spanish Revolution. These events occupied a large place in the popular imaginary. It's like in the US the way people look back on the Civil Rights movement and the Black Panthers. These events were all iconic for us thirty years later. You see what I mean? A segment of our generation of '68 wanted to be part of this. So the events of May 3, 1968, I heard about them that evening, and all I understood was that there was a demo and there was a battle with the cops—which I thought was great. So I knew about this from my parents, from the radio, from the TV. So even if they described them as "rioters," they were talking about battles between students and the forces of order. So for me this was something that was necessarily good. But it didn't go further than that. I remember that very quickly, right after May 3 ... What day of the week was that?

A Friday: almost all the big events happened on Friday.

Hmmm, you're right ... From the next Monday, with some three or four of my high school friends, we heard there were demos, so we said, "Let's go see." But it was more like a game, like we were playing at cowboys and Indians and cops and robbers. The cops, after all, are the cops. But we wanted to see what was going on. I remember the first day we couldn't find the demo, which was no real surprise, since things were going on all over the place. There was nothing. There we were, in the Latin Quarter, place de l'Odéon, like jerks, and we said let's go to boulevard Saint-Michel. So there we were on the hunt for demos. It began like that. Since I didn't find anything I stayed after that for a while in my own part of Paris.

That week the French teacher at my technical school gave us as an exercise the writing out of the first two stanzas of the "Internationale." Now some time between May 6 and May 10 my friends at the Lycée Mallarmé had their first General Assembly at a gazebo in a square. So I went to it, and I didn't really understand everything that was being said.

Were people talking at your high school?

Remember that this was a technical high school, so the discussions were mainly among me and my handful of friends. It wasn't the same—at least at the beginning—at the classical high schools. It was funny, but right away we saw the first fractures: there were the sons of Communists, the sons of Socialists, the sons of Gaullists, and since we weren't very political we were a little stupid. I have to tell the truth. I realized that I was fundamentally anarchist, but I wasn't capable of lining up three sentences on anarchism, aside from shouting, "*Ni Dieu ni maître*" (Neither God nor master) or singing Brassens or a couple of slogans I'd seen on banners at concerts.

And then comes the Night of the Barricades …

And this, there's no getting around it, is the great regret of my life.

May 10, it was a Friday night, and my buddies said, let's go. But it turns out that the morning of May 11, exceptionally, we had classes and a test that counted towards being able to pass on to the final year of high school. And so, my parents and the parents of my pals, all told us, "You can go, but you have to be back early, since you have to wake up in the morning to go take the test." That Friday evening was the big annual anarchist gala with Léo Ferré. So I go to the Latin Quarter with my friends and we get off the metro at Saint-Michel and there's nothing. We ask where everyone is and people point, saying it's straight ahead, everyone's at Denfert. So we walk there and join the demo. It was a huge demo, the first time I saw black flags outside anarchist concerts. And it wasn't only university students: there was a huge crowd, even high school students. I was lucky, because I was able to answer when people asked what's that, and I was able to tell them it's the black flag of the anarchists. It was the only thing I knew. After a while, and this is my great regret, I go home, and when I get there the rest of my family is headed to the anarchist gala at the Mutualité, and my father said, "You stay here, you have a test tomorrow, you have to be in good shape, so you're not going to the concert." I stayed there like an ass.

So you missed both the concert and the barricades.

Exactly.

The concert is pretty legendary. What happened there?

OK, Ferré came to the Latin Quarter in the afternoon and he saw the first demonstrators passing by. He went into a cafe, and from there he saw the black flags and the people chanting slogans. He joined the demo for a while, then went back to the cafe, and it was there that he wrote "Les Anarchistes." The concert began at 8:30—it was a full house—there was an intermission, and it was around 10:00, when a guy came in and said there are barricades outside. There was a big hubbub and Maurice Joyeux got up and said, "We'll finish the concert, and afterwards, those who want to go and join them can go." And that was just what happened. Ferré finished his songs, and then about half the crowd went out and joined the barricades. So my parents came home, since they had my little sister with them, and all night they received phone calls from people telling them about arrests, people who'd been injured, people who couldn't get home. My parents' apartment served as a base to shelter people and take care of the wounded. So because of all the phone calls I was unable to sleep after all, and the next morning I got up to go take the test. Some of my friends, before heading to school, had gone to the Latin Quarter and one of them said, "This is impossible, we can't take the test when there are people like us who've been injured and imprisoned." And to top it off, the test was cancelled.

So you missed the barricades for nothing!

For nothing. Some of us then went with a math and a French teacher to rue Gay-Lussac and rue d'Ulm the next morning, and it was really something. But I picked up a paving stone that I still have at home. I'll show it to you later.

That Saturday and Sunday the phone didn't stop ringing. My father had an urgent meeting of the CNT[1] in exile, my grandfather

---

1 Confederación Nacional de Trabajo, the Spanish anarchist union.

and my grandmother went to the departmental offices of FO to call for a strike for Monday, May 13. Things developed quickly, and it was comrades from the CFDT and FO who pushed the CGT to go out on strike. And in fact, very quickly word spread that Monday the thirteenth there'd be a general strike. On that day I left my own high school behind and went to the local one, where we were informed that all the high school students were meeting at the Gare de l'Est. So I went with my friends. The unions were all the way in the front and we were way, way in the back. My father reached place Denfert-Rocherau while we were still at the Gare de l'Est.[2] After I'd seen rue Guy Lussac I realized that I'd left the realm of cowboys and Indians for something real: the burned cars, the tear gas lingering in the air. When you reached the neighborhood you couldn't help but cry, the tear gas was so unbearable. In fact, I was more shaken than anything.

There were a lot of Maoists in my school, one of them even died in May '68: Gilles Tautin. He'd been at my former high school.

Being at the demo there was this feeling of pride that we felt, even at that time, that what we were doing was as important as what our parents had done during the Resistance and the Popular Front.

You had this feeling from the start?

Very quickly. From the time of the first Night of the Barricades and May 13. In normal times there weren't demos every day or even every month: there was May 1, and the last big demonstration there'd been in France was Charonne.[3] That was '62, and then there'd been anti-Vietnam War demos, things like that.

Did you talk about the events with your parents, who after all were militants?

No, not at all. I was involved in the actions, and they were too. We'd see each other a little, not much. And anyway, I was a zero;

2   A distance of 5 kilometers or 3 miles.
3   Communist-led demonstration on February 8, 1962, against that war in Algeria that resulted in the deaths of nine demonstrators.

I had no real foundation: I saw any bozo with a red or black flag and I followed behind him. After May 13, actually May 14, my high school was closed, since the teachers had gone out on strike. I managed to enter the building, I scooped up some protective helmets for my buddies, and I went to my former high school to see the first GA, and the Maoists were strongly present there. They were all in my class, my age, and I have to say they seemed really intelligent and well informed. But there was a kind of role playing. Like I said, we were a generation trying to do as well as our parents.

So now there are no more classes and you're free. Where did you pass your time?

From time to time I went to my technical high school, but it was closed, so I went to my former high school and to the Sorbonne. And it was at the Sorbonne that I discovered two things. At the Sorbonne, in the courtyard, there were tables, and there was a table with a big black flag hanging over it—it was on the second or third floor—and this was the anarchist corner, where I met with these people, people I knew from the Fédération Anarchiste, people I'd seen with my grandfather and my father, and I found them here as well. And while roaming the Sorbonne I quickly found the Comité d'Action of technical education, which held GAs in one of the smaller lecture halls of the Sorbonne, which I regularly attended. At these assemblies I realized just how much of a zero I was, that I was incapable of stringing together two sentences that made any sense. So I listened, and much of what I heard made me sick: there were a lot of Maoists, of Trotskyists, a few Young Communists. But the Maoists around Geismar, for me they had an interesting discourse because they were interested in direct action. They were a little Situationist, like that. Less formatted than the Trotskyists and the Young Communists. I couldn't stand the Communists. At home there were four groups who were hated: the fascists, the priests, cops and soldiers, and the Communists. For me they were all pretty much the same. I fought—physically and verbally—as often against the commies as against the cops. Though this was mainly after.

I know there were confrontations between the Communists and *gauchistes* in the Latin Quarter.

And in the factories, but I never went to a factory. No, not even to distribute flyers.

There was the festive side to the Sorbonne that attracted me. I know that Thierry passed his time at the Odéon, but I never went there, though I did go once to the Atelier des Beaux-Arts,[4] and that was something I really liked. Because the graphic side, well, you didn't need to have read all of Bakunin, Marx, Engels, or Marcuse to get it. So graphics, drawing, the artistic side, that really interested me. I'd go there and swipe posters.

And I participated in absolutely every demo. As soon as I heard there was one I was off, because I was so angry to have missed the barricades on May 10.

Speaking of which, given that you were young, you were active, you were athletic, the world belonged to the young … Did you pick up women?

Of course. Yes. Oh yeah. Absolutely. Yes. Absolutely: there were babes at the demos and when we'd go over to them, there was our wiseass side, and we picked up girls. Yes, oh yes. Yeah. It's true. Now the demos at night, when things heated up some, well then you couldn't pick up any girls. But I will say that on that front I put up a very good fight.

And on the other one as well. In the demos I was often in the front line and I had no problem fighting the cops. I was athletic …

You threw paving stones at them?

Oh yeah. I had no problem doing that. And I threw marbles as well that we stole from stores. And towards the end we even managed to steal tractors from construction sites and we knocked over trees with them.

So you're the answer to Thierry's question about who knocked down the trees …

---

4 Where many of the famous posters of May were produced.

Yup. The first time I did it was near the Gare de Lyon during the demo on May 23, the second night when things really got hot, the next night, May 24, when we set the Stock Exchange on fire, I was right next to it, though I didn't go inside. There, for example, on May 23 I was with a bunch of guys who called themselves anarchists, and we tore up these huge black curtains at the Sorbonne and made scarves out of them. So on May 23 I had a black scarf. It was funny. And there were guys who had axes, I have no idea where they got them, and I had a helmet and we cut down trees on rue de Lyon, where there's now a promenade.

So you were there when the Stock Exchange was set on fire?

I was right next to it but I got there just when it was all ending. By this point I was also becoming interested in what was happening tactically. After de Gaulle's speech, on the 24th we were all at Gare de Lyon, the university and high school students, and the idea was to seize the Hôtel de Ville and proclaim the Paris Commune. From Gare de Lyon you have to go to the Bastille then rue Saint-Antoine and you arrive behind the Hôtel de Ville. The cops were beginning to catch on, so what they did was they blocked access to place de la Bastille. So there were some guys who arrived and they said, we'll disperse and we'll form several groups and invade Paris. To hide what we were doing from the cops what we had to do was build a high barricade we could hide behind, so we had to cut down trees. I thought this was great and I wasn't at all against it. We cut down a couple of trees between the Gare de Lyon and the Bastille, where the Opéra Bastille is now, but we decided not to hold the position, and the demonstration broke up behind us, though the cops didn't know this.

The cops didn't do anything while you were cutting down trees?

I don't think they understood what we were doing. So right after the demo breaks up we head towards the Seine to reach the Latin Quarter. My friends and I made a large circle and we pass by the Canal Saint-Martin and we try to penetrate from that side and reach the Hôtel de Ville.

There were several thousand of us, and whenever we met up with the cops there were guys who were really clever at the head of us—maybe they were March 22, maybe they were Maoists—who'd divert the march.

And so, in fact, the Stock Exchange wasn't a planned event. It was because as we made our way to the Hôtel de Ville we passed by the Opéra and the Stock Exchange and it was more or less spontaneously that it happened, so I wasn't part of it. But I learned that my father and grandfather were there.

Anyway, there were guys and some girls who said, "Everyone to the Latin Quarter!" So we crossed the Seine and I was on rue Saint-Jacques at the corner of Saint-Germain, I was there until 5:00 in the morning and then I entered the Sorbonne through the windows.

During all this, what did you do about normal daily activities?

I have no idea. None whatsoever. I must have eaten something, but I have no idea what. In fact, I have no idea of anything of daily life during this period. Sleeping, I either did that at the Sorbonne or at home. At the Sorbonne we slept on benches, and there were a few mattresses. We from the collective of technical high schools had rooms that we set up to sleep in. People were given rotating assignments to keep it clean, and I seem to remember there was a nursery as well. Where I spent much of my time, with the other students from the technical high schools, there wasn't any differentiation in assignments between men and women since we were almost all men.

I met Maoists, Trotskyists, but the Communists had left pretty quickly: they didn't understand anything and it didn't interest them. And there were also the libertarians, the anarchists, and plenty of people a part of no group. And at the assemblies the girls spoke every bit as much as the boys. I was at a mixed high school and the girls weren't behindhand in acting up.

You know though, Wally, that when I speak to women they say the opposite.

I think that for the majority of girls that was true and that it was a trigger ...

Given your enthusiasm and all your activity, when masses of people came out in support of de Gaulle it must have hit you hard.

I was in the hospital on May 30.

What happened?

I'd been to too many demos and I'd breathed in too much tear gas and I spent four days in the hospital. It's that all the demos, and especially the big demo of May 24—but the demos, the clashes with the cops, were almost daily occurrences. So I took in too much gas and one night I went home and I was groggy and my mother said I'm taking you to the hospital right away. So that's where I was on May 30 ...

But you must have heard about the demo in any case. You must at some point have felt the world was going to change ...

What I felt was that we, the Rosell family, were the kings of the world. That the people who passed us on the streets shook our hands with joy, and the others looked glum. That was clear. There was a doctor we knew, and with him we trafficked in gasoline.

I didn't so much feel anything at the time, but later, at the end of June, when it was all over and I encountered the world of labor, that I felt the abyss that separated us, the young, the students, from those who worked.

Were you aware at all of Charléty, or as an anarchist was it something outside your interest?

There was a big family discussion about whether or not we'd go to the rally, and I decided to go. There were no black flags, and I went with a few of my friends, and as soon as we got there we saw that it was nothing but political cooptation, and we had to leave. There's a famous photo that was taken there, of a woman on a man's shoulders brandishing the black flag: I was right next to them. They were friends, part of my grandfather's group. But yes, at Charléty you could feel that there was a political battle that was descending over everything. But I listened to what those who had an anarchist political culture had to say: it was more that for me than anything.

Anyway, when I heard about the big Gaullist demo it didn't surprise me all that much. Because I saw in the building where we lived that there were people on the right, but on the other hand, the big change was the death of Gilles Tautin ... I wasn't at Flins when he died ... Me and my friends went to the Gare Saint-Lazare to ask the railroad workers to open a track so we could get to Flins to demonstrate. Obviously, the CGT refused. So I wasn't able to get there. So instead I went back to the Sorbonne, and after he died in the afternoon we went out and put up barricades, burned down commissariats and those kinds of things, and two days later there was another big night of riots, and there we felt a change in the population. That those who'd kept their heads down were now raising them.

Was there anything you did that you thought really odd?

Well, during the events I was a traffic cop.

What do you mean?

What I mean is that the whole stretch from the Sorbonne to the Odéon there wasn't a single cop. There was nothing. Not a cop! The Sorbonne, Censier, Henri IV, and on the other side the medical school and the Odéon, there wasn't a cop; the prefecture had removed them and they didn't set foot in the area. You wanted to know about daily life? Well, posters were put up at the Sorbonne saying they were looking for people to do traffic control, and I volunteered, so I managed traffic at the corner of Saint-Germain and Saint-Jacques, since the traffic lights weren't working in that part of the city. Yup. At the time the garbage pails were made of tin with a cover on top, so we stole all the covers all over Paris and we used them as shields in the confrontations with the cops. And there too, to control the traffic, I had my shield and a billy club a cousin who was in architecture school had made for me.

So for a few hours a day, two days a week, there I was with my shield, my club, and my armband—we'd made them, and since I was an anarchist and pretty much all I knew about anarchism was that the flag was black, my armband was black and not red—and I controlled the traffic. So there were some who worked in the nursery, some who cleaned the Sorbonne, some who stood guard, and I was a traffic cop. And when I'd signal for the cars to stop, they'd stop! That was something that gave me a real hard on! That was really funny ...

No one ran me over, everyone found it normal that it was the Comité d'Action of the Sorbonne that did that. They even found it a good thing, it was something really special. It felt like I was living the Paris Commune.

Was that really the reference you had in your head then?

You're right. The reference at the time for me was the Spanish Revolution and the Resistance and the Popular Front. The Paris Commune came later, when I began to be an activist later in '68.

Did you have any problems getting back into ordinary life?

No, not at all, I went on vacation afterwards. My parents went first, but they couldn't do much since my father and mother had been out on strike for a while, so there wasn't much money to go away ... Even though partial payment of strike time was part of the Grenelle Accords, it was still difficult.

On June 20, through my high school I had a training program to do and I went to Orly to build a new runway. I was there with guys who had been out on strike and what shocked me was when I met a guy from the Confédération Française des Travailleurs Chrétiens (CFTC), from the Catholic union, a scab union, and he was really nice. I found that really bizarre. There I was with my black scarf, and I was confronting the world of labor, and what seemed natural to us as students, as Sorbonnards, as *soixante-huitards*, wasn't at all natural to the people who were working around me.

Then I went on vacation and had to tell my father I'd been thrown out of high school. I'd refused to take the tests that had been postponed because of the events so I was expelled and decided to just go to work. My formal education was over, but through the union I was able to find a job in public works as a designer, and there were all kinds at work: young, not so young, Arabs, immigrant workers, Spaniards, Portuguese, and since I was a designer I worked in an office. But this place had only been out on strike for one day. Me, I'd thought everyone was for the revolution, and suddenly I was facing reality.

For me '68 was more a catalyst for me and my sister than anything else. But looking back I wonder how I failed to do this or that, how I missed this or that event ... I was luckier than friends who lived in the suburbs, I have to say. The RATP and the SNCF closed down so they had problems getting around.

Do you think it had some lasting effect on France?

It was like the French Revolution and the Popular Front. It changed things in at least three areas. First, the role of women in French society. It changed their situation completely, birth control, abortions, things I knew about because my mother worked in this area before '68. Then something very important for us anarchists: the end of Communism. It was May '68 that announced its end. Starting from '68 all the movements in Eastern Europe were anti-Marxist, anti-Stalinist. First anti-Stalinist then anti-Marxist: Solidarity, the Velvet Revolution, all these movements issued from '68. That wasn't seen immediately because the Maoists and the Trotskyists were still important, and the Maoists in France were a particular case. Because though they learned Mao's Little Red Book by heart they were really closer to the anarchists than the Trotskyists or the PCF. They were fundamentally libertarian. The fall of Communism and Marxism, at least in Western Europe, dates to May '68. It's the first time that a Communist Party was overtaken from the left and was seen to be a traitor. That is fundamental. And finally, people's lives. Ecology was from '68. People like José Bové,[5] they

---

5 José Bové (1953–), anti-globalist, anti-militarist farmer activist.

did May '68. Cohn-Bendit of course as well. And even now you can see he was formed by anarchism.

Now I see better that militarily we lost in May '68, but we won politically. Politically vis-à-vis the reactionaries, but also the Communists, even though we lost militarily. It's a little like the Spanish Revolution. Militarily we lost, but at bottom it's like the Paris Commune.

Wait a second, we haven't talked about football and May '68. The football players occupied the offices of the FFF. Now there's something I really regret now, that I didn't go and support the striking football players.

ℰℴ ℭℛ

THIERRY PORRÉ

Thierry Porré, who would go on to be the editor of the anarchist journal, Le Monde libertaire *and head of the historically anarchist union of proofreaders, was a political innocent of 19 in May 1968. During our interview, playing in the background were his great musical loves, American folk and blues music.*

Before May '68 I had no political life, aside from listening to country blues, and sometimes electric blues, but even that I rejected because it was the Twist. I was very much a fundamentalist. And I also read the *poètes maudits*. For the rest ... Well, Marx, I had no idea what that was, Bakunin either; what I'd understood of them I wasn't in agreement with, and that's all. In '68 I'd already failed my bac twice, I'd been thrown out of official high school studies at the end of my fifth year, and was going to private school in '68 with the priests. I played field hockey there, and I later learned it was the national sport of India and Pakistan, but not in France. It was while I was playing field hockey that I met Wally Rosell. I failed my bac for the second time: shame and scandal in the family. So anyway, I was following a course of studies that would allow me to work in the legal field and in May '68 I was in the Université Catholique, hanging out with friends there who didn't have much idea what to do.

So would you say your political education was done during the events?

Yes, they awakened me. The closest I came to politics before May '68 was that I read *Hara-Kiri*. And I also refused to succeed. People would say about me, "Thierry is intelligent, but he doesn't want to learn." I had a cousin I hated who was always first in his class. Oh how I hated him. I'd never want to be that. My mother would say, "You did everything you could to fail your bac on purpose so the whole family would make fun of us." I told her no …

What happened when the events started, in March in Nanterre?

I didn't read the newspapers much, but I'd seen things had exploded at Nanterre, but that was it.

And when things started in Paris?

A friend told me, "Thierry, you've got to come along, there are student demos and we're students too, so let's go. The cops are there, beating up people, even old women." Now I already was used to battles with the cops in the eighteenth arrondissement, where I grew up and lived. Like, one day I was going home and the cops stopped me on Barbès because I looked like a foreigner. They frisked me and when afterwards they saw my ID card they said, "What, you couldn't have told us you were French?" I didn't look like I was French, in fact they thought I was an Arab. It wasn't the only time this would happen to me in my life. So anyway, I knew how the cops were.

So I went to boulevard Saint-Michel and I saw there was a kind of meeting in a big theater and that was how I ended up at the Odéon, which was occupied, and I stayed there until the very end. But again, I knew nothing.

Just to give you an idea, someone asked me while I was there where I was from, and I thought he meant where was I from in Paris, so I told him Montmartre. I had no idea he meant where are you from politically, what party. So anyway, I participated in all the demos, I did the barricades, though I can't tell you where they were or on which days I did them, but I remember being behind one or two. I saw people digging up paving stones to make the barricades, and I thought now here's something I knew how to do.

All this was where I had my first confrontation with the political world. I was with people and I thought they were from the national teachers' union or something like that and I asked them what are you up to and they told me we're building barricades because the cops are busting our balls: I had absolutely no political discourse.

When I got to the Odéon I saw lots of big names, including Hugues Aufray,[6] who was a descendant of Elisée Reclus. But I was a newcomer and I didn't understand much of what was going on, especially at 3:00 a.m. when people were shouting at each other and beating each other up.

There were assemblies there that went on all day?

All day and all night.

What did they talk about?

About everything, Everything. It was so wild. I remember there were people there who knew how to write, with all their grand formulas, but I didn't really get it, and in any event, I don't get hard-ons second hand. Afterwards people would ask me if I'd seen this or that talk by whoever about anarchism at the Sorbonne and I'd tell them I never stepped foot in the Sorbonne. That wasn't my spot. For me, my place was the street and the Odéon. And it was an easy trip to go from Montmartre to Saint-Michel: all you had to do was go straight ahead. I was near metro station Château Rouge so I'd take Magenta then République then Sebasto, and after that you're on Saint-Michel.

---

6 Hugues Aufray (1929–), popular French singer, known, among other things, for his covers of songs by Bob Dylan.

Once I was at a demo and someone asked where I was and I told them I was occupying the Odéon and the guy said, you know who's controlling it? I said no. He said you don't know. And I said, you're going to tell me. And he told me Jean-Jacques Lebel, a comrade who had done a lot of political agitation. And ever after people would say during the events, "you're with Lebel."

So it was a question of convenience that led you to be where you were during the events?

Pretty much. And in my neighborhood I had some political things happening, like near metro Château Rouge every day there were people standing around listening to the radio, and they'd say this is great, the students have handed it to the CRS. I'd ask, where was that? They'd tell me and that's where I'd go. I also talked with my concierge, who was a personnel delegate at a print shop that was on strike: I didn't know a thing about unions and it was my concierge who told me stuff. It was little things, but it added up.

But let me tell you something about the demos, something I remember with horror. This is something I can say now. The first time I saw demonstrators throw paving stones it was at the request of photographers.

Really?

When I say that people look at me the same way you're looking at me. Yeah, the photographers said: "That would be great, you're there, and you pick up a stone and throw it." And what I say now, but not too loudly, is that I have the impression that more than half the people throwing stones were doing it to make the photographers happy.

You saw this with your own eyes?

Of course.

Did you throw any yourself?

Since I was still in school and taking gym class, if there was one thing I hated it was shot-putting. And I found it was the same thing.

So you didn't throw stones?

Never.

Any other dealings with the press?

There are comrades who told me that in an issue of *Paris Match* after May there was a two-page spread of place de l'Odéon with people in front of the theater, and the caption says: "The *katangais*." It seems that right in the middle is me, I never saw that picture and I don't know anything about it.

So you weren't a *katangais*?

No, and it was only later that I learned what they were.

It's said that at the Odéon there were all kinds of people, the *katangais*, homeless people, a bit of everything. Did you see that?

It's true, there was something of everything there. And we had our own health service—there were nurses there, most of them came from Lille and Brussels, I think.

Did your parents worry about you? They knew what you were up to?

My father had died in '57 and my mother worked at Saclay, at the nuclear plant, and from time to time she worked in Tahiti, since she received double her normal wages when she worked there. It just so happened that in May '68 she was in Tahiti, so my brother and I, we did whatever we wanted. I did go to visit my grandfather, who lived near metro Fallières, to reassure him and show him I was still alive.

How would you describe the atmosphere?

Joyful. All tendencies were there, but I don't have many memories of anarchist comrades. Maybe once or twice I saw black flags, and when I went to see the people with them they didn't do much for me: they'd shout, "Raise the black flag high so it's seen!"

Who was there at the Odéon?

There were a lot of artists. I remember things that bordered on the ridiculous. "I demand the floor. I have three things to say to you:

Merde, merde et merde." Either he was making fun of us or he was engaging in Dadaism.

For me, at the beginning—and this too is something that, when I tell it to people they look at me askance—I thought the Situationists were sloganeers. In school I was always a dunce, so the first time I read Debord I thought it was every bit as boring as my philosophy homework. Raoul Vaneigem, on the other hand, his writing was much more enjoyable. But Debord was boring. When I tell people this they all say, you know, no one says it but you're right. Proudhon I've been able to read, but not all; Marx, no way. Bakunin isn't the same thing, he had a real style. But Debord ...

People around you spoke of him at the time?

Oh, they spoke about the Situationists. And when I talk to other people who were involved in May, and they ask were you here or there and I say no, they ask, "What, were you stuck on the Côte d'Azur like Raoul Vaneigem?"

Who cleaned the toilets at the Odéon?

There were assignments, and I did it once. There were the Belgian nurses I mentioned. And to eat we had soup; I have no idea where it came from. I remember once I heard an argument and someone was saying about the leaders, "The bastards, they get French fries and chicken and all we get is soup." You know, these are little details, but it's like archaeology. You dig and from a little thing you can discover major things about a society and the people.

Did you leave the Odéon to participate in demos?

Yes, and I have a funny memory of the first Night of the Barricades, something I never saw in any book. We had our backs to the Luxembourg and someone said, let's go. So we set off—remember, I was 19—along the fence and there were about a hundred of us, headed toward the Senate, and suddenly we heard clicks. It was the Garde Mobile. Later I thought they'd done it to impress us, that they didn't intend to shoot at us. But at the time one of us said, "Let's get out of here." So we went back towards Saint-

Michel, and everyone had tears their eyes from the tear gas ... I'd say I have impressions more than I have memories ...

So you didn't become an anarchist at that moment.

Oh no. And there were days I didn't show up at all: I went home to listen to records. I didn't buy my first issue of *Le Monde libertaire* until two years later. In 1970. And why? Because there was a drawing by Reiser,[7] who I knew from *Hara-Kiri*, on the cover. *Le Monde libertaire* ... I wasn't even sure what that meant. *Le Monde anarchiste* would have been clearer to me.

You were at the Odéon, you participated in demos, and yet you had no real political ideas. What was it that impelled you to do all these things?

Because there were crowds, it was joyful, and the cops were on the other side. I already couldn't stand them since at earlier FEN demos they'd beaten me, calling me a filthy Arab, even though I told them I was French. I'd started experiencing this in 1957, when I moved to Barbès, so it was ten years that I'd been putting up with it on a daily basis. And while the cops were calling me an Arab, the Algerians would yell at me because I didn't understand them when they spoke to me in Arabic. They'd accuse me of being ashamed, and I'd tell them I was French. They'd say, "You're lying, you're Kabyle." All my life there've been Mexicans who've thought I was Mexican, Spaniards who think I'm a Spaniard ...

Did you listen to the leaders?

The only one I listened to was Cohn-Bendit at place Denfert-Rochereau when he stood up by the lion. That I liked. While the Trotskyists, I hated them. At the time I stammered and couldn't get out three words in a row outside the family. Though when I spoke foreign languages I didn't stammer. So anyway, I hated people who spoke like them, but not Cohn-Bendit. He had the gift of gab.

If there's one thing, one image from the time that has remained with you, what would it be?

---

7 Jean-Marc Reiser (1941–1983), French satirical cartoonist.

The felled trees along boulevard Saint-Michel. I don't know who did it or when, but there were felled trees all along boulevard Saint-Michel. I don't know who did it, but that's an image that I've never shaken.

And I think of the demos until 1:00 in the morning, the joyful atmosphere.

Even though there were a lot of people wounded, there wasn't much on the way of deaths. Did you feel tension in the air on the streets?

Not too much. I don't know why. I remember once, I was riding my bicycle—back then I got around by bike—and I was stopped because I didn't have a headlamp. What could I do? There were four cops surrounding me, so I got into the paddy wagon with the bike, and they took me to the commissariat. When I got there it was total confusion, so, just like that, I left. So even that was playful. I mean, when you were at the commissariat they didn't beat you or anything, you just sat there peacefully, and the door wasn't even closed. I went home and told my grandfather what had happened, and he told me, I put some food aside for you. "What, and nothing to drink?" I asked him.

When it was only students, did you think it important that the workers join in?

No, I'm not going to lie to you, it never occurred to me. Afterwards, yes.

While you were in the heat of the event, what did you expect?

[He shrugs.] I can't really say, it was all so day to day. I still believed in government, though at that time the government was a caricature, the government of General de Gaulle.

Did you hate him?

I had no particular feeling; he was an old fool, that's all. But it has to be said he had a certain stature; when he spoke it was impressive. And I was also under the influence of my grandfather, who had fought at Verdun.

You didn't become an anarchist right after. Did you continue your political life after May?

Look, I don't think that in my case we can say that May was a political adventure. It was because of the cops, that's all. I followed along. And I began to read books in 1970 and then I was given an address. And then there was the kiosk at the metro where I saw Reiser on the cover of *Le Monde libertaire*. So I went to see them saying, finally you've formed an organization, knowing nothing about all the splits and disagreements in the anarchist movement. They looked at me strangely: "Where'd this guy come from? Who sent him?" I began to be a little disillusioned.

It must have been a catalyst?

Sure, but if after May anyone would have spoken to me about anarchism I'd have said the anarchists were all individualists, that it wasn't a social movement. And among them there were those who had intellectual positions and those who had class positions. This goes back a long way in the French movement, to the nineteenth century, to *Le Libertaire*, which was a weekly that had syndicalist and anti-syndicalist articles in the same issue. And at bottom the synthesis was that anarchism addresses itself to all classes of society. It's interested in syndicalists, in working men and women.

I'm a fan of Libertad myself.

Ahh, Libertad. He was a union member.

Libertad? The arch-indivdualist?

Of course. Of the proofreaders' union. He would say, "I'm unionized but not a unionist."

You weren't old enough to vote at the time?

In my life I've voted once or twice and I did it out of defiance. So now when people ask if I've voted I answer, no, not often. I voted once or twice for the PCF, back when they frightened the bourgeoisie. In my arrondissement I voted for the PCF. Must have been in '69.

Élections piège à cons?

Not really. It's more that like I said, I read poetry and listened to country blues.

Did May change France?

For sure, but not only in a good way. You know, ten, fifteen years ago it was a subject of mockery: Oh you're an old '68er. It was something utopian, someone with long hair and a beard. And there was something we don't see much, there was a lot of social progress, in union rights, in social movements there was progress, but now when you open the newspaper everything has fallen back into place. There was a moment when it was a brand to sell things. People would ask, did you see this? And I didn't recognize myself in what was written if it was written by members of political committees or phrasemongers. But even so, it changed things. It changed the frame of reference. But there were also counter-currents. When we talk about '68 we can say good things and we can also say things that are not so good. But even so, we made Gaullism wobble, even if that was later, though it's not like what followed was much better.

Did May change you or was it the first step?

It was the consolidation of things that I didn't really understand. People say about me: You're someone who made May, and I answer that it's May made me.

About the Author

Mitchell Abidor is a translator and writer. Among his books are translations of Jean Jaurès, Victor Serge, Benjamin Fondane, and Emmanuel Bove, as well as anthologies on the anarchist propagandists of the deed, the Paris Commune, and the sans-culottes of the French Revolution. He is a third-generation Brooklynite.